Discover
Morocco

Discover

Morocco

Terry Palmer

HERITAGE
HOUSE

DISCOVER MOROCCO
First published April 1989
ISBN 185215.0165
Typesetting by: S.B. Datagraphics, Wyncolls Rd, Colchester
Printed by: Colorcraft Ltd, Whitfield Rd, Causeway Bay, Hong Kong
Distributed by: Roger Lascelles, 47 York Rd, Brentford, Mddx, TW8 OQP, in the UK and major outlets overseas
Published by: Heritage House (Publishers) Ltd, King's Road, Clacton-on-Sea, CO15 1BG

© **Terry Palmer, 1989**

Titles in the 'Discover' series, in print or in preparation, include:

Discover The Channel Islands
Discover Cyprus
Discover The Gambia
Discover Gibraltar
Discover Iceland
Discover The United States: Florida

Discover Malta
Discover Morocco
Discover Tunisia
Discover Turkey

Also by Terry Palmer: *The Cairo Alternative* (Heritage House), *The Ghost At My Shoulder* (Corgi)

CONTENTS

KEY TO MAPS

Terry Palmer's interest in Morocco began in 1963 when he saw the country across the Strait of Gibraltar. He has been there as a package tourist and an independent traveller; in 1988 he toured the country in his own car and by Moroccan public transport, from the Algerian border to the deep south.

1: WHY MOROCCO?

The big country

MOROCCO IS A MAJESTIC LAND OF MAGNIFICENT SCENERY and intriguing cities. In distance, it is the closest African country to Europe — just 14km or 8.5 miles across the Strait of Gibraltar — but its culture places it much closer to the heart of Islam.

The Kingdom of Morocco goes in for superlatives. It has the highest mountain north of the tropics at Jebel Toubkal, south of Marrakech (4,165 or 4,167m; 13,405 to 13,411ft, opinions vary): throughout the continent these heights are beaten only along the Great Rift in Ethiopia and east Africa, and the volcano of Kilimanjaro.

It has the best-preserved medina in Islam, at Fès; it has year-round snows feeding rushing rivers, and yet it has its share of the vast Sahara where daytime shade temperatures regularly exceed 48°C (120°F).

Love-hate reaction. Nobody can have a passing acquaintance with Morocco; it's not that sort of country. Visitors either love it or hate it, sometimes both at once. Some tourists, lured by its charms, go back year after year and always discover something fresh, while others cannot escape fast enough.

Size. The country is big, slightly larger than France, Benelux, Switzerland and Denmark rolled into one — or, in American terms, it's even bigger than Texas. The actual area is debatable because much of the frontier with Algeria is in dispute and there are as a consequence no crossing points along that stretch, but Morocco itself claims to have 710,850 sq km (274,461 sq miles) including the former Spanish Sahara (Western Sahara or Río de Oro) of 252,120 sq km (97,344 sq miles) which it annexed in 1975 when Spain pulled out. This region alone is larger than the UK but has a population no greater than 35,000.

The northernmost headland is Punta Leone near Ceuta at 35° 55' North, on the same latitude as Knoxville (Tennessee), the Grand Canyon and northern Tokyo. The most southerly point is Ras Nouâdhibou, the tip of a long peninsula which it shares with Mauritania, at 21°N — level with the southern tip of the Bahamas and within the tropics. This is also the westernmost headland, at 18°W, not far short of Cap Verde, Senegal, Africa's most westerly point. Morocco's easternmost spot is the oasis village of Iche at 1°0'40"E, just to the north of Figuig.

From north-east to south-west the country stretches 1,360 miles (2,188km) direct — or, for practical purposes, 672 road miles (1,082km) from Oujda to Agadir or 1,067 miles (1,718km) from Oujda to Laayoune. And south of Laayoune, the southernmost town of any size, are the desert walls behind which the Algerian-backed Polisario troops (rebels in Moroccan eyes) have been fighting for independence since 1975. Polisario is gradually losing ground, but meanwhile these southern regions of *de facto* Morocco are no-go areas to all but the most determined of explorers. It's not tourist territory at all.

2: BEFORE YOU GO

Paperwork and planning

VISA REQUIREMENTS

ALL FOREIGN VISITORS need a valid passport, and British travellers must have the full 10-year document. Visas *are* required for Dutch and Belgian citizens even though they may hold the new EEC passports, as retribution for attempts Belgium and The Netherlands have made to restrict the flood of Moroccans into their countries.

No other western European citizen needs a visa, neither do US, Canadian and Australasian passport holders.

South Africans and Israelis. South Africans and Israelis are not allowed into the country, *nor is anybody of any other nationality whose passport carries a stamp from either of these countries*. Passports receive a strict scrutiny (though M'Diq is sometimes relaxed) regardless of the length of queue and you may be asked for further details, such as occupation, with 'student' and 'journalist' sometimes inviting more questions.

Visiting Algeria. West Europeans planning to visit Algeria will not need a visa (US and Australasian citizens will), and have a choice of entry points at Ahfir, Oujda and Figuig. At the time of writing these crossings are open to all traffic at any time of day or night, but regulations vary according to the tension between Rabat and Alger. You will be required to buy 1,000 Algerian dinars at the official rate of exchange (around £100 or $180) which will emphasise the high cost of living in Algeria and force you onto the currency black market.

Not surprisingly, there is very little traffic across the frontier.

EMBASSIES IN RABAT

Belgium: 6 Ave Marrakech, BP 163, (tel 24714); **Canada:** 13bis Rue Jaâfar as-Sadik, BP 709 (71375); **Denmark:** 4 Rue Khémisset, BP 203 (69293); **West Germany:** 7 Zankat Madnine, BP 235 (69662); **Netherlands:** 40 Rue du Tunis, BP 329 (33512); **Norway:** 22 Charia as-Saouira, BP 551 (61096); **Sweden:** 159 Ave John Kennedy, BP 428 (54740); **Switzerland:** Square de Berkane, BP 169 (66974); **UK:** 17 Blv de la Tour Hassan BP 45 (20905); **USA:** 2 Charia Marrakech, BP 120 (62265).

Australia and New Zealand have no direct representation.

BP means 'Boîte Postale,' P.O. Box.

TOURIST OFFICES

The Office National de Tourisme Marocaine, ONTM, has branches in Agadir, Al Hoceima, Casablanca, Fès, Marrakech, Meknès, Oujda, Rabat, Tanger and Tetuan, as well as offices abroad, including:
Belgium: 66 rue du Marché aux Herbes, Bruxelles 1000 (512.2182);

Canada: Suite 1803, 2 Carlton St, Toronto, Ont, M5B 1K2 (598.2208); **Sweden:** Sturegaten 16, Stockholm 11436 (67.9485); **United Kingdom:** 174 Regent St, London W1 (01.437.0073); **United States:** Epcot Centre, Walt Disney World, Orlando, Fla. (827.5337); Suite 503, 5th Floor, 20 East Forty-sixth St, New York 10017 (55.72520).

Offices are planned or already exist in Australia, the Netherlands and Los Angeles. These offices supply brochures on the various tourist areas and a national list of hotels.

In addition, there is a network of Syndicats d'Initiative (say 'sandy cat') in most of the Moroccan cities listed, plus others. The Syndicat, based on the French idea, concentrates purely on supplying local information.

WHERE TO GO

Sun-seekers. The most popular beach resorts for package tourists from Britain are Agadir and Tanger, and if it's purely a beach holiday you want, Agadir is unrivalled, though it can be very hot in summer. The beach is long, wide, and in a slight bay, and most of the time there is a refreshing breeze off the sea, which occasionally can become a strong onshore wind. If this wind pattern shifts in high summer, you can find the shade temperatures reaching 50°C (122°F) for a day or so. Old Agadir was destroyed by an earthquake on Leap Year Day 1960 and the new town is smart but lacking character.

As Tanger faces north across the Strait of Gibraltar and is five degrees further north, its climate is more temperate the year round. Its beach is good without being in the same class as Agadir's, and the historic medina is full of interest. There are also day trips to Gibraltar by air or sea (see *Discover Gibraltar* in this series).

Sunlovers making their own travel plans have a wider choice: picturesque Essaouira, which has a beach approaching the Agadir standard plus a town of character; Azzemour beach and nearby El Jadida town, popular with Moroccans; or cliff-girt Al Hoceima on the Mediterranean coast.

With transport and a tent you could opt for the scenic splendours of Paradis Plage, but there are few basic amenities and you could be carrying water for several miles; or there's the organised spartan life of Club Méditerranée on the coast south of Ceuta.

There are many other beaches in the country, either lacking access or amenities or too close to heavy industry, but there is a vast potential for developing this part of the tourist market without damaging the ecology or making Spain's concrete-ribbon mistake.

The Imperial Cities. The great Imperial Cities of Fès, Meknès and particularly Marrakech are almost straight out of the Arabian Nights: vast medieval walled medinas where it's all too easy to get lost in the maze of alleys; highly ornate mosques (strictly no entry to non-Moslems) and colourful palaces. This is what Toledo, Seville, Granada and Córdoba would still be like if the Christians hadn't reconquered Spain 500 years ago, for this is the true Morocco, a world unlike anything you will find in Europe, and you should not miss it.

Mountains and Desert. Morocco is a land of rugged mountains separated by open plains. Marrakech is the best base for package tourists wanting to explore the mountains in organised comfort, or for independent travellers setting out by bus, hire car or on foot.

South of the High Atlas lies the desert, initially bare rock, including the Drâa Valley with its impressive mountain scenery, but you will need to venture far south of Agadir to find the vast sand dunes that most people associate with the Sahara.

The High Atlas is good hiking country from late spring until autumn, with the altitude tempering the effect of the high-summer heat.

WHAT TO TAKE

On the Beach. Package tourists planning to spend the majority of their time on the beach need little but clothes — but see 'Dress Sense' on page 14. As the sun can be intense, bring your favourite creams and lotions, and an insect repellent for the evenings.

Excursions. For organised excursions, you will need a good pair of shoes, suggestably trainers with a reputable name. Sunglasses are useful, and a hat is essential if you're seeing Morocco in high summer. You will need to guard your money and documents; I recommend a good-quality nylon or canvas moneybelt with tickets, cash, and passport each in separate plastic bags as protection against perspiration. Package tourists may argue that they leave their valuables in the hotel safe, but what of the transit to and from the airport? A heavy-duty screw-top plastic water bottle of at least a litre capacity is a lifesaver on a hot day; look for one that can be clipped to your belt.

Independent Travellers. Members of the backpack brigade don't need to be told what to do, but a few hints are appropriate to travel in Morocco. You need a sleeping-bag — in the cheap hotels sheets aren't changed after each guest — but it should be lightweight; down is the most durable filling but is also bulkier. And make sure your clothes are loose-fitting to avoid sweat sores.

Among your miscellaneous items carry a torch, a luminous clock, a knife which can't be mistaken for a weapon at the customs, and several plastic bags - for wrapping wet swimwear or dirty clothes, for keeping bread fresher, or to wash fruit in when water is scarce. Carry as much water as possible, preferably in more than one container — and don't forget the toilet roll.

WHEN TO GO

Morocco is an anytime holiday destination. There is no closed season for the beaches, and Agadir in winter outclasses northern European beaches in high summer. Tanger's rainy season is from November to March but the showers are shortlived.

The interior can be blisteringly hot in midsummer, passing 110°F (37°C) week after week. Midwinter is a refreshingly cool time to visit the Imperial Cities although sudden rain could flood some of the oueds and make fords impassable for a day or so. From January to April the ski slopes are in business at Oukaimeden, south of Marrakech, and for a shorter season at Mischliffen, east of Azrou.

Unless you love the heat, don't visit the desert between mid June and mid September. Zagora is reputedly the country's hottest town and in

In the Tafilait – ONMT

an August night the buildings radiate the day's heat much like a cooling oven.

Winter nights are usually balmy on the coast but are cold in the interior, with occasional frosts even in the lowlands.

LANGUAGE

The official language is Arabic, but Moroccan Arabic is more different from Arabian Arabic than American English is from English English.

Almost everybody speaks French as an economic necessity, even in the remote areas, and any road sign or official form that is only in Arabic is of no relevance to you. In areas of strong European influence, such as hotel signs and restaurant menus, Arabic takes a low profile, and you will be hard-stretched to see the true Arabic numerals, our so-called Arabic figures having replaced them.

Wherever English-speaking travellers gather, Moroccans have learned the language, which means the package tourist not having a word of French will still be able to communicate. In the medina at Tanger you may hear Cockney and Yorkshire dialects and mid-Atlantic slang coming from Moroccan traders.

Spanish is widely used in Tanger and along the Rif, the former Spanish Morocco, and in the annexed Spanish Sahara. Thousands of Moroccans have worked for years in The Netherlands — many still do

— and inevitably they come back with a working knowledge of Dutch. German is also widely understood in the coastal resorts and Imperial Cities.

Berbers and Moors. The original inhabitants of Morocco were tribes from widely differing backgrounds united only in their languages which, though different, came from Hamitic roots. To the Romans they were foreign, *barbaricus,* which has given us 'barbarian' and 'Barbary Coast' as well as 'Berber.' The Berbers still speak their distinct dialects: Masmouda, also known as Zeutet and Rifi and spoken in the Rif; Sanhadja, a.k.a. Tamazight, centred on Marrakech; and Chleuh or Tashelhait in the south. While the Berber tongues are Hamitic, the Arabic and Hebrew languages are Semitic: remember Shem and Ham, sons of Noah?

The word 'Moor' comes from *Mauritania,* the ancient Berber kingdom, though the name now applies to another land to the south. 'Moor' gives us 'Marrakchi,' an inhabitant of the city of Marrakch, known to Europeans as Marrakech. At the start of this century the English called the entire country 'Marrakech' (Marrakesh) while the Spanish called it 'Marruecos.' English gradually corrupted the Spanish name to 'Morocco.' Or is that pure fantasy? There is a theory which claims that the Berber for 'Keep your distance' led to the city of Marrakech getting its name.

INDEPENDENT or PACKAGE?

If you want a simple holiday on the beach with some leisurely excursions to the Imperial Cities, then take a package holiday and avoid most of the hassle, even though you will see the country through rose-tinted spectacles. If you want more adventure, you may consider going with operators such as Top Deck Travel, who show you a truer picture of the country and its people.

As a totally independent traveller, even though there may be several of you in a party, you will be pestered. If you give way to it this can ruin your holiday, but if you accept it as what Allah ordained for the Moroccans then it will add to the sense of adventure, but either way it is a fact of life you must consider. Morocco is a wonderfully scenic land and if you can tolerate being harassed then a tour of the Imperial Cities is highly rewarding. Better still for the adventurous is to go hiking for a month in the High Atlas. You will be beyond the range of most tourist touts and it will be an adventure to remember for the rest of your years. See 'Streetwise' on page 19.

TOUR OPERATORS

Morocco draws the greatest number of its visitors from France, one of the former colonial powers: 393,000 went in 1986. There were 286,000 visitors from Spain, 166,000 from the United Kingdom, more than the number who visited Tunisia; 156,000 from West Germany, and just 38,000 from the United States. Few Dutch and Scandinavians go to Morocco and the Dutch-registered cars you see on Moroccan roads are driven by migrant workers home on holiday.

This list of British tour operators is compiled from the *ABC Holiday Guide* and other sources but cannot be considered exclusive:

1. Abercrombie & Kent
2. Best of Greece Travel
3. Best of Morocco
4. Cadogan Travel
5. Club Méditerranée
6. Cosmos
7. Creative Leisure
8. Cresta
9. C.L.M.
10. C.V. Travel
11. Dema
12. Ecuador Travel
13. Enterprise
14. Excalibur
15. Explore Worldwide
16. Flair Holidays
17. Global
18. Golden Days (Intasun)
19. Hamilton Travel
20. Holiday Club International
21. Holidaymaker Travel
22. Horizon Holidays
23. Insight International
24. Intasun
25. Just Morocco
26. Kuoni
27. Lancaster
28. Longshot Golf Holidays
29. Martin Rook
30. Morocco Bound Travel
31. Moroccan Sun
32. Moroccan Travel Bureau
33. Pan World Holidays
34. Ramblers Holidays
35. Select Holidays
36. Serenissima Travel
37. Sherpa Expeditions
38. Skyworld
39. Slade
40. Stallard Holidays
41. Sovereign Holidays
42. Sunquest Holidays
43. Supertravel
44. Swan Hellenic
45. Thomson
46. Top Deck Travel
47. Trafalgar Tours
48. Trend Holidays
49. Twickers World
50. Vivair
51. Wings-Sunflight

And these are the resorts they use:

Agadir: 4, 5, 6, 13, 15, 22, 24, 26, 27, 30, 32, 33, 35, 38, 41, 42, 45, 51.
Al Hoceima: 5, 30, 32.
Casablanca: 2, 8, 11, 12, 19, 21, 30, 32, 39, 40.
Marrakech: 1, 2, 4, 5, 8, 10, 12, 13, 14, 18, 22, 24, 26, 28, 30, 32, 33, 35, 39, 40, 41, 43, 44, 45, 50.

Malabata (Tanger): 5.   **Ourigane:** 1, 30.
M'Diq: 5, 22.   **Rabat:** 28, 30, 32.
Mohammedia: 1, 30, 32.   **Smir-Restinga:** 5.
Ouarzazate: 2, 5, 30, 32.

Tanger: 1, 2, 4, 6, 11, 12, 13, 15, 18, 19, 24, 27, 38, 39, 40, 50.
Taroudannt: 1, 2, 10, 30, 32, 43.

In addition, 23 (Moroccan Bound Travel) goes exclusively to: Asilah, Asni, Boumalne, Chaouen, El Kelaa des Mgouna, Er Rachida, Goulimine, Ifrane, Kenitra, Ketama, Khenifra, Khouribga, Laayoune, Larache, Midelt, Nador, Oujda, Ourika, Safi, Sidi Bouknadel, Sidi Harazem, Taliouine and Taza.

Moroccan Bound Travel and Moroccan Travel Bureau both go to: Beni Mellal, El Jadida, Erfoud, Essaouira, Fez, Meknès, Ouarzazate, Tafraout, Tetouan and Zagora.

French Leave? Additionally, these French tour operators go to Morocco, but from departure points in France. They may be slightly more expensive than British operators, who are among the cheapest in Europe, but you will find a variation in resorts: Africa Tours, Airtour, Air Vacances, Cartour, Cédartour, Cosmovel, Fram, Jet Evasion, Jet Tours, Jeunes sans Frontières, Nouvelles, Planète, République Tours, Rêve Vacances, Rivages, Sunair, Touropa, Uniclam.

DISABLED

Morocco makes no special provision for its own disabled people, and wheelchairs are rare. Physically disabled tourists would therefore find themselves in a class apart and likely to regarded as mentally handicapped as well.

As the wheelchair-bound person would presumably draw more satisfaction from sightseeing than from lying on the beach, he will be hit by the high cost of car hire, the unsuitability of public transport and the inevitable hassle for the able-bodied companion.

DRESS SENSE

In a country where many of the women expose only their eyes to public gaze, and men wear the jellaba, that white garment stretching from shoulder to ankle, foreigners must expect to dress, and undress, with consideration.

Young Moroccan women love the beach but invariably wear one-piece swimsuits that cover the thighs; bikinis are for Europeans and only then within the hotel grounds or on the beach nearby. Topless and nude bathing are strictly forbidden, and there are usually armed policemen on duty making certain that beachwear is not worn onto the public road.

Off the sands, men should wear shirt and trousers and women should be covered from the shoulders to the knees, and preferably have sleeves as well. Bare torsos are confined to young Moroccan boys who are alone in being permitted on the streets in swim trunks; it's very rare to see a man's bare chest away from the beach.

European tourists of both sexes can wear shorts with some discretion, but the garments should be loose and large, not only to avoid giving offense but also for comfort.

A woman travelling without a male companion should avoid any hint of femininity or fragility, opting for sober-coloured loose-fitting long-sleeved blouses or an oversized shirt, loose skirts coming well below the knee, and probably wearing a headscarf as well. It would be ridiculous to try to copy the female Berber costume but it's equally pointless to dress in bright touristy clothes.

MONEY MATTERS

The dirham is a soft currency that officially may not be traded outside the country of issue. In practise you can buy and sell dirhams at banks and travel agencies in Gibraltar, at the ferry terminal at Algeciras, on the ferries to Tanger, Ceuta and Melilla, and at shops and currency exchanges in Ceuta and Melilla, which are politically part of metropolitan Spain.

The dirham takes its name from the Greek *drachma* and is divided into 100 centimes. Notes are issued in values of 5, 10, 50 and 100DH, with coins of 5, 10, 20 and 50 centimes and 1 and 5 dirhams. The issuing authority is the Banque du Maroc, founded in 1959 and later renamed the Bank Al-Maghrib. Notes with both names are in circulation.

Inflation. Inflation has not treated the currency too severely. The dirham stood at 10 to the pound in 1982, falling to almost 15 in 1988.

Moroccan banks accept all the world's hard currencies, including the Gibraltar pound, but giving it a lower value than Bank of England sterling. There are at least 14 banking concerns in the country, including several specialist firms such as Crédit Immobilier et Hôtelier. The Banque Populaire has the greatest number of branch offices but you will also see the Arab Bank Maroc, the Crédit du Maroc, the Société Générale Marocaine des Banques (SGMB) and the Banque Commerciale du Maroc.

Banking Hours. Banking hours vary, some businesses opening 0800-1345 Monday to Friday including Ramadan, others 0830-1130 and 1500-1630 Mon to Fri, but not opening in the afternoon during Ramadan or in high summer. To complicate matters, there are some banks whose bureau de change counters open at 1000.

Some banks, notably the Populaire, charge a flat commission of 5DH for changing currency or travellers' cheques, and then add 6% VAT (TVA, Taxe Valeur Additionelle), regardless of the amount of money changed.

Plastic Money. The Crédit du Maroc advances cash for Visa or Access cards, charging the usual small commission, and the SGMB accepts Eurocheques.

The large shops in the cities, and tourist hotels everywhere, accept any kind of negotiable payment from credit and charge cards through International Girocheques to Eurocheques and hard currency, but not personal cheques. In fact, people on a day trip from Gibraltar usually pay for everything in sterling and never even see the local currency.

Changing Back. Moroccan law states that after a stay of more than 48 hours you can reconvert half the dirhams you bought; less than 48 hours and you can reconvert them all, subject to showing exchange receipts. In practise you will usually have to show just one receipt if reconverting fairly small amounts at an airport bank, but there are no formalities at all on the ferries to Algeciras and Gibraltar.

Bank Al-Maghrib or Banque du Maroc; both are legal tender

COST OF LIVING

Morocco is not as cheap as you might expect; the French reckon that a holiday in Morocco is slightly more expensive than one taken at home, assuming standards are the same and ignoring the cost of transport to Africa. These sample prices were relevant in late 1988 when the rate of exchange was 14.20DH = £1.

Standard round loaf .... 0.85—1.00DH
(the price is double if bought in a bar)
Water melon, per kg 2DH
Peaches, per kg 9DH
Bananas, per kg 14DH
Oranges, per kg 5DH
Fillet of beef per kg 54DH
Shoulder of lamb per kg 37DH
Eggs, each 0.70DH
Olive oil, litre 17.90DH
Kim brand marmalade, made in Casablanca, 400gm 5DH
Sidi Harazem mineral water, litre .... 3.50—5DH
Local table wine, 75cl 25DH
Local beer (small bottle) 8DH
La Vaca Que Rie cheese, 200gm 19DH
Cigarettes: Camel, 20s 15DH
-Gitanes, 20s 11DH
Imported foods: Nescafé, 50gm 14.75DH
-Ovaltine, 400gm 36DH
-Kellogg's corn flakes 25DH
-Alpen muesli, 375gm 28DH
-Lipton's tea bags, 50 .... 19.25DH
-VAT 69 whisky, 70cl 150DH
-Martini bianco, litre 85DH
-Cadbury's Fruit & Nut chocolate, 200gm 22DH
Luxuries of life: postcard 1DH
-postage on card to Europe 3DH
-Camping Gaz cylinder, 190gm 10DH
-gent's suit in smart Marrakech shop, off peg   2,100—3,100DH
-fashion sandals in similar shop .... 150—200DH
-quality trainer shoes labelled Power .... 199—229DH
-Ambre Solaire 75DH
-London *Times* or similar, 2 days old 12DH
-Polaroid 'Instant 30' camera 304DH
Travel: Marrakech—Zagora bus fare, 1 way 60.50DH
-Rabat—Tanger rail journey 1 way 2nd class express 71.50DH
-ditto, 1st class 100DH
-petrol, super, litre 6.10DH
-road tax on car, per year 500DH
-Honda MB-5 motor-cycle, new, no extras 19,000DH
Basic wages of unskilled labourer, per day *25DH*

RELIGION

Islam is the state religion as opposed to being just the religion of the state, and 99% of Moroccans are Moslems. There are around 40,000 Catholics, slightly less Anglicans (who belong to the diocese of 'Gibraltar in Europe'), and 30,000 Jews. There have been two mass exoduses of Jews to Israel and Europe, as Independence approached, and around the Six Day War.

Moroccans belong to the Sunni sect of Islam, much less fundamental than the Shi'ites, but the faithful in Morocco are required to pray six times a day, once more than in most Islamic lands. The times are precise to the minute and vary according to the moon's phases, with this being an actual example for one particular day:

Al-Fajr	0413
Ach-Chourouq	0548
Ad-Dohr	1241
Al-Asr	1617
Al-Maghrib	1924
Al-Ichaâ	2057

There is no insistence that people pray at these times, nor that they go to the mosque to do so, but they should do their best to comply on Friday, the holy day.

Muezzin. The muezzin's chant from the mosque minarets is indecipherable to non-Arab listeners but he is proclaiming in Arabic what in English would be "God is almighty. I believe there is no god but God and that Mahomet is his prophet. Come to pray. Come for redemption. God is almighty and there is no god but God."

The word 'Islam' means submission to God's will and Islam is indeed a strict religion, demanding its followers show that submission in their daily life and prayers. The five commandments of Islam are the need for faith, as defined in the muezzin's chant; the need to pray six times a day; the order for the wealthy to give 2.5% of their income to the needy; the observance of Ramadan, the ninth month of the Islamic lunar-based calendar, by refraining from eating, drinking and sexual activity during daylight hours; and to make a once-in-a-lifetime pilgrimage to Mecca.

Mahomet. Mahomet was born in Mecca around 570AD; he began hearing the voice of God around 612 but when he tried converting the moon-worshipping Arabs they drove him from the city and it is this exodus, the *hegira,* which is the starting-point for counting the years in the Islamic calendar. The Gregorian or Christian calendar of 365¼ days places the *hegira* 1,366 years ago, but according to Islam's lunar reckoning 1,410 years have passed since the event.

Koran. Mahomet dictated the Koran, the Islamic holy book, which has 114 chapters each of 6,666 verses. It could be considered as the final volume of a trilogy beginning with Judaism and continuing with Christianity, for it mentions Abraham, Moses and Jesus as earlier prophets, but claims Mahomet as the last and therefore the greatest of them all.

Islam is much stricter than Judaism and Christianity, and those countries proclaiming fundamentalism observe the Koranic law as their civil legal code, which includes such penalties as amputation of the hand of a thief. Morocco is not in this school of thought and has a separate legal code based on the French system — but Moroccan theology still bans all non-Moslems from every one of its mosques.

As a result, crowds of tourists gather ignominiously outside the most important mosques, particularly on Friday, watching the faithful perform their ablutions and their ritual posturing during prayer.

And if you're ever among those crowds, count the women you see among the congregation: none. There are a few zaouias which have special doors for women, otherwise they must pray at home.

HEALTH CARE

Morocco is not in the **malaria** belt, but the British Department of Health and Social Security recommends visitors take antimalarial drugs. I feel this is being overcautious for the usual two-week holiday but worth considering for longer visits or if you're going into remote regions. Malaria is an unpleasant illness carried by the female *anopheles* mosquito, but the prevention involves taking two kinds of tablets beginning a week before your departure and continuing for a month after your return.

Cholera, typhoid and polio immunisation is advisable for the adventurous, but there's little point if you're eating in your tourist hotel. Bear in mind, however, that while the chance of contracting these three diseases is remote, they are potentially fatal. See your doctor for advice on the necessary drugs and injections. The schistomes — tiny worms of **bilharzia** — are in the waters of oases and permanent watercourses in the south, including the Drâa, so avoid paddling, swimming or drinking such water, and be particularly on your guard at campsite swimming pools.

There is no risk of **yellow fever,** and none of **hepatitis** provided you protect any open wounds and avoid drinking suspect water such as from uncovered wells or shared cups.

By now we should all know how **aids** is spread and so how to avoid it. See 'Streetwise.'

Insurance. I would not consider going anywhere in Africa without full medical insurance, including provision for an air ambulance home.

First Aid. The independent traveller should carry a simple first aid kit including as a minimum, two packs of sterilized dressings, antiseptic ointment, adhesive plaster — I prefer Micropore, which peels away cleaner — and some small scissors.

3: STREETWISE

Somebody once said, with feeling, that the trouble with Morocco is that it's filled with Moroccans. An inexperienced traveller choosing this as his first go-it-alone destination outside Europe should prepare for a culture shock, for while many of the people are friendly there is a hardcore of young males whose sole aim in life appears to be the exploitation and harassment of the tourist, even though this is strictly against the law.

For explanation, remember that Morocco was effectively lawless until the coming of the Protectorate in 1912, slaves were sold in the markets in living memory, piracy and banditry have been the way of life for centuries, and there is no welfare state: if you don't work you can starve to death. And unemployment among young males is particularly high, though the actual figure is a state secret.

You *will* be harassed; there is no doubt about it. The intensity of the hustling depends on a combination of factors such as your sex, your age, your dress and appearance, your location, and the opportunity you present as a potential victim.

Package Tourists. Package tourists who stick to the hotel complex and the beach, and travel inland only in organised excursions, will probably experience nothing more than a child demanding a pen or a youth trying to sell them something. But if they wander into the streets or medina of Tanger or Marrakech on their own they will begin to appreciate the situation.

Male Tourists. Independent travellers are, by definition, fair game with no closed season. If you're a man travelling with a female companion you will bear the full weight of the pestering, which ranges from the street vendor urging you to buy, to the self-appointed tourist guide who absolutely refuses to leave you alone.

Acceptance. You have four ways of reacting to such a guide, of which the easiest is to give in and accept his services, after which the harassment stops instantly for guides don't poach each other's clients. If you opt for this solution, agree at the outset what you're to be shown, what it will cost in total — no hidden extras — and where you will be left. Obviously, don't pay anything until the tour is finished.

Resistance. The second choice is to resist. The self-appointed unofficial guide, accustomed to bartering, sees this as a natural response and ignores it. He falls in beside you, pointing out the sights while he judges your response, and if you show the slightest interest you are as good as sold. If you continue like this for an hour and refuse to pay at the end, the guide will produce witnesses who saw you looking where he pointed: you are guilty by default.

The more you resist, the greater the challenge for the guide, as he believes in ultimate success. If you are adamant that you want to be left alone and are reduced to shouting: "Non! Absolument non! Je ne désire *point* vos services! Je vais voir la médina seul, *seul,* SEUL! Comprenez-vous?" he counters with reasons why it is essential you engage him. He offers to show you the town free, out of friendship (the sting comes later); he says it is illegal for foreigners to enter the medina without a guide (nonsense); he says you will be robbed if he's not there to protect you (possible, but remote).

You have, however, let him know you speak French: you have cut off your escape route and your only defence now is to become even more angry. But if you were able to tell him in Arabic the response would be different. "You are one of us! A thousand pardons!"

Ignore. The third option is to ignore him completely. Don't respond in any way at all, and certainly don't have eye contact. It's difficult, particularly when he insults you — but it works.

Simile!* If you and your companion can speak Welsh, Icelandic or Swahili you have a fourth option. You'd love to engage him, but he can't understand a word you say!

Official Guides. Or perhaps you *want* a guide? Remember the basic pay for an unskilled labourer is around 25DH a day and use that as a bargaining point. Boys come even cheaper at 2DH or 3DH for up to 2 hours, and a guide will certainly show you things you would otherwise have missed. But beware the extras: you will be shown interesting places that have no entrance fee — but you have to pay to get out. And by then it's too late to bargain. Official guides, by the way, don't tout for business in the streets; you find them outside the smart hotels or the tourist office and they're recognisable by their big brass badges. Their fee is around 50DH for a day, regardless of how many in the group.

Motorists. Foreign identity plates on a car draw the huckster tourist guides like jam attracts wasps; I've had them driving beside me on their mopeds, shouting offers and parking instructions in the open window.

Guardien de Voiture. The motorist, in his own car or a rented vehicle, quickly learns all about the *guardien de voiture,* the elderly man whose big brass badge shows that he is the official car park attendant. He is the human version of the parking meter, wanting one, two or three dirhams for short-stay parking and 10DH for overnight parking on the street: occasionally the all-night *guardien* will even wash your car for no extra fee.

You'll not escape without paying, even though you protest you never engaged him or you have no money; his badge is official and he has the backing of the police. This is a well-paid job for an ageing man but I often wondered how effective he would be against a determined car thief at 3am, and whether the crime rate warrants his services.

Inevitably there are also the unofficial *guardiens,* usually small boys who will watch you car all day or all night (all *night?*) for a few dirhams — and who will be the first to kick your tyres if you refuse.

Road Directions. Harassment quickly makes you reluctant to ask for directions in case you accidentally engage a guide; at times you need do no more than look at your map or pause at the street corner before you're accosted, invariably by males from their mid-teens to their late twenties. The remedy is simple: if you want to know the way, ask a

Simile is Swahili for "Get out of the way!"

policeman, an older man, a craftsman in the medina, a shopkeeper — anybody incapable of physically escorting you across the city. But don't ask a woman — unless you are one yourself. The response is usually a frigid silence.

Women Alone. The foreign woman travelling with a male escort cannot fail to notice that she is left in total peace, but the moment she ventures out alone, or with another woman, she must expect harassment of another kind. The young men are not so much interested in being guides as in getting her into bed, or in some back-alley, for why should a European female travel to Morocco if it is not to find the man she obviously cannot attract at home?

The suggestions are frequently put into basic language, including English, and the implied threat is sufficient to deter almost all young women from venturing alone into the remote countryside, a sad but wise decision.

Despite this sexual harassment it is feasible for a European woman to see the country on her own, but she must meet the men as equals, which is the first weapon in her armoury. If she speaks French or preferably Arabic, she could say she has plenty of men at home waiting for her favours, then pour scorn on their inferior offers — but do it carefully.

The Law. It is worth knowing the law is on your side on the matter of harassment, with the police having the authority to question any young man who appears to be a self-appointed guide. The problem is that the law is not enforced as the police recognise the unemployment problem.

Homosexual acts and prostitution are also illegal and punishable by stiff prison sentences. The man-to-man gay approach can come at any time, and a slightly shocked refusal is enough.

Bargaining. Bargaining is still fundamental to the Islamic way of life despite so many fixed-price items on the market. Whenever you're buying anything that could remotely be considered a souvenir you must enter into the spirit of the game and never show enthusiasm even if you're determined to have that item. Various theories exist on what proportion of the asking price you should pay, and if you've had more than your share of harassment set your ceiling at a half: it's an excellent way of getting your own back at the system.

Souvenirs. Some of the souvenirs you will see are of such poor quality that any price is too high: examples are mock-antique daggers in curved brass sheaths padded with tissue paper, and ornate boxes made of thuja or cedar wood from the High Atlas that fall to pieces before you get them home. The camelskin bags of Tanger are reasonable souvenirs though they will develop holes within a few months. I can't comment on the silverware beyond assuring you it's silver plated — but how thick is the plating? My experience of the souvenir market is that the best quality is to be found in the ceramics and pottery; if the workmanship is bad, it shows. But for the best souvenirs of all, ignore the souvenir stalls and buy in the domestic market in the souks; if you can see the craftsman at work you're certain of good quality — it's just up to you to strike a bargain.

This 'sell-'em-junk' attitude to souvenirs is just as unfortunate as the hassling, both having adverse effects on the tourist industry which the country so desperately needs. Morocco has some excellent craftsmen who turn out superb woodwork, as you will see in any medina, and with more attention to quality Morocco could find a useful export market.

Beggars. There are few beggars, most of them women with infants, sitting on the pavements in the newer parts of town and holding out their hand.

Petty Crime. I saw no evidence of street crime, but ample proof that it exists. Shopkeepers don't hang merchandise where they can't see it, and official guides showing parties of tourists around the medinas urge them to keep everything in front of them, in full view, and with bags hung around the neck. At the other extreme I have seen self-service supermarkets with dark and unsupervised areas where shoplifters could take their pick.

Several tourist hotels advise their guests to buy strings of beads for use as currency within the hotel complex, and then lock their cash in the safe. The explanation is that this avoids pilfering by the staff, but it also induces guests to make all their purchases in the hotel.

Security. It is definitely not safe for foreigners to wander the streets after dark unless there is good lighting and the safety of crowds, and anybody who goes onto the beach of a major resort by night is asking for trouble, starting with assault and progressing to rape. Several hotels stress this need for caution.

Hashish. Probably the greatest threat to the individual traveller lies among the drug pedlars of the Rif. Dozens of boys and young men stand on the roadside offering tiny packets of cannabis resin wrapped in plastic and shouting "Fumez! Smoke!" to the passing motorists. Backpackers who find themselves on foot on this main highway between Chaouen and Al Hoceima should be particularly careful not to buy any drugs and to avoid the risk of hash, or even goat dung packed to look like it, being planted in their luggage.

Kif, hash, hashish, cannabis — call it what you will — has been grown in these mountains for decades, and it is still a thriving business, with the drug now being sent to Europe cleverly hidden in the hulls of small ships: two such vessels were arrested in British waters in 1988.

It's not illegal to cultivate cannabis, and indeed the plant grows wild here, but it is illegal to possess the drug in any form, or to handle it by any means, with a 250,000DH fine and five years imprisonment as the maximum penalty, plus seizure of the means of distribution — which means your car. Once again, the law is not enforced, and when you visit the Rif you will undersand why. Instead, I have heard unsubstantiated rumours of dealers giving the police the car registrations of people who've bought hash, and of police posing as dealers to trap tourists.

4: MOROCCO BOUND

Air, sea and land connections

THE OBVIOUS WAY TO GO IS BY AIR, certainly for a conventional holiday, but there are arguments in favour of taking the sea crossing for people planning a longer stay.

BY AIR

Agadir and Tanger are the main airports for package holidays and charter flights.

AGADIR. Agadir's Inezgane Airport, AGA on your luggage label, is 4 miles (6.5km) south of town, around $4\frac{1}{2}$ hours flying time from England.

Package tourists are, of course, met by chartered coaches, but for the flight-only traveller there is no airport bus. If this is you, expect to walk to the end of the service road and catch a number 5 or 6 bus (labelled in our style 'Arabic' numerals, not the real Arabic) which will take you to Boulevard Hassan II, near the Royal Palace. Or share a grand taxi for around 5DH a seat. Or hire a car from one of the several companies represented.

Check-in times for independent travellers are 1 hour for Royal Air Maroc and 40 minutes for all other airlines.

Scheduled services fly in summer to Casablanca (around 28 a week), Dakhla (3), Fès (1), Frankfurt (1), Geneva (2), Gran Canaria (1), Laayoune (6), London, Heathrow (1), Marrakech (8), Milan (1), Ouarzazate (2), Paris, Orly (4), Tanger (7), Tan Tan (1) and Zürich (2).

TANGER. Tanger's Boukhalef Squahel Airport, TGN, is 9 miles (15km) south-west of the city, around $2\frac{1}{2}$ hours from Heathrow.

There is no bus service to the airport but buses stop at the end of the airport approach road, a mile away. The alternative is to take a grand taxi for 6DH per person from outside the terminal door; if you're travelling solo you'll be expected to pay for all the seats.

Check-in times are 1 hour for Air France, Royal Air Maroc and GB Airways (Gibraltar); 45 minutes for Sabena and 40 minutes for all other airlines.

Summer scheduled services go to Agadir (7 weekly), Amsterdam (4), Barcelona (1), Brussels (4), Casablanca (many), Copenhagen (1), Düsseldorf (1), Fès (1). Frankfurt (3), Geneva (1), Gibraltar (5), London Heathrow (3), Lyon (3), Madrid (4), Marrakech (2), Marseille (1), Paris Orly (2), Vienna (1) and Zürich (1).

Amenities. All Morocco's airport terminals are smart and clean, including the toilets, though these are sometimes poorly signed and invariably without paper.

Travellers arriving on international flights will find banks for changing currency and cheques, usually including Eurocheques, and frequently handling Visa credit cards. There are telephones; refreshments, mostly at a snack bar; and car rental desks, though these are not always manned and you will have to wait for the car to be brought out from the city. Car parking space and taxi ranks are just outside the door.

Departing travellers will find few check-in desks, except at Casablanca Airport, beyond which are security arches leading to the departure lounge. Duty-free kiosks stock the usual line of merchandise, including spirits.

With Casablanca the exception, most terminals would comfortably fit into Westminster Abbey — one at a time.

Other airports
Al Hoceima. (AHV). The Côte du Rif Airport is 10 miles (17km) south-east of the town, with scheduled services to Amsterdam and Brussels for the Club Méditerranée clients at the resort, and to Casablanca, Marrakech, Tanger and Tetouan.

CASABLANCA. The Mohammed V Airport (CAS) 19 miles (30km) south of Casablanca is Morocco's main aerial gateway, with scheduled services to many cities in Europe, though long-haul flights have transfers at Frankfurt or Orly. Check-in times are occasionally up to three hours in advance of take-off.

The airport bus, number 6, starts from the CTM-LN depot in Rue Léon l'Africain in the city centre, south-east of the Old Medina. The fare is 20DH, travelling time is 45 minutes, and departures are every 30 minutes from 0530-0800 and every hour from 0900-2300. Or from Ave Mohammed V, **Rabat,** for 45DH; it's cheaper to use the normal bus to Casablanca then take route 6.

Dakhla. (VIL) Dakhla is a small coastal town midway between Laayoune and Nouâdhibou. It handles internal flights only — Agadir, Casablanca and Laayoune — and as it's in the politically sensitive area of the former Spanish Sahara you may need permission to go there.

Errachidia. (ERA) The airport is on the edge of the town more usually spelled Ar-Rachidia, in the Ziz Valley and convenient for hikers destined for the High Atlas or for people trekking into the Tafilalt.

Fès. (FEZ) Saïs Airport is at the village of the same name 6 miles (10km) south of town. Its European flights are to Lyon, Madrid, Marseille and Paris Orly.

Laayoune. (EUN) Villa Bens Airport is 2km from Laayoune, the southernmost resort. It has three flights a week to Gran Canaria and daily links with Agadir and Casablanca, used by Club Méditerranée customers.

Marrakech. (RAK) Menara Airport is 4 miles (6km) south of the city. The 11 bus from the main Post Office (PTT) connects with the end of the airport service road. There are regular links with Paris Orly and once-weekly flights to Brussels, Geneva, Strasbourg and south European cities.

Ouarzazate. (OZZ) One mile out of town, this airport is convenient for hikers into the High Atlas and trekkers down the Drâa Valley. There are three summertime flights weekly to Paris Orly, and links with Agadir,

Casablanca and Marrakech.

Oujda. (OUD) Les Angads Airport 9 miles (15km) north of Oujda has scheduled services to Amsterdam, Brussels, Düsseldorf, Frankfurt, Marseille and Paris (Orly).

Rabat. (RBA) Rabat-Salé Airport 6 miles (10km) east of Rabat. Internal flights to Casablanca only; long-haul flights transfer at Paris (Orly), Frankfurt or Copenhagen.

Tan Tan. (TTA) The Plage Blanche Airport is 5 miles (9km) west of this desert town. Services to Agadir, Casablanca and Laayoune only.

Melilla. (MLN) Remember that Spanish regulations apply; flights to Almería and Málaga only, the latter daily, by Fokker Friendship which does not fly in bad weather.

European Airports

If you've left it too late to get a seat on a flight direct to Morocco, if you're heading for Tanger and the Rif, if you drop everything and decide to go to Morocco tomorrow, if you're looking for a touch of adventure, or if money is short, you could consider flying either to Málaga or Gibraltar. There are usually some tempting flight-only discounts to Málaga from where you can catch the Portillo bus to Gibraltar or Algeciras for the ferry (see below); or you can go to Gibraltar on a standby flight from Gatwick and complete the journey by sea or air. (More details of these airports and buses are in *Discover Gibraltar*, 2nd edition.)

BY SEA

The choice is by car ferry from Algeciras to Tanger or Ceuta; by ferry from Málaga and Almería to Melilla; by hydrofoil from Tarifa to Tanger; by high-speed catamaran from Gibraltar to Tanger or M'Diq; by car ferry from Sète or Port Vendres (France) to Tanger; or from Naples to Tanger.

FROM ALGECIRAS. The car ferry to **Ceuta** has the quickest crossing (90 minutes) and the most frequent sailings. Departures from Algeciras Monday to Saturday in high summer are: 0700, 0800, 1000, 1100, **1200**, 1300, 1500, 1600, **1730,**, 1830, 2000, 2100.

Sunday sailings are 1000, 1300, 1600, 1830, 2100.

From **Ceuta** sailings Monday to Saturday in high summer are: 0830, **0930,** 1030, 1230, 1330, 1500, 1600, 1730, 1830, **2000,** 2100, 2230.

Sunday sailings are 0930, 1330, 1600, 1830, 2100.

(Times given in **bold** do not apply on Saturdays.)

Foot passengers can virtually walk on the Compañía Trasmediterranea's ferries as if the *Herald of Free Enterprise* tragedy had not happened. Motorists can reserve a crossing (you'll see many agencies from Málaga to Algeciras but I hear rumours that some of these are bogus) or join the queue; even in high summer you'll seldom wait more than two sailings. **Fares** are around £10 per person, £25 per car, one way.

In a hurry? Note that Ceuta and Melilla are Spanish territory; you will not need to show passport or motor insurance. Entering Morocco at the land frontier outside the enclaves is chaotic *and will take you at least an hour on foot or 90 minutes with a car*. I suspect this is a protest at Spain's continued presence in these two ports.

Sailings to **Tanger** take 2½ hours; there are three crossings per day in each direction in summer, and one or two in winter. The **fare** is from 2,550ptas to 3,300ptas per person, with cars less than 6m at 7,500ptas (more than 6m, 11,200ptas) one way. Passports are checked during the crossing and there is no delay on disembarking at Tanger.

FROM TARIFA. The hydrofoil from Tarifa reaches Tanger in 30 minutes with three flights a day in summer, one in winter, but never on Sundays. Transtour operates the service with a fare of 2,400ptas, 150DH or £12 per adult, one way: *vehicles are not carried*.

FROM GIBRALTAR. *Gibline One* carries 226 passengers but *no cars* to **Tanger** on Mon, Wed, Thurs and Sat (high season) at 0900, at 1730 on Mon, 1830 on Fri and 1100 on Sunday; and to **M'Diq** at 0900 and 1730 on Thursday, but these last-mentioned sailings are often block-booked. Fares are £16 single, £22 day return. Once you've got a ticket, M'Diq is your easiest point of entry.

FROM MÁLAGA and ALMERÍA. One sailing daily each way to Melilla, operated by Compañía Trasmediterranea (Isnasa).

OTHER FERRIES. The General National Maritime Transport Co operates the Tanger — **Naples** run, calling at Malta and Libya. The Compagnie Marocaine de Navigation, Comanav, runs the 38-hour crossing from **Sète** to Tanger with fares for car and passenger at £90 each, one way. The Nador — **Port Vendres** route costs 800fr per person and 890fr per car.

Time. *Note that Morocco is on GMT the year round. This means a two-hour time difference between Spain and Morocco in summer and a one-hour difference in winter.* All sailings are given in local time.

BY LAND

Europabus runs long-distance coaches from France to Morocco in association with Iberbus and CTM, the Moroccan national carrier. Departures are from Paris (Mon, Thur, Sat), Lyon (Mon, Tues, Fri), Toulouse (Tues, Sat), Brussels (Tues, Fri), and Marseille and Lille (Tues). Fares from Paris are 1,500DH one way, 2,700DH return.

Morocco's frontier with Algeria has crossings at Ahfir, near the coast; north-east of Oujda; and at Figuig. Diplomatic relations between the two countries have been strained for years, and frequently broken, so there is little traffic. See 'Visas.' The road running inland, south of Laayoune, crosses into Mauritania through territory formerly held by the Polisario fighters and is certainly beyond the scope of the average tourist.

5: TRAVELLING IN MOROCCO

Car, bus, taxi, train

MOROCCO'S ROADS ARE GOOD. Main roads are well-built and maintained, despite the rigours of the climate. Minor roads often have steep gradients and broken edges but the standard is better than in Tunisia. Tourists should avoid the unmade tracks wherever possible. In 1984 there were 35,824 miles (57,651km) of roads, of which 46% were paved. And there were just 36 miles (59km) of motorway, from Casablanca almost to Rabat.

In 1983 the country had 477,000 private cars and taxis, almost 8,000 buses, and 180,000 lorries and vans, giving 47 persons per car — and yet almost all the *grands taxis* are Mercedeses.

TAXIS. Morocco has two kinds of taxi; the **grand taxi** is similar to the *louage* of Tunisia in that it runs on specific routes between towns and leaves as soon as there is a full load of six passengers; on busy routes

This railway timetable at Rabat says it all

DEPART الذهاب

ESTINATION	M.T Express	1.10 Direct	12 TC Rapide	CT-FC Rapide	MK Rapide	128 TNR 1.2	CT-18 Rapida	Rapida	1-16 Direct	5.8 Direct	8 Rapide	MF-FM Rapide	8.2 Rapide	13-14 Rapida	16.12 Direct	جاء
NITRA	0.10	7.22		8.16			9.05	13.26	14.09	15.57		18.14	18.53	21.54	23.17	طرة
JI KACEM	0.10	7.22					9.05	13.26	14.09	15.57		18.14		21.54	23.17	ى قاسم
NGER	0.10			8.16					14.09				18.53		23.17	جة
KNES		7.22					9.05	13.26	14.09	15.57		18.14		21.54	23.17	ناس
A		7.22					9.05	13.26	14.09	15.57		18.14		21.54	23.17	اس
DA		7.22							14.09					21.54	23.17	دة
ABLANCA	4.22	22.52	21.11	20.43	19.35	19.15	18.19	17.59	16.40	14.34	11.53	11.03	8.45	6.50	5.10	يضاء
RAKECH	4.22		21.11	20.43			18.19			14.34		11.03	8.45		5.18	كش
ZEM	4.22									14.34			8.45		5.18	زم
							18.19						8.45		5.18	
JADIDA					19.15				16.40	14.34				6.50	5.18	يدة

HANGEMENT DE TRAIN A SIDI KACEM   القطار بسيدي قاسم
HANGEMENT DE TRAIN A CASABLANCA   القطار بالدار البيضاء
ANGEMENT DE TRAIN A CASABLANCA ET BENGUERIR   القطار بالدار البيضاء وبن جرير

there is a continuous service but on quiet routes you will have to wait for that sixth person to arrive. Fares are up to 150% of the corresponding bus fare but the travelling time is less.

The *petit taxi,* usually a Simca or Fiat and always sprayed a distinct colour peculiar to that city, operates within the city limits and carries three passengers. These cars are normally recognised by the slogan *petit taxi* painted on the roof-rack. Only in Rabat do the petits taxis have meters; elsewhere you should agree the fare before the journey begins, and bargain if you think it is too high, as it often may be if you look an affluent tourist.

BUSES. The *Compagnie de Transports au Maroc - Lignes Nationales,* known as CTM-LN or just CTM, is the national carrier with services to virtually every town in the land. The head office is at 303, Blv Brahim-Roudani, Casablanca (phone 25.29.01)

There are plenty of other bus companies, many of them running just one vehicle. Standards of service and comfort therefore vary enormously, and private buses on quieter routes leave when they have enough passengers. The railway, ONCF, now runs express coaches on important routes that aren't served by trains, notably to Agadir and Laayoune; fares are at the grand taxi level.

Gare Routière. Problems often arise with towns that have more than one bus stop — *gare routière* - with CTM coaches using one and local buses another.

Luggage. Passengers are responsible for seeing their luggage is stowed aboard the bus, and are sometimes expected to pay for the privilege of having it unloaded from the roofrack. I find an outburst of indignation stifles more demands.

RAILWAYS. The *Office National des Chemins de Fer,* ONCF, is the Moroccan state-owned railway company which in 1987 had 1,176 miles (1,893km) of track, and plans to double it. From Casablanca, lines run to Rabat — Meknès — Tanger; Meknès — Fès — Oujda — and down into the desert to the mines at Bouârfa; and Casablanca — El Jadida — Safi — Marrakech.

Extensions are planned to Nador, Agadir and Laayoune, which is why ONCF runs its own buses on those routes.

Fares. Second class rail fares are more expensive than CTM bus fares, Rabat to Tanger single costing 71.50DH, but third class rail travel is considerably cheaper. The photograph on page 27 shows the day's departures from the main station at Rabat.

Caution. Avoid travelling on night trains unless one in your party can stay awake to check against pilfering of luggage.

CAR HIRE. Car hire is not cheap in Morocco but there is no shortage of companies with cars to rent. To drive a hire car you must have had your 21st birthday (25th for driving a hired minibus) and have held a full licence for at least a year; your home driving licence is valid with no need for an International Driving Licence.

Most hire companies accept payment by charge or credit card; all ask for the estimated cost in advance, sometimes with a refundable deposit — and the bill will be subject to 19% VAT (TVA).

These rates, charged by Europcar in 1988, are typical of what you must expect:

Renault 4: daily 170DH, weekly 1,190DH, plus 1.80DH per kilometer, *or* 2,170DH weekly, unlimited mileage.

Peugeot 505: daily 380DH, weekly 2,660DH, plus 3.80DH/km, *or* 5,880DH weekly, unlimited mileage.

Rental Companies. Hertz has 12 branches in the country, Europcar has 13, and InterRent has seven. Avis, Afric Cars and Budget have offices in the major cities, and there are numerous small companies.

Take Your Own Car. People planning a longer stay in Morocco or who want to see as much as possible may find it worth taking their own car. If this is for you, you will need to carry proof of ownership and your vehicle will be entered on your passport — which means you cannot leave the country without exporting the car as well. British insurance companies are not keen to issue cover for Morocco so it's more convenient to buy 'assurance frontière' when you arrive.

Cover is for *third party only* at these prices, plus a small stamp tax:

Time in days	5	10	20	30	90	
Mo-cycle, moped	72	112	146	179	336	.... Dirhams
Cars	112	154	225	280	560	
Caravans	car plus 10%					

Take Your Own Motor-cycle. If your own car gives you the advantage of near-total mobility, your own motor-cycle will give you even more mobility at less cost; many young French people see the country this way. The disadvantages are the problem in repairing punctures at the roadside and the need for security.

Port of Entry. On the map, Ceuta appears to be the cheapest and quickest way into the country, but you must allow at least 90 minutes to get through Moroccan frontier formalities, entering and leaving. The process is theoretically simple: you go to a small window, ask for the appropriate form, hand it in with your passport, then collect the stamped passport. But 100 people are doing the same thing at the same time and the result is bedlam in the noonday sun. Try Tanger; the only hassle there is from tourist guides.

MOTORING REGULATIONS

The **speed limit** is 40kph (24mph) in towns, with certain semi-rural areas limited to 60kph (37mph) or 100kph (62mph) as shown by international symbols. On the Casablanca — Rabat motorway the limit is 120kph (74mph). There is no compulsion to wear **seat belts,** nor crash helmets when driving mopeds.

Motorway. There is no practical way of avoiding the 36 miles (59km) of motorway which is toll-free. Pedestrians cross it, cyclists use the hard shoulder, and boys sell fruit at the roadside, but it's all illegal.

Petrol is readily available north of Agadir, though you seldom find service stations in the open country. Stations are open on Fridays and Sundays, but be prepared for some to be out of stock and for many to close on Friday afternoons during Ramadan. The main brands available are Mobil, Total, Agip, Petrom, Elf and Somepi, offering the choice of 'super' or 'essence,' the latter being around 92 octane. Many accept credit cards, notably Visa, with Diners Club coming a poor second, and in late 1988 a gallon of super cost the equivalent of £1.95.

The *guardiens de voiture*, 'car guards,' supervise and charge for **parking** in towns and cities — see 'Streetwise' — but you should not park beside kerbstones alternately painted red and white or red and yellow, nor by international no-parking signs. It's not difficult to find a space, even in Casablanca.

The **standard of driving** is poor, with Moroccan drivers overtaking on blind corners and even overtaking vehicles already in the fast lane on the Casablanca — Rabat motorway. Instant response is demanded when the traffic lights change to green.

Avoid **night driving**, mainly for the hazard of boulders on the road. During the day, motorists use rocks as cones to warn of a breakdown ahead, but they never bother to remove them before driving away.

A Portuguese doorframe survives in the old Portuguese city of El Jadida

6: ACCOMMODATION

Hotels, caravanning or camping?

MOROCCO'S TOP HOTELS ARE AMONG THE BEST IN THE WORLD, and it needn't cost you the earth to stay in reasonable luxury. At the bottom of the scale, some of the most colourful hotels are in the medinas, but if you're in this class you should definitely view the room before deciding. Hotels base their charges on the number of persons using the room rather than charging a set price per room, regardless.

Tariff. These are maximum permitted prices, in dirhams and including tax, from the 1988 season:

Rating	4 A	4'B	3'a	3'B	2'A	2'B	1'A	1'B
2 pers, WC, bath	125	103	78	68	50	41	35	30
1 pers, bath	81	68	51	44	34	28	23	20
continental b'fast	10	10	8	8	6	6	5	5
set dinner	$35\frac{1}{2}$	$35\frac{1}{2}$	$27\frac{1}{2}$	$27\frac{1}{2}$	$23\frac{1}{2}$	$23\frac{1}{2}$	$20\frac{1}{2}$	$20\frac{1}{2}$

Hotels have their ratings changed frequently so to simplify the situation we have ignored the A and B distinctions; even so, some of our quoted gradings will be outdated.

Medina Hotels. The vast majority of the medina hotels are unclassified and usually cheaper than the one-star 'B' rating, but they may increase their prices in high season and become dearer than classified hotels. Don't choose a place down a narrow and poorly-lit alley if you plan to get back to it late at night and remember that sheets are not changed after each guest in the majority of these hotels, so a sleeping-bag is useful.

Fiche de Police. Each guest must fill in a *fiche de police*, a questionnaire, which is forwarded to the police, much as was done in France years ago.

Holiday Villages. Three firms share the holiday club market: Club Méditerranée, with holiday villages at Agadir, Al Hoceima, Marrakech, Malabata, M'Diq, Ouarzazate and Smir-Restinga; Club Salam at Agadir and Casablanca; and Club des Dunes d'Or in Agadir. Club Med trades in Britain but if you want to book through its French office, it's in Place de la Bourse, Paris 2.

Club Salam is at Blv Mohammed V, Agadir, and Club des Dunes d'Or is at Centre Balnéaire, Agadir.

Caravanning. Going to Morocco for three months? If so, a caravan is a cost-effective option, but it insulates you from the Moroccan way of life. Avoid travelling in high summer — both car and caravan will be intolerably hot — and keep out of the mountains during the winter. You

Don't drop the other melon! Khenifra's Sunday market is purely for the locals

will need to be prudent in choosing where to park overnight as you may well be pestered with children demanding dirhams, pencils or sweets. Security is therefore a problem, but a caravan can certainly open up new vistas.

Camping. Several tourist cities have camp-sites — *un camping* is the site, not what you do there — often close to the centre of activity. Security is less of a problem at sites that are completely fenced, but you should never leave valuables unattended.

The fee should be 3DH to 5DH per person if you supply your own tent, but Camping Sinbad at Zagora asks 20DH per person for sleeping in a mud hut: the local Hotel des Amis is cheaper!

Camping sauvage, pitching your tent in the open countryside poses distinct security problems and you should never do it in sight of the road or where children might find you. I recommend that you never make camp in the wilds out of sight and sound of at least two other tents, which ruins any ideas of privacy. The alternative is to camp on private and fenced property, paying the landowner for the privilege — but don't let up on security.

7: DINING OUT

And Nightlife

WHO HAS EVER GONE TO MOROCCO and not tried couscous? Couscous is made from semolina and is tasteless and insipid on its own, but it forms the basis of many dishes as *pilav* does in Turkey and rice does in Spain; usually it is topped with mutton, poultry or fish, with appropriate vegetables.

Couscous is reserved for the main meal of the week, usually after prayers on Friday, or for a special occasion, and is traditionally eaten with the right hand, rolling it into a ball with some meat or vegetables.

You will certainly meet *harira*, a thick soup of meat and veg; the name actually means 'soup' and it is often a meal in itself, particularly after sunset during Ramadan. Similarly, *tajine* is the name of an earthenware pot with a conical lid which was plunged into hot ashes to cook its contents, but the term now applies equally to the vegetable stew made in a tajine.

Bstilla or *pastilla* is not so common because it's difficult to prepare — it's pre-cooked pigeon, crumbled and re-cooked on thin flaky pastry. You will find *méchoui* only if you go to a major festival or if your tourist hotel plans a celebration, as it is a complete lamb roasted over charcoal in an open pit. The Turkish specialities of shish-kebab and doner-kebab are seen everywhere, particularly in the cheaper cook-houses in the medinas which are something of an endurance test for your digestive system. Another one to try is *kefta*, spiced meat balls.

Sweets. The Moroccans love sweet dishes. *Haloua* is a honey-cake and *kâbel-el-ghezal*, literally 'gazelle horn,' is a sweet cake decorated with almonds. *Dattes farcies* are dates stuffed with a marzipan-like paste.

Restaurants. The majority of restaurants in the *villes nouvelles*, the French-inspired towns, offer a menu indistinguishable from what you would find in France, and you must go closer to the medinas to find Moroccan dishes on offer, but venture too far and you find the standard of hygiene drops. You should also be prepared for VAT of 14% on your bill, plus a service charge. And don't pay until you've checked every item.

Drinks. Mint tea is the national drink, and its preparation has become as much a ritual as wine-tasting is with Europeans. The teapot is filled with boiling water, emptied, and filled again, then green tea is added with a liberal helping of fresh mint leaves: you will see these on sale in every medina and growing wild wherever there is permanent water.

The tea is then poured into a glass, which is emptied back into the pot. The second pouring, done from two or three feet above the glass, is the one that's drunk, with three or four lumps of sugar.

Devout Moslems who interpret the Koran as forbidding all alcohol (it doesn't; it merely cautions against excess) alternate mint tea with espresso coffee and mineral water flavoured with orange blossom, but relaxed Moslems like their native wines.

Wines and Spirits. At around 25DH for a 75cl bottle of *vin ordinaire,* wine is not cheap by local standards, but there are some good brands. Ksar, brewed in Meknès, is a tough red to go with Cabernet and Valpierre. Gris de Boulaouane and Cardinal are rosés, Chaudsoleil is a good white, and Beni Snassen is the Moroccan version of muscat. Few spirits are distilled in the country, but Berger Sport, a pomegranate liqueur, appears popular.

Lagers. Beer as north Europeans know it, is not to be found in Morocco, but Brasseries du Nord Marocain produces a good lager, Speciale Flag. Others that drown a thirst are Store and the ever-present Heineken. If that's not to your taste, try the mineral water Sidi Harazem, claimed as beneficial for kidney ailments and arthritis, or Sidi Ali. Si Harazem, by the way, is bottled in the town of that name near Fès, and Si Ali comes from Oulmès, south-west of Meknès.

NIGHTLIFE

Morocco is not noted for its nightlife but it is much livelier than Tunisia. In any of the big towns you can join the crowds thronging the streets as soon as the sun goes down, much like the Spaniards did in their *paseo* until television began eroding the custom. Tanger has the best general nightlife, a hangover from its days as a free port and international zone; there is life after dark in Jemaa el Fna, Marrakech, and at Aïn Diab, Casablanca. The only casinos are at Marrakech and Mohammedia.

The tourist hotels and the syndicat d'initiative are responsible for organising most of the tourist entertainment, including the occasional snake charmer, and package travellers' evening fare therefore will usually be a show of folk dancing or belly dancing at a smart restaurant, or a western-style disco in the tourist hotel.

There are exceptions. Moroccans enjoy themselves during Ramadan after the sun has set, and there are several important festivals — see page 37

8: FILE ON MOROCCO

Facts at your fingertips

AFFILIATIONS

Morocco is a member of the United Nations Organisation, the Non-Aligned Movement, the Islamic Conference and the Arab League.

ARMED FORCES

The Army was created in 1956, shortly after independence, and currently stands at 170,000 men, equipped with 110 main battle tanks and as many light tanks, and 1,400 armoured cars in 7 squadrons. There are still 2 desert cavalry and 3 camel battalions — and the Royal Guard.

The air force was founded in 1959 and now has 15,000 men who fly 279 aircraft ranging from the Mirage fighter to the Boeing 707 and the Gazelle helicopter. The navy was created in 1960 and its 6,000 men have a guided-missile frigate and 25 other vessels.

Collectively these are the *Forces Armées Royales*, commemorated in the name of a major road in almost every town. And conscription? Eighteen months for every male.

BUSINESS HOURS

Banks. Banks do not have consistent hours of business. You can assume that every bureau de change *will* be open 1000-1130, Monday to Friday, but most bureaux open at 0900 (the banks themselves at 0800 or 0830). They close at 1130 or 1345 in Ramadan and high summer, and might be open 1500-1635. None opens Saturday or Sunday.

Tourist offices. 0830-1200 and 1430-1800, with local variations. Usually open Mon-Sat but sometimes Mon-Fri. Some Syndicats d'Initiative are open 0800-1200 and 1400-1700, Mon-Fri.

Shops and Offices. 0830-1230, opening again at 1430. Closing times vary: offices, including car hire agencies, 1700; shops, 1900; food shops 2000 or 2100. Offices are closed on Saturday, shops are open. Some shops and car hire companies open 0900-1300 Sunday.

Museums and Palaces. 0900-1200, 14330-1800 daily, but each museum has its own variation of these hours and may change its times at random. 'Standard hours' in the text must be interpreted very loosely.

Post Offices — postal. *Smaller offices:* high summer (undefined): 0830-1400 and 1600-1900, Mon-Fri, 0830-1230 Sat. Remainder of year: 0830-1200, 1430-1830, Mon-Fri, 0830-1230 Sat. *Larger offices* do not close for the midday break.

Post Offices - phones. For operator-controlled international calls in small towns, 0830-2100 daily; in large towns the office never closes.

ECONOMY

Morocco mined 21,391,000 tons of phosphate ore in 1986, much of it in the former Spanish Sahara, which explains the country's determination to control this otherwise hostile territory. Most of the phosphate was exported — and in that same year Morocco owed $12,500,000,000 abroad.

The country produces around 750,000 tons of coal, 200,000 of iron ore and 23,000 of crude oil in a year, with small amounts of copper, lead, magnesium and zinc.

For a land that's mainly scrub and desert, Morocco's agriculture is impressive: around 3,500,000 tons of wheat and the same of barley each year, and 2,500,000 tons of sugar beet. It also grows potatoes, tomatoes, onions, melons, and 800,000 tons of oranges — but only 45,000 of dates.

There are 2,500,000 cattle, 4,500,000 goats, 12,000,000 sheep — and 35,000,000 chickens. Being a Moslem land, there are few pigs. The fishing fleet nets 400,000 tons a year, half of the catch being sardines.

ELECTRICITY

Voltages of 110 and 220 are often found side by side; check which socket you use. Sockets are of French design and therefore need adaptors for British appliances. There are still a few towns on 127v.

FESTIVALS

Many towns and cities hold their own festival to mark some local event, usually relating to the land. Here are some:

Early morning bread delivery in the medina at Chaouen

February: Tafraoute; Festival of the almond blossom.

March: Casablanca; Amateur theatre.

June: Marrakech; National folklore festival. Sefrou; Cherry festival. Goulimine; Camel fair.

September: Marrakech; Tourist fortnight. Rabat; Arab theatre. Meknès; Fantasia. Agadir; Folklore. Imilchil (remote High Atlas village); *Moussem* des Fiancès ('marriage market'). Moulay Idriss; Morocco's leading *Moussem*.

October: Erfoud; Dates. Tissa (in the Rif); Horses. Fès; *Moussem* of Moulay Idriss (folklore). Meknès; *Moussem* Sidi Aïssa at Mouloud (Mahomet's birthday).

December: Rafsaï (Rif, between Ouezzane and Taza); Olive harvest.

Moussem. A moussem is a religious gathering at the tomb of a marabout (holy man). People come from miles around and stay up to three days in tents, making a pilgrimage but enjoying tribal dances and singing. Tourism is tainting some moussems but you should try to see one nonetheless.

FILMS

Among the cinema films shot in Morocco are Hitchcock's *The Man Who Knew Too Much*, the Marx Brothers' *A Night in Casablanca*, Orson Welles as *Othello*, Alec Guinness in *Lawrence of Arabia*, John Huston's *The Man Who Would Be King*, Zeffirelli's *Jesus of Nazareth*, and the classic *Ali Baba and the Forty Thieves*.

FLAG

Thousands of Moroccan flags fly in the country but seldom do you see two which are exactly alike. The flag should be red with a hollow green five-point star in the centre but on many the green has given way to gold and the star is leaning. See the rear cover.

GAS

Camping Gaz is available in 190gm cylinders, mainly from backstreet hardware shops. The price is 10DH.

GOVERNMENT and CONSTITUTION

Morocco is a democratic and social monarchy with a single chamber parliament. Under the present Constitution, issued on 10 March 1972, all citizens are equal before the law, all adults have the vote, and there is guaranteed freedom of movement, opinion, speech, and the right of assembly.

Islam is the state religion, but other religions are respected.

Independence. The former French Morocco became independent on 2 March 1956 with the former Spanish Morocco gaining its freedom on 8 April 1956; on that same date Tanger lost its status as an international zone and joined Morocco. It took several years for both sections of the country to achieve full political and financial unity, with the Spanish pulling out of Sidi Ifni as late as 1966 and the Spanish Sahara (Río de Oro) in 1975.

Monarchy. King Hassan II, born 9 July 1929, came to the throne on 26

February 1961. He is commander-in-chief of the Royal Armed Forces, he can appoint and dismiss his Prime Minister, and he presides over the Cabinet.

Parliament. The single-chamber parliament, the Chamber of Representatives, has 306 members elected for six years, two-thirds of them by direct vote and the remainder by an 'electoral college' of local government councillors and heads of the trade unions and industry.

Politics. Twelve political parties contest the seats and after the election of 14 September 1984 the *Union Constitutionelle* had 83 seats, but the Collective Independents had 61, the Socialists 36, the *Mouvement Populaire* 47 and *Istiqlal* ('Independence' — a word you often see on street maps) had 41. The others, including three trade unions, shared the remaining 38 seats.

HOLY DAY and REST DAY

It bears repeating that Friday is the holy day throughout the Islamic world, but the influence of Christian colonialism means that Sunday is the official day of rest.

MAP

The best map of Morocco is in the Red Cover series published by Roger Lascelles, 47 York Road, Brentford, TW8 0QP, at £3.95. It covers northern Morocco on a scale of 1:800,000 and the former Spanish Sahara on 1:2,500,000. It also has street maps of five cities.

Kümmerley & Frey's map is at 1:1,000,000 with the southern provinces at 1:2,000,000, and with six town insets.

There are several variations on spelling Moroccan place names, such as Marrakesh, Marrakech, Marräkush, Marrakch. I have followed the style of the Lascelles map except for Chefchaouene which I call Chaouen.

NEWSPAPERS

The three French-language provincial daily newspapers have near-nationwide distribution but still sell in relatively small numbers. *Maroc Soir* and *Le Matin du Sahara* are published from Casablanca, and *L'Opinion* from Rabat. The press is uncensored.

European daily newspapers are on sale in the large towns and tourist resorts one or two days after publication, for 12DH.

POLICE

The *Gendarmerie* in blue uniforms are in charge of state security and set up the occasional road checks; the *Sûreté Nationale* in smart khaki uniforms control the traffic in cities and fill the role of the police force in Britain. I find the *Sûreté* friendly and obliging.

POPULATION

Morocco has had a population explosion. In July 1971 there were 7,670,000 inhabitants. By September 1982 the number had risen to 20,419,555, including the few thousand occupants of the former Spanish Sahara. The UNO estimate for July 1986, of 22,476,000, showed a considerable reduction in the rate of increase; the birth rate is now 36 per 1,000 and decreasing. A million women are in the 5,450,000 workforce.

Casablanca has had a phenomenal increase in size and population from 20,000 at the start of the century to 2,408,000 in 1981, making it by far the country's largest city. Rabat and Salé together come second with 841,800.

POST OFFICE

The Post Office is the *Poste, Téléphone, Télégraph,* modelled on the French system. Postal and telephone services operate from the same building but using different doors, and in large towns the telephone office and kiosks never close.

At the moment it is easier to make international calls via the operator and the telephone office, but coin-operated call-boxes are being introduced. Place several 5DH coins in the slot on top of the apparatus, dial 00 for the international code, pause, then dial the national code and the local number, omitting the first zero.

PUBLIC HOLIDAYS

Morocco's public holidays are based on two calendars. Those on the Gregorian (Christian) calendar are fixed, but those on the Islamic calendar move back 11 days each year, except leap year, and are themselves subject to variation as most are governed by the moon's phases, like our Easter . Those marked with an asterisk (*) are in the Islamic calendar and are approximate for 1989; the dates were to be finalised within weeks of the event and after we went to press.

To complicate matters more, Islamic feasts are not held on the same dates throughout the Arab world, with Ramadan and the Islamic New Year as prime examples.

January	1 New Year's Day
April	12* Beginning of Ramadan
March	3 Fête du Trône (Accession of King Hassan II)
May	1 Fête du Travail (Labour Day)
	11* Aïd es Seghir, 'Little Feast' (end of Ramadan)
July	9 Fête de la Jeunesse (Youth Day)
	19* Aïd el Kebir, 'Great Feast' (Feast of the Sacrifice)
October	16* Mouloud en Nabi (Birth of the Prophet)
November	6 Marche Verde (Green March; civilian occupation of Spanish Sahara)
	18 Independence Day

PUBLIC TOILETS

There are extremely few public toilets in the towns. You will find them in all airports, almost all railway stations, on trains and in major bus stations, and they will be either acceptably clean or spotless.

Customers at service stations have to share the staff toilets, which are usually dirty.

The accepted answer, inherited from colonial days, is to use the toilet in a café or hotel, but in practice this is possible only if you're a client.

RADIO and TELEVISION

The government-controlled **Radiodiffusion Télévision Marocaine** operates from Rue El-Brihi, Rabat. Its radio broadcasts are on long and medium waves with a different band for each of the 22 towns with a transmitter; most of these towns have a television booster station as well — and most programmes are in Arabic. It also transmits on short wave in French, Arabic and Berber for west Africa and the Near East.

Radio Méditerranée Internationale, also government-controlled, is a commercial station operating from Tanger and broadcasting in French and Arabic on 1233KHz from Tanger and on 171KHz from Nador.

The **Voice of America** is heard from Tanger on a stream of channels: 5995, 7190, 9530, 11710, 11855, 15245, 17855KHz and 18 others.

Radio Ceuta broadcasts round the clock in Spanish on 88.5MHz FM, and **Radio Melilla** is on 96.6MHz FM.

Radio Gibraltar comes over loud and clear, in English, on 91.3, 92.6, 100.5 and 206m FM, between 0645-2400 daily, but reception doesn't penetrate far inland in Morocco. Neither does the **BFBS** station in Gibraltar with a 1kw transmitter on 93.5 and 97.8m.

The **BBC World Service** broadcasts daily in English from 0500-0730 on 48.43, 31.88 and 24.80m; from 0700-2115 on 19.91m; 0900-2300 on 24.80m again; 1615-2300 on 31.88m again, plus other bands. French and Arabic bands are additional. And you can occasionally pick up **BBC Radio 4** after dark as far south as Essaouira, provided there are no mountains on your northern horizon.

SPORTS

Surprisingly for a country of hot deserts, Morocco has a **ski season** lasting several months. Few Europeans ski here and no major winter sports operator features the country in its brochures; accommodation ranges from poor to good but access to the resorts relies on normal bus services or grands taxis, there is not much equipment for hire, tuition is unavailable, and après-ski is the inevitable disco or bar. But if you're a solitary skier looking for the unusual, then Morocco offers the only skiing on the African continent north of the equator.

The resorts are at **Oukaimeden** in the High Atlas 47 miles (75km) south of Marrakech and at **Mischliffen** in the Middle Atlas near Azrou, with solo skiing possible elsewhere.

Oukaimeden. (For transport, accommodation and a description of the area, see 'Marrakech Excursion.') The winter resort of Oukaimeden has the highest ski lift in Africa, which doesn't claim much, but when it was built it was the world's highest, at 10,739ft (3,273m). The lift is almost a mile long (1,600m), rising 2,500ft (750m), with six smaller lifts in the neighbourhood. There are five main slopes with names that sound eerie when translated into English...or Welsh: *Big Cwm, Route of the Crest, Big Route, Cwm of the Dead,* and others. A teleski is a recent addition, with a 975ft (297m) cable rising 256ft (78m).

Mischliffen. Mischliffen is not a village; it's a shallow volcanic crater around 2,000m altitude, accessible along the 1934 road from Ifrane, north of Azrou. Access from Ifrane is by taxi; to Ifrane from the world at large, by an adequate bus service.

The main ski lift is 1,520ft (463m) long, rising 633 ft (193m), with a secondary lift of 760ft (232m) rising 177ft (54m) for the nursery slope. The main slopes are colour-coded, red and black being difficult, blue moderate and yellow easy; they run a little more than 200m.

Accommodation is no problem provided you have the funds. Azrou has the Panorama (2*, 36 rms), the Azrou (1*, 10 rms) and Les Cèdres (1* 9 rms), but Ifrane offers the Michlifen (sic) (4*, 119 rms), Grand (3*, 44 rms), Perce-Neige (3*, 29 rms) and des Tilleuls (1*, 20 rms). They all have bars and restaurants but no après-ski life at all. There is limited equipment-hire in Ifrane. Other sports? Morocco has **golf** courses at Rabat (45-holes, 8 miles south-east of the city); Mohammedia (18 holes, par 73); Marrakech (18 holes, par 72); Tanger (18 holes); Agadir (18 holes) and Casablanca (9, going round twice, par 67). Casablanca also has the country's best football matches, at the Marcel Cedan Stadium.

There are **watersports available at the larger resorts, including windsurfing, parascending, water skiing and sailing.**

TELEPHONES — see POST OFFICE

TIME

Morocco is on GMT the year round. You therefore put your watch *back* an hour if you're going from Britain or Ireland when Summer Time is in force; from the remainder of western Europe, as well as from Ceuta and Melilla, you put your watch back *two hours*.

TIPPING

It's customary to tip restaurant waiters 10% if there's no service charge, with a similar tip to hairdressers and cinema usherettes. Hotel staff who do you a genuine service could expect a few dirhams.

WATER

North of Agadir, tap water is perfectly safe to drink but is occasionally heavily chlorinated, particularly in Marrakech. In remote areas in the south be careful not to drink water that has been exposed to possible contamination.

WEATHER

These weather statistics come from the Moroccan National Tourist Office:
Temperatures in °F/°C:

	JAN	APRIL	JULY	OCT
Agadir	69/20	75/23	80/26	78/25
Al Hoceima	61/16	67/19	83/28	74/23
Casablanca	63/17	68/20	81/27	77/25
Essaouira	64/17	66/18	72/22	70/21
Fès	61/16	72/22	97/36	81/27
Marrakech	66/18	79/26	102/39	82/27
Ouarzazate	63/17	80/26	102/39	80/26
Tanger	59/14	66/18	80/26	73/82
Zagora	69/20	86/30	108/42	86/30

Average hours of sunshine:

	JAN	APRIL	JULY	OCT
Agadir	249	313	330	251
Casablanca	163	249	331	239
Fès	157	241	375	237
Marrakech	209	278	364	241
Ouarzazate	214	305	342	239
Tanger	165	253	379	252

Figures, of course, don't show the drama of the weather: hold your bare arm out of a moving vehicle in midsummer and the 'scorch factor' verges on the painful. And these figures show nothing of the vast amount of hot air which rises off the land by day, bringing those onshore winds that occasionally give mists along the Atlantic coast.

WILDLIFE

There are scorpions and snakes in Morocco, but you won't come anywhere near them on a conventional package holiday. Hikers in the mountains and trekkers into the desert, particularly those who sleep in tents, stand a small chance of meeting a scorpion; its sting is extremely painful but seldom fatal. Wild boar live in the Atlas ranges, but you are much more likely to see the monkeys of the cedar forest south of Azrou.

The most visible bird in Morocco is the little egret, but you may also see an eagle riding the thermals or a pair of storks nesting on a tall building.

Hunting is allowed on the lake of Sidi Bourhaba (Boughaba) north of Rabat and on the Oued Massa south of Agadir, from October to February inclusive. Permitted targets include migratory birds which use these feeding places to build up reserves before the Sahara crossing.

Trees. Some strange mixtures of trees are found in the High Atlas, such as aspen, juniper and northern conifers growing beside olive, evergreen oak, mimosa, fig, the African thorn tree, and the eucalyptus. The *arganier*, an unusual tree found mainly between Essaouira and Agadir, looks like an olive but is grown for its foliage, used as fodder for goats — and the cloven-hoofed creatures climb these trees to get at the best shoots.

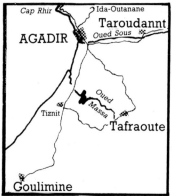

DISCOVER MOROCCO
9: THE MAJOR RESORTS

Agadir and Tanger

MOST EUROPEAN VISITORS SET FOOT ON MOROCCAN SOIL at Agadir on the desert's fringe, or at Tanger in the far north. We, too, begin our discovery of Morocco at these main resorts.

AGADIR

On Leap Year's Day 1960, at 13 minutes to midnight, an earthquake struck Agadir, killing 15,000 people and obliterating the town. On 3 March, King Mohammed V vowed the city would be rebuilt — and what you see today is the result of that promise.

The Agadir that rose from the ruins is a smart city of 250,000 people catering mainly for the tourist trade. With its infrastructure, it is the best beach resort in the country; it has a benign climate with day temperatures ranging from 70°F to 80°F — except when winds of high summer blow off the desert and send the heat soaring to 115°F. The town planners have avoided the grid system and the architects have ignored the high-rises that have spoiled so much of Spain, with the result that Agadir is interesting and attractive.

New Agadir. But it is no longer Moroccan. There is no medina, there are no souks, and the very atmosphere of Morocco has gone from the town. The only parts to survive the earthquake are the foundations of the Kasbah, on the hilltop to the north of town — but even here the walls have been rebuilt.

Modern Agadir is divided into sectors, like the old medinas — the residential quarter is to the north, and inland, the commercial district is in the centre, the smart hotels and the holiday villages of Club Med and Dunes d'Or (Golden Dunes) are on the beach, the Tafoukt district was created to house the boutiques selling leather goods with internationally-known brand names, and the cheaper hotels are clustered around the bus station.

The port is to the north, and the industrial area to the south, around the suburb of **Inezgane** and the airport. And in modern Agadir there is nothing to remind us of that Berber word *agadir*, which is a multi-storey fortified warehouse for farm produce.

Old Agadir. The Portuguese traders landed here in 1505 and added another fortress to their chain of castles along the African coast; they had captured Ceuta in 1415, sailed up the Gambia River in 1456, (see *Discover The Gambia* in this series), seized the Canaries, the Azores and Cape Verde, and early in the 16th cent they established several fortresses along the Moroccan coast. They called this latest settlement

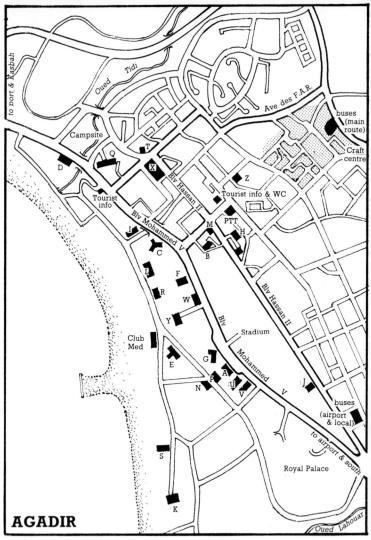

AGADIR

Santa Cruz do Cabo de Vao and when its builder sold his interests to the Portuguese king, Santa Cruz became an important trading station.

The Kasbah. Sultan Mohammed ech Sheikh built the kasbah on the hilltop to the north of town in 1540, 700 feet (215m) above the Portuguese-held city, which he seized the next year. Santa Cruz continued to prosper under its new owners, trading in sugar cane, leather, wax, dates, and a little gold, all drawn from the hinterland, but it took the name Agadir, the Berber word for a fortified granary. A century later the cultivation of cane sugar went into decline, taking the 'fortified granary' of Agadir with it.

In 1746, with commerce in decline, the Moors granted trading rights in Agadir to the Dutch, and both nations combined in the rebuilding of the kasbah in 1752, as shown by an inscription in Dutch and Arabic, carved above the main entrance which survived the earthquake. By 1760 trade was again thriving, but the Sultan Sidi Mohammed ben Abdallah, suspecting too much Spanish influence, closed the port to European merchants and built the rival Essaouira on a better natural harbour.

Gunboat diplomacy. Agadir was doomed, and a traveller in 1819 commented that there were only a dozen dwellings left standing. France expanded its colonial interests elsewhere in Africa later in that century, prompting a German consortium to buy large territorial concessions from the Sultan of Marrakech in 1910, if only to keep the balance of power. On 1 July 1911 the Germans sent their gunboat *Panther* into Agadir to warn the French not to seize too much of the country, an action which almost started the First World War three years early.

Treaty of Fès. France offered to give 100,000 square miles of the Congo to Germany in return for a free hand in Morocco, and war was averted for the moment. But this concession prompted the Treaty of Fès on 30 March 1912 which led to the creation of the French Protectorate of Morocco. The Franco-Spanish Convention of 27 November 1912 then gave Spain control of the northern part of the country, like two robbers sharing their spoils, and on 18 December 1923, France, Spain and

Britain agreed to set up the International Zone of Tanger.

Verdict. Agadir is an outstanding resort for beach-based holidays, with windsurfing, water-skiing, scuba diving and sailing available from the beach, and riding (camels or horses) and golf elsewhere; organised excursions go to Tafraoute, Taroudannt, and Marrakech via the scenic Tizi n'Test route. This is a smart and clean town, but is not the place to come if you want to see local colour. As in all of Morocco, the nightlife is confined to the hotel's entertainments — discos, ethnic dancing, and more discos — and is much more sedate than on the Costa del Sol, perhaps leaving the energetic younger generation bored.

HOTELS: see map for town hotels. The more expensive ones are block-booked by tour operators. Hotels in **Inezgane:** Hacienda (4*), 50 beds in bungalows in 17 acres; Pergola (2*), 23 rms; Provençal (3*), 40 rms (both on Rte d'Inezgane); Pyramides (3*) 25 rms, Rte Oued Souss; Orient (1*), 22 rms, Rte de Tiznit.

PENSIONS: The tourist office lists 20 'touristic residences' in the town. These would be *pensions* elsewhere, and offer basic accommodation with no meals.

HOLIDAY VILLAGES: Club Méditerranée; Dunes d'Or; Club Salam at Hotel Salam.

CAMPING: at north of town on Blv Mohammed V; good security but expensive; also takes caravans.

RESTAURANTS: not much choice, despite the tourist office's optimism. Mille et Une Nuit and others are near the main bus station and cheaper hotels, or for class try Les Arcades at Ave Allal beni Abdallah, between the bus station and the PTT.

NIGHTLIFE: most of the larger hotels have self-styled night clubs which are mainly discos with Bibylos's laser show probably topping the bill. Spectator entertainment includes the expected belly dancing, jugglers, and acrobats. **BUSES:** the main bus station for CTM departures is on Blv Mohammed Sheikh Saadi (see map); the SATAS depot is at Rue Yacoub el Mansour nearby. Local and airport buses and **grands taxis** go from Place Salam near the Royal Palace.

CAR & MOPED HIRE: more than a dozen car hire companies operate in the town, most with offices on Ave Mohammed V or Blv Hassan II and several with agencies at the airport. MotoRent on Blv du 20 Août has mopeds and small motor-cycles on daily or weekly rentals.

FESTIVALS: an African Arts Festival, usually in July.

TOURIST INFO: ONMT in Immeuble 'A' opposite the PTT; go up steps, walk 50 paces and look to your right; S.I, Ave Mohammed V.

AROUND AGADIR
Taroudannt

Taroudannt, with 30,000 inhabitants, offers a glimpse of historic and colourful Morocco within easy reach of Agadir. The rust-red mudbrick walls which completely encircle the town have been kept in good repair from the 18th cent until modern times, though the walls around the kasbah are older.

Within the walls there is plenty of open space, evidence that the town has known past glories. The built-up area is centred on two squares,

Place Assarag and Place Talmoklate, connected by the main street. The souks house a wider range of crafts than most, although they occupy only a small area. Here you can browse undisturbed among carpet weavers, jewellers, a few silversmiths (most of the Jewish craftsmen have gone to Israel) and leather workers — though the tannery is outside the town. Near the kasbah you may notice the Dar el Baroud, a palace built in 1909 but not open to visitors.

Old Capital. Taroudannt commands the Oued Sous, a rich valley which grew the produce the Portuguese shipped through Agadir, but the town was far enough from the sea to avoid being sacked. Founded in antiquity, by 1030 Taroudannt ruled the region until the Almoravides seized it in 1056. Its fortunes waxed and waned: it was destroyed in 1306, but the rebuilt town became the capital of southern Morocco from 1520 until Mohammed ech Sheikh drove the Portuguese from Agadir in 1541. Mohammed then unthroned his brother in Marrakech and moved himself and his new Saadian dynasty to the traditional capital.

Massacre. In 1687, at the end of the Saadian era, the town revolted against the new Sultan Moulay Ismail, who massacred much of the population and replaced them with tribesmen from the north. Agadir's fall from glory brought economic ruin to Taroudannt, but it had a brief spell of notoriety in 1912 and '13 when it relied on German support to defy the French administrators of the Protectorate.

Golden Gazelle. Despite this apparent treachery, the colonial bosses came here to escape from the pressures of city life. The French jet set still comes, patronising the out-of-town Hotel Gazelle d'Or, a five-star establishment that is one of the most exclusive in the country: it has just 28 rooms but offers all the luxuries you could wish for, including riding in the private grounds. The four-star Hotel Salam is in part of the old Saadian palace in the kasbah, and retains many of the original features.

Taroudannt today lives from its olive and citrus plantations, and it is probably the most northerly place in the country for seeing the 'blue people,' though most of the women wear all-enveloping black.

HOTELS: La Gazelle d'Or (see above, closed in August); Salam (see above); Saadiens (2*); Taroudannt (1*); de la Place (unclass). All but the first are in town.

BUSES: for Agadir, Casablanca and Marrakech (via Tizi'n'Test), Pl Assarag and Pl Talmoklate; for Ouarzazate, local buses and **grands taxis,** outside the town walls.

Tafraoute

Set in a spectacular sun-trap in the Anti Atlas mountains, Tafraoute offers an insight into a world remote from European customs; the package tourists at Agadir could come here by bus (five hours each way) or by hire car, spend one or two nights, and truly claim an experience to remember for years. If nothing else, the sunsets are a blaze of colour.

The town is distinctive, with 1,700 people of the Ammeln tribe living in two- or three-storey houses, sometimes with the projecting upper floors supported on stilts. Most of the men have left Tafraoute and its surrounding villages, forced to work in the cities to the north where, strangely, most run tiny grocery shops in the medinas, coming home for a few weeks each year.

But it is the countryside which cries for attention, with its arid rose-and-ochre granite outcrops rising to the rugged Jebel Lekst to the north, forming the sun-trap.

Tafraoute grows plenty of almonds and dates, carob and argan trees, and a little barley, and the best time to come here is in February when the almonds are in blossom and the temperature has yet to soar; there is a large almond festival at the end of the month.

Around 27 oases in the valley form the core for the outlying villages; there is no organised public transport and the minor roads are bad, so getting around is mostly on foot. Agard Oudad to the south is built at the base of a tapering rock known as the Finger, while at Oumesnat the houses cling to a steep rock face with arm-width streets cut into the granite.

HOTELS: Les Amandiers (4*) is a mock-fortress and over-rated, 60 rms; Redouane (unclass).
MARKET: Wednesday.

Tiznit

Tiznit is a garrison town of 40,000 people, begun in 1882 by Moulay el Hassan as a base for subjugating the tribesmen of the Sous valley and the Anti Atlas, and the 3 miles (5km) of pisé walls are a continual reminder of recent history. Strangely, these walls enclose eight or nine older ksour which are now lost in the medina.

In 1912 the upstart El Hiba proclaimed himself sultan here in opposition to the French and Spanish protectorates, and rallied the

support of the blue men to the south, so earning himself the title of the Blue Sultan.

The town's chief attraction is the Jewellers' Souk, to the left of the Mechouar — the principal square, formerly the parade ground — and just inside the main entry, the Three Gates (Trois Portes, Bab Tlata). The craftsmen are noted for their fine sabres and daggers, but don't try taking any through the customs.

Beside the Great Mosque is the *Source bleue de Lalla Tiznit,* the spring which feeds the Saint Tiznit river. It's now just a cement lining to a bubble of water, but legend claims that it marks the spot where a reformed prostitute established the first community of Tiznit, now named from her.

HOTELS: Tiznit (3*), 40 rms, Rue Ksebt n'Tafoukt; Mauritania (1*), 16 rms, Rue Goulimine; several unclassified hotels around the Mechouar.

TRANSPORT: buses leave from the Mechouar or Bab Oulad Jarrar; *grands taxis* from Mechouar or the main roundabout outside town.

FESTIVAL: Moussem of Sidi Abd er Rahman, August.

MARKET: Thursday, on Tafraoute road.

Goulimine

Goulimine's attractions are its blue men and its Saturday camel market, both of them more myth than fact although the market still draws coachloads of tourists on pre-dawn departures from Agadir. Sadly, it now seems to be· kept alive for the tourists, and it ceases altogether during summer. The reasons are clear: the government is trying to make the nomads settle down, the truck has displaced the camel, and the route to the south lies through the disputed territory of the Polisario. And the blue men don't come here in great numbers any more, either.

There is a better camel market of sorts at Asrir, 7 miles south-west, as part of the Moussem of Goulimine held once a year in June, but this is also in decline.

Forget the camels and accept Goulimine for what it was, the gateway to the Sahara and the starting point for caravans to Timbuktoo from the coming of Islam until our own generation. The town traded in salt going south, the northbound traffic being gold from Guinea (which is how the guinea coin got its name), and slaves from west Africa. If you feel the spirit of adventure you could hire a Land Rover and driver at an extortionate fee and sample the desolation that lies to the south.

There is nothing else to attract visitors to Goulimine, now an administrative town of 145,000 people, but the 125-mile (200km) journey from Agadir goes through some wild and rugged scenery. With your own transport you might visit the small oasis of **Aït Boukha** watered by a canal from the Oued Mait, or the 30-mile long **Plage Blanche,** 'White Beach,' 15 miles (25km) from Goulimine down a bad road. The beach, not surprisingly, is deserted.

Blue Men. You will hear much about the celebrated blue men of southern Morocco, but you will need to travel off the tourist trail to find a genuine one: there are plenty of fakes selling equally dubious souvenirs. The true blue men were nomadic Berbers who dyed their woollen clothes in indigo, which rubbed onto their skin and made them almost as blue as their clothing. The indigo plant is a perennial, its leaves and branches being crushed, then soaked in water which becomes the dye.

HOTELS: Salam (2*), 27 rms, Rte de Tan-Tan at town entry; the hotel might arrange a *guedra*, a dance by the blue women, with sufficient audience and advance notice. Several cheap hotels from here into town.

FESTIVALS: Moussem of Goulimine held in June at Asrir.

Immouzer des Ida Outanane

A 37-mile (60km) expedition into the mountains to the north leads to Immouzer des Ida Outanane, a spectacular journey that would warrant a party of people hiring a grand taxi. The road is tarred but narrow as it winds through the Gorge of Asif n'Tarhat, formerly known by hippies as Paradise Valley and forming their mountain hideout until Morocco decided it didn't want long-haired foreign men. The white houses of the Ida Outanane tribe cluster in a palm-grove at journey's end, and from the edge of the village of Immouzer there's a view over rugged mountains to the sea.

Immouzer produces honey, and visitors in July or August may find themselves at the Honey Festival; if you come in spring, cross the ridge to the next valley and see the waterfall tumbling into a tiny gorge filled with almond trees. The nearby **Auberge** des Cascades (3*, 28 beds) is a bit pricey but has a splendid setting.

The Petit Socco in the medina at Tanger

Paradis Plage

Paradis Plage stretches for miles from Tarhazoute almost to Cape Rhir. It's a splendidly scenic stretch of coast with rocky headlands breaking the beach into separate sections, all ideal for swimming and all lacking any basic amenities.

Tarhazoute village has a few shops and bars, plenty of roadside stalls selling the short Muscat bananas from the local plantations, but there's no water: a near-continuous file of young men carries it for miles. Almost everybody staying on Paradise Beach is camping, and to appreciate this type of holiday you must accept the privations and the lack of security — and bring your own tent.

TANGER

Tanger was English territory from 1661 to 1684, and when you hear the amount of English used in the medina you could be excused for thinking it still is under British rule.

If this is your introduction to Morocco you will certainly get a crash course into the country's culture, for Tanger is a mix of Europe and Africa, of French and Arabic — with quite a bit of Spanish and English thrown in — of the old medina with its rambling alleys and of the new town built to European design.

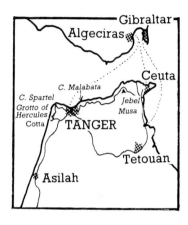

Tanger is larger than life, for it was a free-spending, easy-going international city from 1922 to 1956, with no taxes or duties, a growing reputation for financial deals that would be frowned on anywhere else, and an expatriate community that included the big spenders, the lesbians and the gays whose lifestyle was illegal in other cities, and the inevitable shady characters dodging the law of their native land. Take a tour of the town with an official guide and you will learn of other notable past residents, including the Marquis of Bute who built The Rock Hotel on Gibraltar.

Tighter Code. The loss of independence has ended the free port status, and the Islamic authorities have closed the brothels and the gay bars...most of them, at any rate. Tanger today is therefore living in part on its reputation, but with 305,000 people and a busy port and textile industry, it is also re-emerging as an important tourist centre.

First Impressions. If you come by sea as an independent traveller on foot you will get the impression that much of the population has turned out to greet you and show you the town, find you a hotel, or sell you everything you don't want. This is the harsh reality of the self-appointed tourist guide and until you learn to control it, it will inevitably control

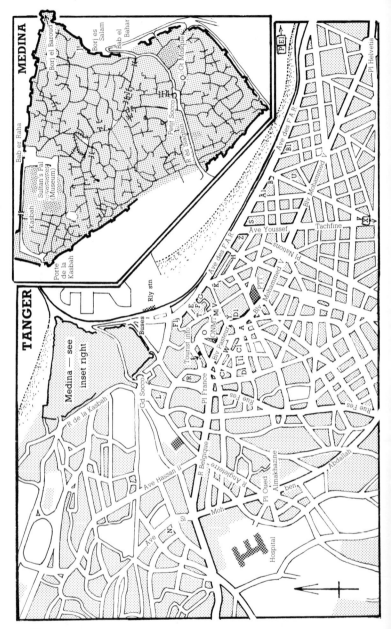

MEDINA

Bab el Baroud
Borj es Salam
Bab el Bahar
Gt Mosque
Borj er Raha
Bab er Raha
Kasbah
Sultan's Pal (Museum)
Pt Socco
R ès Siaghin
Porte de la Kasbah

TANGER

Medina — see inset right

R de la Kasbah
Gd Socco
Tourist info
Pl France
R France
Rue Fès
Blv Pasteur
Buses
Rly stn
Ave des F A R
Ave des F A R
Ave Youssef
Tachfine
Pl Nations
PTT
Blv Mohammed V
Blv Mohammed V
Pl Helvetia
Ave Hassan II
R Belgique
R Angleterre
Pl Oued
Almakhazine
ben
Abdallah
Moh
Ave
Hospital
Hospital

52

you. The independent air traveller who has come into town by bus will alight in the Grand Socco and avoid most of the hassle, only his luggage marking him out as a potential victim.

Grand Socco. The Grand Socco is the prime landmark of the *ville nouvelle* and its name shows how cosmopolitan the city is: *grand* is French and *socco* is the Spanish way of pronouncing the Arabic *souk,* 'market.' But the Grand Socco is no longer a souk; the markets have been moved to the south side of the medina on Rue Portugal, and the square is now a drop-off for buses and taxis, and is also known as Place du 9 Avril 1947 and the Souk Bar Ra. By the way, you will still see plenty of Spanish street signs such as *Calle* Magallanes alongside *Rue* Magellan though the Arabic *Zankat* is increasingly in use — in Latin characters as well as Arabic.

Budget Hotels. Magellan Street leads off the seafront Avenue des Forces Armées Royales near the second landmark of the new town, the Place de France. This part of the Avenue des F.A.R. has the cheaper hotels such as the Ibn Batuta, and is where you'll find the 'English pub, Tanger Inn.' A tangerine is not only a type of orange developed here, it's also an inhabitant of Tanger.

Place de France. The *place* leads east into Charih (Boulevard) Pasteur and gives access to a little square with a splendid view over the port and across the Strait of Gibraltar to Spain; on a clear day with binoculars you can pick out individual buildings in Europe. The third landmark is the Place des Nations Unis, also known as Place Oummame.

Mendoub. Opposite the Grand Socco are the Gardens of the Sadad Tribunal, still known as the Mendoubia Gardens from the *Mendoub,* the sultan's agent in Tanger during the rule of the International Commission. It was in the Mendoub's residence here, now the Law Courts, that Sultan Mohammed V announced in 1947 the start of the campaign for independence. Several 17th-cent cannons in the gardens are reminders of past naval battles in the strait.

Medina. On the north side of the Grand Socco an archway leads to Zanket al Kasbah (Kasbah Street), with an opening to the right leading

KEY TO HOTELS

A Africa (4*)	Q Mamora (2*) (in medina)
B Almohades, les (5*)	R Minzah, el (5*)
C Astoria (2*)	S Miramar (2*)
D Atlas (3*)	T Munira, el (1*)
E Biarritz (1*)	U Oumnia, el (4*)
F Bretagne (1*)	V Panoramic Massilia (2*)
G Cecil (1*)	W Paris, de (1*)
H Charf (2*)	X Pasadena (4*)
I Chellah (4*)	Y Rembrandt (4*)
J Continental (3*) (in medina)	Z Rif (5*)
K Djenina, el (2*)	A1 Sheherezade (3*)
L Grand H, Villa de France (4*)	B1 Solazur (4*)
M Ibn Batouta (1*)	C1 Tanger (3*)
N Intercontinental (5*)	D1 Tanjah Flandria (4*)
O Lutetia (2*)	E1 Tarik (4*)
P Malabata (5*)	F1 Valencia (1*)

into Rue des Siaghînes (Zanket es Siaghin, Silversmiths' Street), the main thoroughfare of the medina.

Cathedral. On the right, the Spanish Cathedral built in 1880 is now abandoned, and most of the Jewish silversmiths have left for Israel and Europe. Rue des Synagogues is still there on the right, leading to the Mellah, the Jewish quarter, and as you enter the Petit Socco you may see Rue des Chretiens (Christians' Street) on your left.

Petit Socco. The Petit Socco, Little Souk, or in Arabic the Souk Dakhil, was twice its present size until a collection of cheap hotels was built early this century, masking the sex parlours behind them. Here, in the heart of the International Zone, the pimps and drug pushers did their business, and during the Second World War the area was the unofficial meeting place for British and German secret agents.

An alley leads south to the far corner of the medina and the building which housed the United States legation from 1821; you might be able to go in and see some of the rooms.

Great Mosque. Rue de la Marine leads out of the Petit Socco, past the Great Mosque. Each town of size has one mosque more important than the others, the so-called 'grand' or great mosque, but this one is also great in size, filling a complete block. However, as non-Moslems are not allowed inside any Moroccan mosque, we must content ourselves with a glimpse at the highly-decorated main door and learn a little history: Sultan Moulay Ismail commissioned the building in the late 17th cent to mark the English withdrawal from Tanger in 1684, and Sultan Moulay Sliman enlarged it in 1815.

Kasbah. The main road turns left and wanders across the medina to the Kasbah, dominated by the Dar el Makhzen, the Sultan's Palace, built by Moulay Ismail shortly after the English pulled out. The English, in their 22 years of occupation, levelled the original medieval kasbah and destroyed much of Tanger's other defences.

Dar el Makhzen. Moulay Ismail (1672-1727) enlarged the palace but it was extended again in 1735, then Moulay el Hassan added to it in 1889, lending a hint of Italian influence in the architecture. Sultan Moulay Hafsid took up residence here in 1912 when the French forced his abdication, but he found the palace too cramped for his needs. More recently it has been converted into the Museum of Arts (standard opening hours, closed Tuesday), with the Museum of Antiquities in the neighbouring palace, Dar Chorfa.

All north Moroccan art and craft is represented in the larger museum, including weaving, basket-making, pottery, ceramics, carpet-weaving and, in the hall devoted to Fès, illuminated manuscripts, brasswork and silks.

The Antiquities Museum has a few palaeolithic exhibits but strongly features the Roman era, with an original mosaic from the House of Venus's Cortège in Volubilis and copies of several bronzes from there (these originals are in Rabat). On the first floor there is a collection of lead and clay-pot coffins, one of them containing the remains of a child.

Forbes Museum. While on the subject of museums, Zankat Assad ibn al Farrat, formerly Rue Shakespeare, leads from the kasbah main gate one kilometer to the Forbes Museum (open daily, 1000-1700), where American millionaire Malcolm Forbes's collection of 115,000 toy soldiers is on display, re-creating the Green March of 1975 and the battle of Dien Bien Phu in 1954, among others. There's a small display devoted to the works of British army officer Major Henry Harris.

Tingis. According to Greek mythology, Tanger was founded by Tingis, son of the sea-god Poseidon, and the Romans chose to know it by this name. After the sacking of Carthage in 146BC, Tingis became part of Mauritania which later had its capital at Volubilis, but by the 3rd cent AD political needs had brought the capital back north and the province became Mauritania Tingitana.

Gibraltar. The Vandals crossed over from Europe in 429, led by their king Genseric who made Tingis his capital. The Romans came back in 533 and stayed until the Islamic flood swept across north Africa under Musa ibn Nosseys in 706. Four years later Musa sent a scout across to Europe and in 711 he dispatched the Persian warrior Tarik ibn Zeyad from Ceuta to begin the Islamic conquest of Europe. Tarik landed at the rock which in Arabic is still called Jebel Tarik though we know it as Gibraltar. (See *Discover Gibraltar* in this series for the full story.)

The Arab chieftain Idriss ben Abdallah, fleeing from the new Abbaside dynasty in Baghdad, settled in Volubilis and became the target of the old Umayyad dynasty still in Spain. In the internecine battles that followed, Tanger changed hands several times — and was snatched in 958 by the Fatimites from Tunis.

Ibn Batuta. Other dynasties rose and fell, most of them occupying Tanger for a while: the Almoravides, the Almohades, the Hafsids and finally the Marinites in 1274. The geographer and explorer Ibn Batuta was born here in 1304 and later went on to visit Timbuctoo and China.

By the 15th cent the Portuguese, under their stay-at-home explorer Prince Henry the Navigator, were trying to sail around Africa to the east and so needed to develop outposts along the coast. They added Tanger to their collection in 1471, but in 1578 Portugal's king Sebastião I attacked the Moors at Ksar el Kbir (Alcazar-Kebir) and was killed in the Battle of the Three Kings. Spain absorbed Portugal, and so took control of Tanger which it held until 1640 when Portugal re-emerged as a free country.

English Colony. But Portugal didn't hold onto Tanger for long; the city joined Bombay as part of the dowry that the child-bride Catherine of Bragança brought to her marriage with England's Charles II in 1662. England couldn't make a success in Tanger, particularly with Moulay Ismail's troops laying a near-permanent siege to the city, and decided to pull out.

Samuel Pepys. Samuel Pepys, the secret diarist, was secretary to the commission sent to supervise England's withdrawal in 1684, but his Tanger diary lacks the forthright personal touch of his earlier jottings though there's no doubt he found the African experience very distasteful.

Morocco's monarchy went into an irreversible decline in the 19th cent and Tanger in particular became the town every European power wanted but none could justifiably seize. Germany had sent its gunboat *Panther* into Agadir and prompted the eventual partition of Morocco into French and Spanish protectorates in 1912 — but what of Tanger? Spain had held Ceuta and Melilla for centuries and so wanted to keep

Tanger as well. Britain felt it would go nicely with Gibraltar. France thought it would help in the administering of Algeria and French Morocco. And Germany didn't want anybody else to have it.

International Zone. And so came the compromise: nobody should have it. In December 1923 the International Commission — Britain, France and Spain — created the 140-square-mile International Zone and appointed 27 members to administer it: six were Moroccan Arabs, three were Moroccan Jews, and there were others from the signatory countries plus Italy, Belgium, Portugal and the Netherlands. Germany, which had tried to check French influence in the region but had lost the Great War, was not represented.

Free from the constraints of Islam — free, in fact, from almost all constraint — the International Zone flourished for everybody who wanted to live slightly outside the law, be it the law on taxes, finances, prostitution or general morality. And it also drew those who liked to sit and watch, with Ian Fleming, Camille Saint-Saëns and Tennessee Williams among those present.

In later years Allah el Fassi came to the zone to run the Istiqlal, the party formed in Fès in 1943 with independence as its aim. The Nationalist newspaper, *La Voix du Maroc*, set up its presses in Tanger, but still the party went on.

It stopped abruptly on 8 April 1956 when Spanish Morocco became part of the Kingdom of Morocco, and Tanger lost its international status. But if you go to some of the backstreet nightclubs you can still find a hint of what life used to be.

Verdict. Tanger offers variety and is very popular with one- or two-day trippers from the Costa del Sol and Gibraltar who want a cautious look at Africa. The city is cosmopolitan, with much of its activity along the Avenue des F.A.R. and its backstreets. The modern town has a busy port and ferry terminal, and beaches which are good but no rival to the Agadir strand.

Sights to see are concentrated in the moderate-sized medina and kasbah and will occupy a full day at most, but the immediate countryside offers some splendid scenery, notably across the Strait of Gibraltar to Europe, and the intriguing Hercules Caves near Cape Spartel.

Tetouan and Chaouen are within easy reach, but are not as spectacular as Tanger itself; Meknès and Fès are overpowering and warrant at least a two-day excursion. Ceuta is worth a visit only if you can tolerate the delays at the frontier — or why not fly to Gibraltar for the day?

The climate at Tanger is less extreme than on the Costa del Sol, and its beaches face north. Although this is Africa, it is a long way from the Sahara and the dramatic and extreme conditions of Agadir and its environs. Tanger is a good place for combining beach and culture, but if you venture out alone you must be prepared for some harassment.

HOTELS: the majority, regardless of their star rating, are between Blv Mohammed V and the Ave des Forces Armées Royales: see map for locations. There are several pensions in the medina and along the Ave F.A.R.

Hotels worthy of note include the unclassified Gran Socco on that square, convenient for incoming buses if somewhat noisy; the Continental at Rue Dar el Baroud in the north-east medina, once the town's top hotel and still full of character; the Fuentes in the Petit Socco where Saint-Saëns used to stay; and the Grand Hotel Villa de France for slightly decrepit charm.

Out of town hotels: Malabata (5*), at Malabata village 6km east, 600 beds; Ahlen Village (3*), Route de Rabat, 5km, 400 beds; Grottes d'Hercule (3*), 270 beds; Residence Ritz (2*), 1 Rue Soraya, 90 beds; Marco Polo (2*), Ave des F.A.R, 21 beds.

HOLIDAY VILLAGES: Club Méditerranée at Malabata, 7km east of town, 800 beds.

CAMPING: International-Miramonte, 500 sites, 3km west of town near seafront, bus 2 or 21; Tingis, near Club Med at Malabata, 6km east, and classy.

RESTAURANTS: there is no shortage of places to eat in Tanger, assuming you don't patronise your hotel's kitchens. For dining *à la marocaine* with a panorama, you could try Le Détroit (the Strait) in the kasbah, looking out over the medina walls and with Spain in the distance on a clear day.

For straightforward Moroccan-style eating try Damascus on Ave Prince Moulay Abdallah, Hammadi on Rue de la Kasbah or Ibn Batouta on Rue es Siaghîn in the medina. La Grenouille at Rue Jabha al Ouatania (formerly Rue Rembrandt, off Blv Pasteur), is a good French restaurant, or there's Claridge at 54 Blv Pasteur.

Romero at Ave Prince Heitier (Ave Prince Moulay Abdallah, also off Blv Pasteur) is a good Spanish restaurant for fish dishes. Indian dishes are the speciality of Khayam at the Almohades Hotel on Ave des F.A.R.

For dining with a floor show try the restaurants at the Minzah, Almohades or Solazur hotels, or take lunch with a miniature fantasia at the Ahlen Village.

NIGHTLIFE: pretty well confined to the first three hotels just mentioned. It's good, but no more than you would expect in Morocco, with belly-dancing the main attraction. The major hotels also have discos, but if you've seen one you've seen them all. For something a bit off-beat and a little down-market, join the late-night drinkers at the Tanger Inn on Rue Magellan. Ignore tales about the Tanger casino: there isn't one.

SPORTS: 18-hole **golf** course at the Royal Country Club; phone 389.25 for details. The yacht club at the port can put you afloat (385.75), and the Chellah Beach Club (404.59) on the Ave des F.A.R. offers windsurfing.

BUSES: CTM bus station is by the port, amid a cluster of smaller depots run by independent companies. **Grands taxis** also start from here and from Grand and Petit Socco.

RAIL: five daily train departures for Casablanca, with connections for Meknès and Fès.

FESTIVALS: Music Festival of the Strait (of Gibraltar), July; Moussem of Dar Zhirou, September.

TOURIST INFORMATION: ONMT, 29 Blv Pasteur; SI, Rue Khalid ibn el Oualid, a backstreet to north of Blv Pasteur.

AROUND TANGER
Hercules's Cave & Cape Spartel

The Grotto of Hercules is a popular call on organised tours but is difficult to reach on your own: you must either share a grand taxi or walk from the airport.

The caves are impressive but not spectacular; they were started by wave action in the cliffs and served as a shelter for prehistoric man, but later visitors found that the rocks were pure millstone grit and for centuries masons have been cutting small grinding stones from the cave walls, creating a bizarre effect as if you're looking inside a mould.

The last stones were scraped away about the time that Tanger went international, after which the licentious lot moved in.

Access nowadays is through shafts some little way inland (0900-1800 daily, for a fee) but as the high tide still surges into some of the caves, be careful.

Cotta. Half a mile inland lie the ruins of the Punic settlement of Cotta, later occupied by the Romans. The visible remains are the unimpressive foundations of a temple and some public baths, but history has a brighter story: Cotta produced garum, a vile concoction made from fish left to rot for months in clay jars.

Cape Spartel. The organised tour, or a long walk, will take you north to Cape Spartel, Africa's northwestern promontory, guarded by a stubby lighthouse (no access). The view is interesting on a clear day but your main concern will probably be the youths selling kaftans and camelskin bags. Inevitably somebody will tell you this is where the Atlantic and the Mediterranean meet, but that's not so.

Royal Palace. The most direct route back to Tanger goes through La Montagne, the smartest suburb and where there is yet another Royal Palace, though surprisingly with some squatters' shacks not far away.

Coast road to Ceuta. If you have your own transport and choose a day when there is no mist in the strait, the 54-mile (87km) drive along the S704 to the Ceuta frontier at Fnideq will reward you with some marvellous scenery.

The road is very twisty, with some steep gradients and patches of bad surface, but there are several parking spots for admiring the view. Cape Malabata offers a look back at Tanger but your main interest will be Spain and the shipping in the strait. As you pass Jebel Musa — Ape's Hill, one of the two Pillars of Hercules — you will see the other pillar, the Rock of Gibraltar, like a rugged island in the channel, and with binoculars you can pick out individual buildings on The Rock. The road ends with a bird's eye glimpse of Ceuta itself.

Ksar es Seghir. Midway along the coast run is the colourful fishing village of Ksar es Seghir, showing traces of its earlier Portuguese rulers. Its beach is visible from Europe on a clear day.

10: MINOR COAST RESORTS

Not in the major brochures

EVERY SUITABLE HOTEL NEAR A BEACH is in somebody's holiday brochure, but the resorts in this chapter are for the specialist visitor. Some are hedonists' delights, such as the Club Méditerranée hideouts, while others are historic towns such as Essaouira which is a working Moroccan town rather than a resort. In these locations the package tourist will be in much more contact with local culture, seeing the country as it really is — and that includes the self-appointed guides, though in fairness I must stress that they are only a passing irritant in the minor resorts. The list is alphabetic.

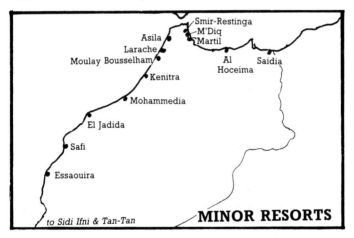

MINOR RESORTS

AL HOCEIMA

Al Hoceima is a strange town. It was founded by the Spanish in 1926 as Villa Sanjurjo, a fishing port on the Mediterranean coast and which could also serve the Peñon de Alhucemas, the fortified island in the bay which had been under Spanish sovereignty since 1660 — and still is, with absolutely no access from Morocco. A few Spaniards remained in Villa Sanjurjo after independence but the majority of foreign visitors now are French package tourists who join Moroccans on the beach, with the Club Méditerranée bringing in the Britons.

It's an attractive resort, with a heavy Spanish influence in the architecture in the old part of town, though the modern hotels are the inevitable characterless blocks. The town beach is small, set in a deep, cliff-girt bay and extremely crowded in high summer, though the police still maintain the strict ban on beachwear being worn anywhere but on the sands.

To the east of town, a wide beach stretches for several miles around the main bay, where you will find Club Med and the camping sites.

Peñon de Alhucemas. The main island in the bay, the Peñon de Alhucemas, is heavily fortified and totally impregnable to anything short of heavy artillery. The two lesser islands are just rocky crags, but they're all out of bounds to Moroccans and are a continual source of friction between Rabat and Madrid.

With the collapse of the Saadian dynasty in the 17th cent, European powers planned to carve up Morocco. In 1661 the French Cardinal Jules Mazarin realised the English had designs on these rocks and suggested France should seize them or, failing that, urge Spain to do so. Merchants from Marseilles tried to establish an outpost in 1666 but couldn't reach an agreement with Moulay Rachid, then the Spanish announced the Saadians had granted them a concession in 1660 and the French had better stay away. Spain occupied the peñon in 1673 and built the tower which still dominates the fortress today.

Spain also holds onto the Islas Chafarinas near the Algerian border and the Peñon de Velez de la Gomera, a tiny rock west of Al Hoceima, as well as Ceuta and Melilla. I'd love to know why!

HOTELS: Quemado (3*, 102 rooms, Apr-Oct, night club) is on the beach and has the tiny **tourist office** as neighbour. All other hotels are at the top of the steep hill into town: Mohammed V (4*) and its annexe (3*) with 95 rooms total, on Ave Mohammed V; Maghreb el Jadid (3*, on same avenue); National (2*, Rue Tetouan); Karim (1*, Ave Hassan II) and unclassified Essalam, Marrakech and Turismo.

HOLIDAY VILLAGES: Club Med, 1,200 beds, May-September; on the main beach with a good view of the Peñon de Alhucemas.

FURNISHED FLATS: Maroc-Tourist Villas. Write Boîte Postale 408, Rabat, well in advance of your journey.

CAMPING: Plage el Jamil and Plage Cala Iris; Jamil has a restaurant and electricity and prefers caravans on its 2.5-acre site.

TRANSPORT: CTM depot in town centre, but check departure times as some are *very* early. Also an airport; see Chapter 4.

ASILAH

There are two interesting facets to Asilah. The obvious one is the beach, stretching southwards almost to Larache, and to the north almost without a break to Cape Spartel. The less obvious feature is the story of Raissuli, the 'Pasha of Asilah,' and his 20th-cent palace.

Asilah is a town of around 20,000 inhabitants, 28 miles (46km) south of Tanger and on the Atlantic coast. The beach is excellent and the main attraction for tourists, but you will need to bring all your gear, from bucket and spade to windsurfer.

Founded by the Phoenicians as Zili, the town was minting its own coinage before Carthage, but the Romans rounded up the entire population and shipped them to Spain, sending back Spaniards to fill the gap.

Portuguese Occupation. Shortly after Portugal had captured Tanger, it sent 477 ships and 30,000 men who seized Asilah on 24 August, 1471. During their occupation the Portuguese built the ramparts which still encircle the medina, and you might just see the weatherworn arms of Alfonse V over the Porta da Terra, 'Landport Gate,' now the Bab Homar.

King Sebastião I of Portugal landed his army of 20,000 soldiers here in 1578 when he set out on his grand scheme to conquer Morocco, but he was killed at the Battle of the Three Kings at Ksar el Kbir, which led to Spain taking Portugal and all its possessions, including Asilah.

The Moroccans Arrive. Moulay Ahmed al Mansour seized Asilah in 1589 but the bloodthirsty builder of Meknès, Sultan Moulay Ismail, built two mosques and a Koranic school and brought in forced migrants from the Rif. The Europeans continued to harass, with naval bombardments in 1829 and 1860, but worse trouble was on the way.

The Pirate Pasha. Er Raissouli was born in the Jebala mountains near Chaouen in 1858. Starting as a rustler at the age of ten, he quickly made his reputation as a brigand and terrorist, and in 1876 was thrown into prison. On his release 18 years later he went back to his mounain home and soon kidnapped the *Times* journalist Walter Harris and two Americans, ransoming them for £14,000 and using this power to become the accepted head of the Jebala tribes.

In 1906 Raissouli moved into Asilah and declared he was a direct descendant of the Prophet; two years later the sultan had to acknowledge him as the town's pasha. In 1909 Raissouli built his palace in the medina, overlooking a jagged cliff, bragging that he used forced labour.

The Spanish sent him thousands of guns and millions of pesetas in the hope that he could overthrow the sultanate, but Raissouli was already bargaining with the Germans who had promised that he should be the new sultan. "The Berbers are my servants, the Spanish my slaves, the French my enemies and the Germans my allies," he boasted.

But Germany lost the First World War and in 1918 the disillusioned

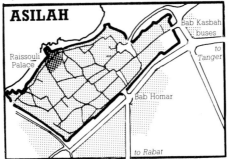

Spanish drove Raissouli from Asilah. He died in 1925, unknown and unlamented.

Raissouli's Palace. His palace is now officially the Palace of Culture and home of a festival in August, and is open to the public at other times with some persuasion and a few dirhams.

HOTELS: Al Khaima (3˙), out of town on Rte de Tanger; Oued el Makhasine (2˙), Ave Melilla, near beach; Oasis (2˙), Place Nations Unies; Asilah (1˙), 79 Ave Hassan II, outside ramparts near Bab Homar; Marhaba (unclass), Ave Hassan II.

CAMPING: near the railway station.

TRANSPORT: buses and taxis leave from outside Porte de la Kasbah at end of Route de Tanger; the railway station is 2km along this road.

EL JADIDA

In 1502 a Portuguese ship was wrecked off this coast, 60 miles (98km) south-west of Casablanca. There were European merchants only a few miles away at Azemmour and the local tribesmen were paying tribute to Portugal, so the survivors put up a small fortress to start another colony. Four years later (or eight or twelve years, according to other chroniclers) the Portuguese began building a walled town around it, calling it Mazagan. From the outside it looked like a medina, but inside those sturdy walls, Mazagan had reasonably wide streets set at right-angles and was nothing like a traditional Arab town.

Soured Relations. With the creation of Mazagan, relations between the Europeans and Moors began to turn sour at Azemmour, where both races shared the tiny town, so the Portuguese made this exclusively-European venture their main commercial port on the north African coast, and built a vast underground cistern in the town centre to help them survive the threatened sieges from Sultan Moulay Abdallah.

Spain controlled Mazagan after the Battle of the Three Kings in 1580, but the Portuguese were back after their homeland regained its independence from Madrid in 1640, and they stayed until Sidi Mohammed ben Abdallah seized the town in 1769.

The Moors renamed their trophy El Jadida, 'the new,' and converted the lighthouse into the great mosque, but they retained the European character of the old town and even allowed the churches to remain.

Mazagan Again. Under the French Protectorate the old title of Mazagan came back into fashion and cast-iron plates went up on the street corners, restoring the original Portuguese names. European merchants increased their business, leading to the creation of the new port beside the old *Cité Portugaise*. After independence the name reverted to El Jadida, the town continued to expand to its present 150,000 population, and it became a popular beach resort for Moroccans.

The *Cité Portugaise*. The old Portuguese city still retains enough character to distinguish it from an Arab medina; look at the street plan, the elaborate Portuguese doorway of a house in Rua da Nazareth or, more particularly, the Portuguese cisterns on the main street, Rua da Carreira, also called Rue Moamed al Ahchemi Bahbah.

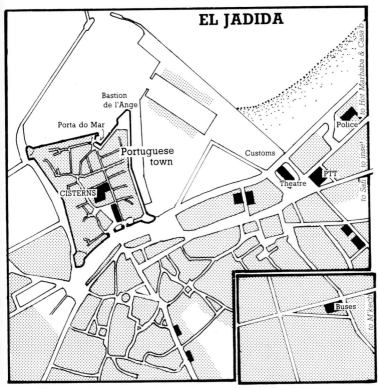

Cisterns. The Portuguese began digging this underground chamber in 1514, but authorities again disagree on the original use: was it an early warehouse or arms store, or was it always designed as a reservoir? Certainly it was soon brought into use for storing water, and with a floor area of 108 by 112 feet (33m x 34m) it could hold 600,000 gallons if filled two metres deep.

The vaulted roof is supported on 25 columns and nowadays there is usually only a thin film of water on the floor to provide bizarre reflections, such as those which created an unusual effect for a sequence in Orson Welles's *Othello*. Opening hours are nominally 0700-1300 in summer, 0800-1230 and 1400-1600 in winter, with a 2DH admission fee.

Ramparts. If you want to walk along the ramparts, buy your admission ticket at the cistern then walk back to the Bastion St Espirit near the town gate and look for a man to unlock the big brown double doors to the left of a souvenir shop. You'll be able to walk along the top of the walls from here to the Bastion de l'Ange (Angel's Bastion) and to the Porta do Mar, the old Portuguese Sea Gate, now closed by a wrought-iron door.

ESSAOUIRA (Mogador)

Bab el Bajar
North Bastion
Kasbah Sqala
KASBAH
Museum
R Derb Laalouj
R Si Moh ben Abdallah
Ave l'Istiqlal
R Moh Zerktouni
R Moh el Gorry
Bab Doukkala
buses
Boul Moulay Youssef
PL Moulay el Hassan
buses
Tourist info
Port Sqala
Fishing port
Gt Mosque
MEDINA
Bab/Marrakech
Bab es Sebaa
South Bastion
PTT
Boul Mohammed V
way out of town
↓
to Purpuraire Is

KEY TO HOTELS
A Atlantique
B Beau Rivage
C Iles, des (4*)
D Mechouar, du (1*)
E Remparts, des (1*)
F Sahara (2*)
G Tafraout (1*)
H Tourisme, du
(Tafouket (3*): *on Blv Mohammed V*)

The Church of the Asssumption, completed in 1628 and standing just inside the town gate, is now an assembly hall and theatre, devoid of any Christian relics.

Beaches. El Jadida's beach is good, though there are rocks to the north. It's popular with Moroccans in high summer, which puts pressure on the accommodation. There are several other beaches to the south, notably at Sidi Bouzid and, 7 miles (11km) from town, Moulay Abdallah, both within reach by taxi.

Tit. Moulay is close to the near-vanished walls of Tit, a fortress village built in the 12th cent to subjugate the local Berber tribe of the Dukkalah. The ribat of Tit incorporates a minaret similar to that of the Koutoubia Mosque of Marrakech, and another which has been dated to 1060 and was possibly a defence against a Norman conquest — the Normans had seized southern Italy and Sicily and were soon to take Malta out of the Islamic world.

Lighthouse. A few miles further on you might be lucky enough to climb the 248 steps to the top of the Cap Blanc lighthouse. The Syndicat d'Initiative in town used to grant permission but now the tiny office is closed and you're on your own.

Transport to Cap Blanc isn't easy, your options being grand taxi or the bus to Jorf-Lasfar and walk. Jorf-Lasfar isn't a place to linger in; Spanish and Japanese finance is building a large port here to ship out the phosphates of the hinterland rather than route them through Casablanca.

Azemmour. The Portuguese had been established at Azemmour, 10 miles (17km) east of El Jadida, since 1486, on the site of what may have been the Punic Azama, buying wheat, horses and textiles, some of which they bartered for slaves on the other side of the Sahara. But when their kinsmen built Mazagan, relations with the Moors deteriorated and the Europeans pulled out of the town in 1541.

The only remaining sign of Portuguese presence is in the kasbah which they built and which is now in ruins, but the small medina to the south is Arab and much later.

A half-hour walk through the medina takes in all the town has to offer, but if you go to the bridge over the Oued Oum er Rbia ('Mother of Springtime') you'll have a grand view of the old walls. The oued, by the way, is one of Morocco's largest rivers and one of the few which flow all through the year.

HOTELS: see map. Off the map is the Doukkala (4*), Rue Jamaia al Arabia. There are no cheap hotels in the old town. Azemmour has only one basic hotel, near the bus station beside the main gate.

TRANSPORT: see map for bus station, off Ave Mohammed V. Grands taxis are available outside the town gates. The railway station is south of town, on the new branch line from Casablanca.

ESSAOUIRA

As with so many fortified towns along this coast, Essaouira owes its origins to European intervention. Today it's a pleasant place 125 miles (200km) north of Agadir, with a good beach close to the town centre, an unusual medina, and a fishing port. Quiet and with little hassle, it is worth a stopover of two or three days.

Purple Islands. The Phoenicians came here in the 7th cent BC, built a small settlement on the coast and used the two rocky isles to the south for collecting salt. The Romans found the isles were a breeding-ground for the shellfish which produced the rich purple dye used on the imperial togas, and so gave rise to the name by which the rocks are still known in French, Les Îles Purpuraires. They are a sanctuary for gulls and the Eleanora falcon, and if you convince the tourist office staff you're an ornithologist you might buy a *permis*, haggle for a boat, and visit the Purple Isles, one of which is now crowned by the hulk of a prison — the place where Raissouli was jailed from 1876 to '94, before he became the pirate pasha of Asilah.

Mogador. The Phoenicians probably built a lookout tower, a *migdol* in Punic; by the 11th cent the Moors were calling the little settlement Amogdoul and the town's Islamic holy man took the name Sidi Mogdoul: he is Essaouira's patron saint to this day. The Portuguese corrupted Mogdoul to Mogdoura, and from 1580 the Spanish called it Mogador, the name that stuck until independence in 1956.

The Portuguese built a fortress at Mogador in 1506 but lost the town to the Moorish Moulay abd el Malik in 1628. Mogador slumbered on until 1760 when Sultan Sidi Mohammed ben Abdallah developed it as an alternative to Agadir, then in revolt.

French Architect. Surprisingly, he chose a European to design his new town. His French prisoner, Theodore Cornut, based his plans on two intersecting main streets and so managed to implant the symbol of the cross in an Islamic community, but history doesn't record whether this was accident or intent. Around this time the town began to be called Essaouira, which some authorities claim is Arabic for 'well-designed' or even 'little ramparts,' but linguists at the tourist office insist the name has no meaning in Moroccan Arabic.

According to an inscription, a renegade Englishman built the small port in the year of the hegira 1184 (1769), and it is now the nation's third largest handler of sardines.

Essaouira Today. The distinct European style of architecture, and the grid pattern of the main streets, give the Essaouira medina a character found nowhere else in Morocco; El Jadida is a medieval European town dropped in Africa, but Essaouira is Islamic African with heavy European overtones. The main souks are around the centre of town where the Rue Mohammed el Gorry (Qory) meets Ave de l'Istiqlal and Rue Mohammed Zerktouni, and at the base of the Sqala de la Kasbah where woodworkers produce high quality furniture and delicate marquetry: if you want a genuine Moroccan souvenir, buy it at a place such as this where there are few other European tourists to induce low quality work.

Sqala. The fortified town has two sqalas (artillery platforms) of which the Kasbah Sqala is by far the larger. This is an impressive raised platform around 40 feet by 600 feet (14m by 200m) which allowed cannons to be mounted at the top of the ramparts and fired between the merlons (crenellations). The impressive collection of 16 cannon, plus two in the north bastion, was cast in bronze or iron in Spain from the late 16th to the mid-18th cents, and most came as presents from European merchants anxious to trade in the town. The dramatic setting, with the view over the parapet to the sea-washed rocks, was used for several location sequences in Orson Welles's *Othello*. The other sqala? It's much smaller and guards the port.

Sidi Mohammed Museum. Leaving the Kasbah Sqala by the Rue Derb Laalouj, you will find the Sidi Mohammed ben Abdallah Museum which, like the next street, is named from the sultan who created the modern town and who is almost revered as its second patron saint. The museum (standard times excluding Tuesday), has exhibits of musical instruments and Berber sheet music, and of the tools and clothes of daily life in past ages.

HOTELS: see map. Hotel des Iles (126 beds) is the smartest and most convenient for the beach, but is characterless. Hotel des Remparts (45 beds) has plenty of character but no restaurant.

CAMPING: municipal camping site on Boul Mohammed V on edge of town; showers and toilets available.

RESTAURANTS: Chalet de la Plage caters for European palates; Chez

The Spanish cannons in the Sqala de la Kasbah at Essaouira were cast in the 16th to 18th centuries

Sam in the port serves unbeatable fish dishes; other restaurants are around Place Moulay el Hassan where you can also buy freshly-grilled fish in the street.

TRANSPORT: CTM office is on Place Moulay el Hassan; CTM and other buses leave from Bab Doukkala.

FESTIVAL: Moussem of Sidi Mogdoul in summer.

TOURIST OFFICE: S.I, in a small island-office by Place Moulay el Hassan.

Around Essaouira

From the roundabout outside of town the road branches left for Marrakech, offering some good views of Essaouira as it climbs. The right branch to Agadir was closed in 1988 due to a collapsed bridge and may remain closed. It still gives access to **Diabat,** a Berber village with unhappy memories of European drug-addicts.

You'll really need a car to reach the **dunes** inland of Cap Sim, now 40 road miles (65km) from Essaouira due to that broken bridge. The persistent onshore winds have created this duneland which is a cameraman's dream of what the Sahara ought to be — and with the sea in view and civilization not far away. No wonder the area is popular with film-makers.

Near the mouth of the oued on which Diabat stands, the dunes have almost covered the 18th-cent palace and the nearby fortress of Sultan Sidi Mohammed ben Abdallah, who wanted to watch over his creation from a comfortable distance.

Haha. The main coast road, P8, leads south to Agadir through some splendid semi-arid coastal scenery where you'll again see goats clambering up the branches of the argan trees. Around 22 miles (35km) from the Diabat turning, a sign points inland to the village of Tnine Imi n'Tlit. The track wanders into the mountains for around 10 miles (17km) and is not suitable for saloon cars, but if you are in the mood for a long walk, preferably in winter, you can reach the lookout post on the top of **Jebel Amsittene,** 2,970 ft (905m) above the hazy sea. The view extends all round, and is particularly impressive to the south, into the High Atlas. To the north are the lands of the Haha, a Berber tribe almost wiped out during 14th-cent feuds.

Inspecteur Watler. A few miles north of Essaouira the Lascelles map marks 'Inspecteur Watler,' a forester's hut with a good sea view; north again, is the **Belvédère du Chicht,** another spot for splendid cliff panoramas, but accessible only by car.

KENITRA

Kénitra has a tourist office, but it's not a resort by any stretch of the imagination. The beach is wide, but 7 miles (12km) away at **Mehdiya Plage,** and the sand is fine-grained but greyish. Mehdiya Plage is popular with Moroccans seeking a break from Rabat, 25 miles (40km) south-west, but there's little to interest the European sun-lover. The beach is rather exposed and *currents can make it dangerous for swimmers.*

Mehdiya itself has another of those kasbahs built by Europeans: the Spaniards in this case, who seized the estuary of the Oued Sebou in 1614 to drive out the Barbary pirates who were lurking there. The original kasbah was built in the late 13th or early 14th cent by the Almohade sultan, Abd el Moumen, on the site of the 5th-cent Carthaginian settlement of Thymaterion. Moulay Ismail, builder of Meknès, drove the Spanish out of the kasbah in 1681, but most of their masonry and several of their cannon are still in place today, with the addition of a monumental gateway built on Moulay Ismail's orders; you'll probably find a badge-wearing official guide on duty here.

Port Lyautey. Kénitra itself is a port on the Oued Sebou, with 800 metres of quayside for loading Mamora wood and cork for export, and 450,000 people in the town — a rapid rate of growth for a community that didn't exist before 1913 and was created by the French for their own benefit: indeed, from 1933 until independence in 1956 it was known as Port Lyautey, named from the first French resident general.

Two points of history. In 1942 the United States landed troops at Mehdia at the beginning of their North African Campaign, and in 1972 Moroccan troops at the nearby air base staged a *coup d'état* which failed.

Mamora Forest. Between Kénitra and Salé, the cork oaks of the Mamora Forest stretch from the coast 40 miles (60km) inland, covering the sandy plain. Wild pear, laburnum, mimosa and pines are scattered in the forest, with increasing plantations of eucalyptus to feed the paper mills of Sidi Yahya du Rharb, east of Kénitra. The cork oaks are also exploited: the first peeling of cork, the so-called male bark, is discarded, but thereafter the thicker female bark is harvested every nine or ten years.

Lake Sidi Bourhaba. Having criticised Morocco for allowing the shooting of migratory birds on Atlantic wetlands I cannot ignore the wildlife reserve of Lake Sidi Bourhaba (Boughaba) south of Mehdiya. The country urgently needs more such sanctuaries.

Thamusida. Thamusida is 10 miles (17km) north-east of Kénitra and close to the main road to Tanger, which is fortunate, for the ruined 2nd-cent fortified camp is not signposted, is difficult to find, and is not spectacular.

Turn west off the road onto a poor track near the 'Kénitra 14km' stone and keep straight on. Thamusida is around 150 metres square and offers the ground plans of a Roman army camp with the supporting services of a small civilian community.

HOTELS: Mamora (2*), Ave Hassan II, with night club; La Rotonde (2*), Ave Mohammed Diouri; Ambassy (sic, 1*) Ave Hassan II; Astor (1*) Ave Mohammed V; Europe (1*), near La Rotonde. **Mehdiya Plage:** Atlantique (2*).

RESTAURANTS: Camping La Chênaie, Kénitra; Auberge de la Forêt, Mehdiya Plage.

TRANSPORT: railway station south of town; buses from Ave Mohammed V; taxis near the market.

LAAYOUNE

Laayoune is at the back of beyond — and at the frontier of the Sahara. This is positively the end of the road as far as regular public transport is concerned, and for the casual tourist: if you venture south of Laayoune you're a traveller and you need the equipment, the stamina, and usually the permission of the Moroccan authorities.

Around 100,000 people live here in a town created in the past decade to exploit the phosphates of Boukra, 75 miles (120km) south, in the province the Spaniards once called the Río de Oro, 'River of Gold.' Morocco didn't seize this vast expanse of sand and rock purely for territorial claims: it wanted the mineral wealth.

Laayoune is built to a European-inspired street plan along the bank of the Oued el Hamra and has absolutely nothing to inspire the visitor but, as tourists are rare, you may see several blue men and know them to be the genuine thing.

Laayoune Plage. Twelve miles (20km) west of town the Sahara meets the Atlantic and provides a good beach with occasional surf, but there are no resort facilities yet. A little to the south is Laayoune-Port, from where ferries sailed to the Canary Isles until Laayoune airport took over the link. The port is now busy with the phosphate trade, and both are expanding.

HOTELS: Al Marria Khadra (4*); Parador (2*); Residencia (2*); Marhaba (unclass).

TRANSPORT: Buses to Agadir, including express coaches; also to Smara, 150 miles (250km) inland. Air links with Agadir, Casablanca, Tan-Tan, Gran Canaria and a few others.

LARACHE

The Spanish influence is still strong in Larache, though it was founded in the 7th cent by Moslem invaders, the tribe of Beni Arous. They established a vineyard here — *el araïch* in which the modern name has its origins. And don't be misled: early followers of the Prophet loved their grapes even if later interpretations of the Koran led to the banning of alcohol.

An 11th-cent Moorish scribe wrote of a 'great city' here, 38 miles (62km) south of Tanger, and the Portuguese considered it the maritime capital of Barbary. But it was the Spanish who sailed into the port in 1471 and seized the place, shortly after the Portuguese had captured Asilah and Tanger.

The Portuguese grabbed Larache in 1489, but lost it within weeks to the Sultan of Fès, Mohammed es Said. His brother, Moulay en Nassir, built the kasbah in 1491 and allowed Algerian and Turkish pirates to operate from it, their ships being protected by the sand bar forming across the mouth of the Oued Loukos.

See-saw. João de Meneses, Portuguese governor at Asilah, didn't like that and seized the pirate galleys in 1504, burning some and taking the others as prizes. The Spanish attacked the town in 1546, and in 1610 Sultan Moulay el Mamoun gave Larache to Felipe III of Spain in return for favours. Portuguese, Dutch and Turks attacked, but Moulay Ismail snatched it back in 1689; the French bombarded the kasbah in 1765 and prompted the Moors to strengthen the defences. Even the Austro-Hungarians had a go in 1829, with the Spanish having the final say with a bombardment in 1860 while their main force attacked Tetouan. And with the partition of Morocco in 1912, Spain again took Larache, staying until 1956.

Castillo de la Cigüeña. Traces of the Spanish occupation are all over town in the bars, the Casa de España restaurant and even the Spanish Consulate, but the main landmark, Castillo de la Cigüeña, the Stork's Castle, was built in 1578 by Moulay Ahmed al Mansour, using Portuguese prisoners taken at the Battle of the Three Kings — and it's still an impressive monolith on the approaches to town.

Beach. Larache is a reasonably pleasant place of 70,000 people, but the port and the strong smell of decaying fish tend to dominate the river front. The excellent Plage Rasrmel is on the peninsula across the Oued Loukos, accessible either by a number 4 bus and several miles of terrible road, or by fishing-boat ferries which at weekends depart in an endless flotilla.

HOTELS: Riad (2*), Rue Mohammed ben Abdallah, former home of a French duchess; España (1*), Ave Hassan II, Spanish charm; Cervantes (unclass) nearby, dull. Several budget hotels in the medina.

LIXUS. Lixus, two miles east of Larache, is one of the two most important historical sites in Morocco, marking the first known settlement of Neolithic man in this part of Africa 10,000 years ago, yet you'd be forgiven for thinking it an insignificant heap of old stones. It's not fenced, and the only sign saying 'Lixus' points down the rutty road to Larache beach although the ruins are conveniently at the junction itself. Being unfenced, there are no opening hours; you just walk onto the site.

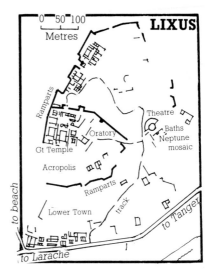

There are no self-appointed guides either, but there is a badge-wearing old man who'll politely point out everything, in French.

Garden of the Hesperides. Lixus is probably the site of the Garden of the Hesperides, the three nymphs who guarded the golden apples of Hera, the Greek goddess of childbirth and wife of Atlas. Finding the gardens, and the sacred apples in them, was one of the twelve labours of Hercules. You, mere mortal, can find the Pillars of Hercules and the Atlas Mountains, but not the Gardens of the Hesperides: they belong to mythology.

Moving into tangible history, the ruins of the Lixus we see today may have been built by Phoenicians from Tyre around 1100BC, but the city was certainly thriving in the 7th cent BC under the name of Makom Shemesh, Sun City, according to Punic coins found on the site. Shemesh ceased minting coins around the time of Christ, when Juba II was the King of Mauretania, but the name *Shamush* has survived here to modern times and now means 'sunburnt.'

Romans. The Romans came around 43AD and made Lixus one of their colonies and a major producer of garum, the vile sauce derived from fish left to rot for months in clay pots. Diocletian reorganised the empire in the 3rd cent, sending Lixus into a gradual decline. It was already deserted and in ruins when the Islamic conquest swept the land in the 7th cent.

Lixus Today. The head-high walls you see by the road junction are the remains of the garum factories, conveniently downwind of the main town on the hilltop. A track climbs to the amphitheatre which has a circular arena, unusual for the time but ideal for staging those grim fights to the death between man and animal. A spear-throw away are the ruins of some baths, with a remarkable mosaic of the sea-god

71

Neptune still guarding the tepidarium.

The acropolis (fortified city) stood on the hilltop, with the Great Temple in pride of place on the highest point, commanding a view in almost every direction. This temple was pre-Christian but the site has also yielded several Christian churches and an oratory, and even a mosque, although a number of buildings have proved impossible to identify.

Ksar el Kebir. The P2 road leads south 22 miles (36km) to a crumbling town with a history set to rival that of Lixus. Ksar el Kebir, the 'Big Fort,' has entered European history as Alcazar-Kebir, site of the **Battle of the Three Kings,** or the Battle of Oued el Mokhazine as the Moors prefer it. Portugal had been raiding the Moroccan interior from its base at Asilah so King Sebastião I decided in 1578 to mount a major onslaught that should seize a large chunk of territory.

The king personally led his army of 20,000 men into battle, with the former sultan Mota-ouakil commanding a batallion. Mota-ouakil's nephew, Abd el Malik and his army of 50,000 Moors, met the invaders between Oued Loukos and Oued el Mokhazine just north of Ksar el Kebir. It wasn't so much a battle as mass slaughter; Sebastião and Mota-ouakil were killed, with almost every man in their army being either slain, drowned, or taken into slavery.

But as Abd el Malik, the third king on the battlefield, also lost his life, his brother, Moulay el Mansour, became Sultan of Morocco. Portugal, however, still without a king in 1580, was annexed by Felipe II of Spain.

Ksar el Kebir, near the site of the Roman Oppidum Novum, was founded in the 11th cent. Yakub el Mansour, who built the Koutoubia minaret in Marrakech, added the walls but Moulay Ismail, who created Meknès, destroyed them as punishment after a local uprising. Further unrest in the 19th cent added to the town's decline, but it has a thriving Sunday market.

Souk el Arba du Rharb. Twenty-three miles (38km) south is Souk el Arba du Rharb, a strange town with a part French, part Arab name: Wednesday market of the Rharb (Plain). It has a **hotel,** the Gharb (2*, 36 rms).

MARTIL

Martil is a small fishing village 9 miles (15km) from Tetouan, in the middle of a splendid beach which seldom sees a foreign tourist but which is popular with the people of Tetouan. Once a haven of Barbary pirates, the village is beginning to show its age.

The **Hotel** Nuzha and a few pensions offer the only lockable accommodation, or there's the 7-acre (3ha) Camping Martil with basic amenities. **Buses** ply between Tetouan and Cabo Negro.

The beach extends northwards to **Cabo Negro** with its 670-bed Club Med mini-resort and the **Hotel** Petit Merou (3*, 42 beds). For self-catering apartments on week or fortnight lets, write to the Société Africaine de Tourisme, 52 Blv Hassan II, Casablanca.

FESTIVAL: Martil has its Water Moussem in July.

M'DIQ

M'Diq, pronounced 'muh-deek,' is only a few miles from Cabo Negro and is far busier, with foreign and Moroccan sun-worshippers camping on the edge of the beach. The sands are also popular with day-trippers from Gibraltar who come over on *Gibline One*, a high-speed catamaran carrying 226 passengers. It's no good for day trips in the opposite direction but it is a convenient point of entry and exit for Morocco as there's less customs hassle here — day trippers are processed easily. Crossings are only on Thursdays and are likely to be block-booked in high summer.

ACCOMMODATION: Hotels; Golden Beach (4* with bar and disco); Kabila (4* with so-called night club). Both are north of the village and by the beach. Playa (1*) is in the village and not near the beach despite its name. **Holiday village;** Yasmina (Club Med), 600 beds. Plenty of *camping sauvage* but watch your valables.

MOHAMMEDIA

A huge petrol refinery, a busy textile industry, a fish-processing factory and a large port are scarcely ideal neighbours for a holiday resort, but they all come together in Mohammedia. When you consider the lack of scenery inland and the uninspiring coastline, you can seriously ask: why have a resort here?

The answer lies 18 miles (30km) to the south-west: Casablanca. Mohammedia provides the escape valve for Morocco's largest city but is in only three British tour operators' brochures, gaining mention because of its specialist appeal.

Specialist? Mohammedia has an excellent beach protected in part by causeways leading out to two rocky islets; then it has a racecourse, a marina, an 18-hole golf course and, in the Hotel Miramar, one of the two casinos in the country: the other is in Marrakech.

It also has docks capable of handling Morocco's entire crude oil imports and most of its oil-based exports, and there is the refinery of Samir, the Société Anonyme Marocaine de l'Industrie du Raffinage, established in 1959 and now capable of processing 4,500,000 tonnes of crude oil a year. The port can handle all this plus much more, and has the third-busiest docks in the country.

Fedala. The old port of Fedala, now absorbed in Mohammedia, was little more than a tiny creek but it exported cereals and dried fruits to Europe in the 14th cent; the Portuguese seized it in the 15th and held it into the 16th, but the reconquering Moors let pirates take over the harbour. The Christian world reacted with violence and in 1773 Fedala opened once more to legitimate trade with Europe, but expansion and commercial success had to wait for the earth-moving machinery of the 20th cent.

HOTELS: Miramar (5*), Rue de Fès, 300 rooms, casino, night club. Formerly in the Meridien chain but still among Morocco's top hotels. Samir (4*), Blv Moulay-Youssef, night-club. Several other luxury hotels catering for Moroccan visitors. A few cheap hotels near the kasbah.

CAMPING: along the coast road north-east towards Mansouria;

International Loran, smart and pricey in 9 acres; Oubaha, and Mimosa. All well out of town.

TRANSPORT: buses, grands taxis and trains along the coast.

Beaches to Rabat.

Maps mark the beaches: Mansouria, Dahomey Plage, Bouznika Plage, Skhirat Plage, Ech Chiahna, Sables Eddheb and Temara Plage. They all have good sands but their off-beach amenities vary enormously.

Temara. Temara is the smartest, being the closest beach to the embassies and executive villas of Rabat, as well as to the Dar es Salaam royal palace, built by Mohammed V. Discos and flashing neon line the beach, but a little way inland at Temara village is the Golf Royal de Dar es Salaam, a complex covering 1,012 acres (410ha) with three 18-hole and a 9-hole golf course.

Access to Temara Plage is by taxi from Rabat's Ave Hassan II; the bus which leaves from the same depot goes only to the village. The beach resort has the Hotel La Felouque (3*, 20 rooms, night club) and Hotel Casino (unclass), as well as Camping La Palmerai at Plage de Sidi el Abad.

Skhirat Plage. Still in the luxury class is Skhirat Plage, dominated by the royal summer palace which a group of Berber cadets stormed in July 1971 in an attempt to overthrow King Hassan II.

The Hotel Amphitrite (3*) at Skhirat Plage has 72 beds; Skhirat village is on the main coast railway and bus routes to Rabat and Casablanca.

Ech Chiahna. Ech Chiahna comes a little down-market with its Hotel Kasbah-Club (3*, with night club and hammam) at Plage Rose-Marie; or you can go further down-market to the Camping Rose-Marie with its bar and restaurant.

MOULAY BOUSSELHAM

The tiny fishing village of Moulay Bousselham is 23 miles (37km) down the coast from Larache, but 57 miles (91km) by road, or 90 miles (144km) by bus route via Souk el Arba du Rharb, from where buses leave when they have enough passangers to warrant the journey. The road to Moulay Bousselham is narrow, and the village is merely a cluster of houses between the shallow cliff and the lagoon of Merdja Zerga, but it has the reputation of offering the best diving in Morocco — watch the currents and take note of the beach patrol.

The original Moulay Bousselham, the 'man with a burnous' who gave his name to the village, was a *sufi*, a Moslem mystic, who came here from Egypt early in the 10th cent. Although he died around 951, pilgrims still come to the village each summer — and in September the people celebrate the Moussem of Sidi Ahmed ben Mansour.

Accommodation is a choice between the Hotel Lagon (3*, 30 rooms) or the 37-acre Camping, open all year.

SAFI

Don't come to Safi town if you're looking for beaches. The sands are to the north of Cape Safi; beautiful, wild, and totally without any infrastructure — including food, water and lodging, and offering only a simple bus service. Come by motor-cycle bringing your tent and all your provisions and you could almost become Robinson Crusoe II.

Superphosphates. But Safi itself, midway between Essaouira and El Jadida, is a sad town, for all its 250,000 inhabitants. Its southern suburbs are swallowed in the phosphate factories of Maroc-Chimie and Maroc-Phosphor, said to be the largest such complex in the world.

If you're interested in statistics, here goes: the complex was begun in 1965, tripled in size in 1975, and has doubled since then. It produces nearly 1,000,000 tons of superphosphate a year, plus 2,000,000 tons of phosphoric acid, lesser quantities of sulphuric acid, and even extracts uranium ore from the raw phosphates mined around Youssoufia and hauled down to the coast by rail. At the beginning of the decade the port could handle 5,000,000 tons of cargo a year, mostly phosphates and their derivatives, but by the time you read this the port's capacity could be doubled.

In addition, Safi has a sizeable fishing fleet and processing plants, exporting thousands of tons of tinned sardines a year. No, it's not my idea of a holiday resort.

Old Safi. Safi's first mention in history was in the 11th cent under the name of Asfi. The ribat was built in the 14th cent and the tiny port opened to European merchants in the 15th cent. By 1450 Portugal was taking Safi's products down to Guinea and trading them for gold and slaves, and in 1508 when they realised the Safian rulers were in dispute, they seized the town and built two fortresses. Their glory was shortlived, however, for when Agadir fell in 1541, the Portuguese withdrew from Safi.

At the end of the century Safi again welcomed European traders and 200 years later it was the busiest port in the country, an astounding fact

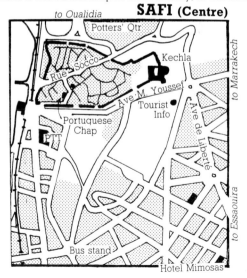

SAFI (Centre)

to Oualidia

Potters' Qtr

Kechla

Rue Socco

to Marrakech

Ave M. Youssef

Tourist Info

Portuguese Chap

Ave de Liberté

PTT

to Essaouira

Bus stand

Hotel Mimosas

considering that the harbour was rudimentary and exposed to the prevailing winds off the Atlantic.

Kasr el Bahr. The Kasr el Bahr, 'Castle of the Sea,' sometimes called the Dar el Bahr, 'Palace of the Sea,' was built by the Portuguese as a fort and as the governor's residence. It's part-restored and is occasionally open to visitors. *Kasr*, by the way, comes from the Latin *cacer*, 'prison,' and is allied with the word 'incarcerate.' The Moroccans used is as a prison until switching the jail to that other Portuguese relic, the Kechla.

Kechla. The Kechla, or the Borj el Dar, 'Palace Fortress,' is at the eastern end of the medina walls and was used as a royal palace in the 18th cent.

The choir of the original Portuguese cathedral still stands in the centre of the medina but is now called the Portuguese Chapel. Your other points of interest lie east from here along the Rue du Socco — call it 'Market Street' — where there are several basic **hotels.** Out through Bab Chaabah you're on the Rue des Forgerons, the ironworkers' souk, leading to the Quartier des Potiers, the Potters' Quarter, a fairly large area producing tiles on a co-operative basis using local clay.

HOTELS: Atlantide (3*, out of town); Les Mimosas (2*), Rue Ibn Zaidoun, off Ave de la Liberté, 1km south of Hotel de Ville (Town Hall). Budget hotels on Rue du Socco.

TRANSPORT: rail station south of town (take Ave Liberté); change at Benguerir onto main line. Buses from Place Ibnou Sina, 1km south of medina.

TOURIST INFO: S.I, south of Kechla.

Around Safi You need your own transport, preferably a motor-cycle, to explore the lonely coast south of Safi. The road runs along the flank of a mountain and gives good sea views, though the beach is usually out of reach. Beyond the Oued Tensift, impassable during the winter rains, stands the **Kasbah Hamidouch,** (49 miles, 78km) one of several fortresses built by the bloodthirsty Moulay Ismail (1672-1727). This one is square, each massive wall 150 metres long and studded with watchtowers. Inside, despite the ravages of three centuries, a moat guards a near-identical inner fortress.

North of Safi and Cap Beddouza, the road parallels the coast right to El Jadida, with **El Oualidia** a tempting midway stopover. El Oualidia grew around the kasbah that Sultan El Oualid built in 1634 to defend the little harbour against European attack, and has splendid mooring for its fishing boats in the Lagune d'Aïr, sheltered by a natural sandbar. Access to the sea is somewhat treacherous, a point to remember if you go swimming.

The town is a mini-resort popular with the aspiring middle-class of Marrakech, many of whom settle in for the summer under canvas, ignoring the **hotels:** L'Hippocampe (2*) by the beach, and the Auberge de la Lagune (1*). Both are small, but they both serve alcohol, which says something about Moroccans' tastes when they're off their home territory. There is a **holiday village** of sorts, the Société Touristique Amal which also runs one of the two camp sites.

SAÏDIA

Saïdia, pronounced 'Sa-*idd*-ee-ah,' is on the Mediterranean shore, a mile or so from the Algerian border and sitting on the edge of a first-rate beach that stretches 8 miles (12km) from the Oued Kiss at the frontier to the Oued Moulouya in the west, and continues past Cap de l'Eau and the Spanish-held Chafarinas Islands. The wetlands at the mouth of the Moulouya are a haven for birds.

The village rambles around its kasbah, built in the 19th cent by Moulay el Hassan and now occupied by some of the villagers.

Accommodation is very limited; the Hotel Al Kalaa (2*) on the beach has 33 rooms, the Hamour (2*) has nine and the Select (1*) 18. There are two campsites, but plenty of Moroccans pitch tent on the edge of the beach.

SIDI IFNI

South of Agadir and on the same latitude as the northern Canary Islands is Sidi Ifni, a crumbling community of 20,000 people that the Spaniards began in 1934 and which has been Moroccan only since 1969. The Spaniards landed here in 1476 and built the town and fort of Santa Cruz de Mar Pequeña ('Holy Cross of the Little Sea') to protect their routes to the Canaries. The Moroccans drove them out in 1524; the Spaniards re-established their right to the site in 1860 with the Treaty of Tetouan, but delayed their return until 1934 when the French were developing much of the southern sector of the country. As the Tetouan Treaty had no connection with the creation of the Protectorate, the Spanish stayed on after 1956.

The town they had created was in true Castillan style and commanded a coastline of some 50 miles (80km), but Morocco sealed the land access in 1966, two years before Spain did the same to Gibraltar, and the Spanish eventually pulled out. Might the same happen at Ceuta and Melilla sometime?

The **Hotel** Ait ba Amran (1*), 20 rms, is on Ave de la Plage; Bellevue (1*), 16 rms, is on Place Hassan II, the former Plaza de España; Suerte (Spanish for 'luck,' and some is needed), unclassified. Sidi Ifni is not on the tourist trail but its state of decay creates its own character — and there's a good beach. **Buses** connect with Goulimine.

SMIR-RESTINGA

Smir-Restinga is not a place. It's the name of a stretch of beach south of Ceuta and reaching to the northern side of M'Diq's little harbour, and it's occasionally known as Restinga-Smir. The sands are good but not outstanding, and there is no infrastructure at all unless you patronise the holiday clubs or find an enterprising native setting up a food stall. Water? Toilets? This is the open beach!

Maroc Tourist has a large stake in the available accommodation, running the hotels Boustane and Karabo (both 3*) and its own holiday village with chalets, self-catering apartments, a scattering of shops (boutiques would be more apt a description) and a night club. You can try to make reservations by writing to Maroc Tourist, Immeuble Dalil,

Tour D, Sahat Moulay el Hassan, Rabat (B.P. 4.403), which the London office of ONMT assures me is correct, but I'm still waiting for a reply.

Club Med corners most of the remaining market with its 650-bed complex, open only during the summer, leaving the Hotel Playa (1*) as virtually the only other choice — unless you choose to pitch your tent on the edge of the dunes: personally, I'd feel safer sleeping in my car.

TAN-TAN PLAGE

Tan-Tan is on the edge of the Sahara and was the frontier post with the former Spanish Sahara (Río de Oro) until 1975, when Morocco invaded the territory with an army of 350,000 civilians. Fifteen miles (25km) from the sea at Tan-Tan Plage, and 77 miles (125km) south-west of Goulimine, Tan-Tan is an administrative outpost of 42,000 people, many of them military, controlling a large territory which is arguably unpopulated: there is 0.6 of a person to each square mile.

A few miles north of town the road crosses the Oued Drâa, the outfall of the river that makes the upper Drâa Valley into an oasis. Normally the river loses itself in the sands before it reaches the Algerian frontier, but once in a generation it actually spills into the Atlantic Ocean.

If you come to Tan-Tan it will probably be by bus from Agadir (I never drove my car down this far) and you'll probably have to explain yourself to the gendarmerie; not a bad idea if you're in or on your own transport and are headed even further south.

You can describe the road from Agadir how you please: bleak, empty and hostile, or crossing the threshold of normal experience and taking you through rugged country to the adventure of a lifetime. Certainly, on this road it is better to travel than to arrive, for Tan-Tan is a one-horse (and a few camels) town where Saharan sand drifts down the streets and where the only saving virtue is its tax-free status. Unless you come in October, when the locals hold their camel races.

Tan-Tan Plage. If you fly from Agadir or Casablanca you will see that Tan-Tan Plage is a resort in the making, with concrete skeletons going up for the hotels and holiday villages that should soon attract the tourists. There is, of course, a good beach.

HOTELS in Tan-Tan: Royal (2*; it has a pool and a bar); Angala (1*) and Sahara (1*).

TRANSPORT: buses, including an express service, between Agadir and Laayoune; also the airport.

11: FÈS

The oldest imperial city

FES EL BALI, THE ORIGINAL WALLED CITY, is like nothing else on this earth. It is the largest and best-preserved medina in the Arab world, a living museum where 200,000 Fassi — the people of Fès — earn their daily bread, the seat of the world's oldest university, the first capital city of the land that became Morocco, the hub of Moroccan religious, artistic and intellectual life — and the city that gave the world the funny red hat.

Fès el Bali,'Fès the Old,' is an experience that must be seen to be appreciated. It owes its survival to French influence at the start of the Protectorate, but the Western world has given it little else except electricity and the motor scooter. Its streets wander without plan across several hilltops, sometimes paved with cobbles and going down steep slopes, at other times lined with tiny shops and shaded by bamboo canes or canvas.

If you venture into this maze of alleys without a guide it is almost impossible not to get lost, as you would need a large-scale map to follow every twist and turn and blind-alley. One way to appreciate Fès el Bali is, indeed, to wander in and lose yourself, so coming unexpectedly upon a mosque doorway, a water-carrier posing for pictures (at a price; these days he makes his living as a model), or a view over the city skyline, none of which you will ever find again.

And then, hire yourself a guide and see the medina as a tourist. You'll have no problem in finding somebody to show you the way; the problem lies in trying to take ten paces inside the old city *without* an escort. You can engage an official badge-wearing guide at any smart hotel or the tourist office, or take your pick from the young lads offering their services — but agree a price and an itinerary before you set off, and pay at the end.

Fès: a potted history.

Moulay Idriss. Moulay Idriss ibn Abdallah ben Hassan ben Ali was a descendant of Mahomet through the Prophet's daughter Fatima and her husband Ali. Defeated at the Battle of Fakh in Arabia in 786, Moulay Idriss and his Fatimite supporters came to the Maghreb and in 789 established his Idrissid Caliphate centred on a tiny Berber village. Legend claims that during the enlargement of the village he was offered a token pick-axe — a *fas* in Arabic — made of gold and silver, which led to the community being called Fas, eventually becoming (with the French-added accent) Fès.

Moulay Idriss died in 792, probably from poison, and in 808 his son Moulay Idriss II founded his own city on a hilltop a short distance away but on the other side of a small stream — today's Oued Fès. In this new capital Idriss II built a mosque in his own honour; it is now a zaouia and holds Idriss's tomb.

Kairouan Mosque. Eight hundred Moslem families fled from Córdoba in Spain in 817 to settle in Moulay Idriss I's Fès, so creating the district known today as the Andalous Quarter. Soon afterwards, Fatma led an exodus of refugees from her native Kairouan in Tunisia and settled them in the growing community of Moulay Idriss II's Fès, where she founded the Jemaa Qaraouiyyn in 857. A *jemaa* is strictly a meeting place, not only for prayers but also to exchange ideas and learning. Soon the Kairouan Mosque became more important as a seat of learning and evolved into what can be considered the world's first university where people who had knowledge passed it on to others in informal gatherings.

Arabic Numerals. One of the early students was later to become Sylvester II, the first French Pope, born around 945 and head of the Christian Church from 999 to 1003. Sylvester studied mathematics at the Kairouan Mosque and took back to Europe the concept of Arabic numerals to replace the cumbersome Roman numerals then in use. Europeans altered the numerals beyond recognition, brought them back to north Africa in the 19th cent, and they've now replaced the Arabic originals.

With the fall of the Idrissid Caliphate in 923, Fès was caught in the struggles between the Umayyads in Spain, and the Fatimites, the original Shi'ites, followers of the Mahdi in Tunisia. Fès continued to grow regardless of who ruled, and saw several mosques and medersas founded, as well as some fondouks. Later in the 11th cent Yusef bin Taxfin, the sultan of the Almoravides, the people 'vowed to God,' merged the two areas of Fès into one, sitting astride the oued that ran through its middle. And then he moved his capital to Marrakech.

But Fès was not finished. Abd el Moumen, sultan of the Muwahid dynasty, also known as the Almohades or the unitarians, seized the city in 1145. Moslems coming over from Europe brought the idea of the water mill to north Africa, in return for the Arab invention of the windmill now gaining support in the Christian world. Jews and wandering Arabs brought their dyeing, pottery, metalwork and textile skills to Fès, helping the city to grow in commercial importance.

Capital Again. Sultan Abu Yusef Yakub created the Marinite dynasty in Fès in 1269 and made it his capital city as he swept away the Muwahids. The Marinites lost most of Spain to the Christians and ruled no further east than Melilla, but they lavished attention on their homeland, particularly Fès. By 1273 it was obvious the city was too small so Abu Yusef began another, outside the city walls.

Fès el Jedid. This new city had a vast royal palace, the Dar el Makhzen; its own great mosque; its own souks, hammams and medersas; barracks for its own garrison of troops; and a medina that was not such a rabbit-warren as in the original Fès. This city was called El Medinet el Baïda, 'White Town,' but it became better known as New Fès, Fès el Jedid, which meant old Fès became Fès el Bali.

Building Boom. Abu er Rabi and Abu Saïd Otman (1308-1331) built sumptuous palaces and houses, and their successor Abu el Hassan

Ceuta from the lower slopes of Jebel Musa, one of the Pillars of Hercules

In the bustle of a medina, a 'snatch' shot from waist-level

The busy ferry from Larache to the beach across the Oued Loucos

This spectacular 'Grand Cañon' is in the High Atlas

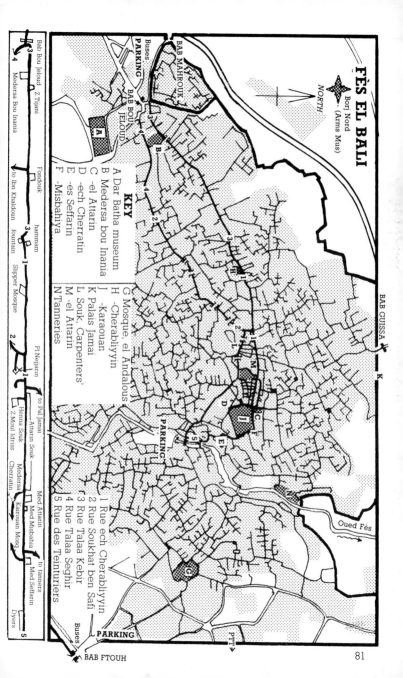

(1331-1351) founded the Cherabliyyin Mosque, which takes its name from the Turkish-style leather shoes to be made in later ages in the neighbouring souk. And by now the best brains in Islam were gathering at the Maghreb University.

Under Abu Inan, between 1351 and 1358, the country extended its boundaries east to Tunis, and in Fès the sultan built yet more medersas, notably the Bou Inania and the Attarin, while the Jews moved from Fès el Bali to Fès el Jedid and established their mellah near the Royal Palace. Around this time the population of the two Feses may have reached 200,000, making it one of the largest cities in the world and one of the most powerful in Islam.

Earthquake. When the last Marinite sultan, Abd el Hak, was killed in a riot in 1465, the city was at the peak of its power. From here it began a gradual but not irreversible decline, hastened in 1522 with an earthquake which did considerable damage to the older buildings, and helped again in 1554 by Mohammed ech Sheikh who founded the Saadian Dynasty in Marrakech, where he made his capital. Fès went into greater decline, and anarchy began destroying its reputation.

The Oudaia tribe moved into Fès el Jedid, staying until 1833 when Abd er Rahman evicted them; they were unperturbed when Moulay Abdallah, the third sultan of the Alaouite Dynasty, moved his capital back to Fès and began the city's greatest era of public works, building bridges, paving the streets of New Fès, and improving several of the mosques and medersas.

During the 18th cent Morocco's sultans moved their capital several times, to Marrakech, to Meknès, to Rabat, and back to Fès, where in 1909 Mohammed V, king from independence until 1961, was born.

Treaty of Fès. European influence in Africa grew throughout the latter part of the 19th cent, corresponding with internal disputes among the sultans which weakened Morocco. On 28 April 1912, at the Treaty of Fès, Spain and France partitioned the country at the start of the Protectorate, and on 28 April the French appointed General Lyautey as the first Commissioner and Resident General of French Morocco. In order to minimise resistance to his scheme he declared Fès to be a national monument and conservation zone, and moved the seat of government to Rabat.

He started a third city, la Ville Nouvelle, the 'New Town,' built on European lines for European administrators, leaving Fès el Bali and Fès el Jedid devoid of power and of purpose. It proved to be the right decision for the wrong reasons, for Fès el Bali is now the largest and best-preserved old-style Arab medina to be found in the world, and the three cities together had a population of 562,000 at the 1981 census.

FÈS EL BALI

The practical routes into the medina — on foot, of course — are from the west via Bab Bou Jeloud and from the east via Bab Ftouh, this latter suggestably for the Andalous Quarter only; cross the Oued Fès and you're lost.

A third route is suitable only for cars; leave the southern ring road, the Route du Tour de Fès, for the narrower Boulevard Mohammed el

Alaoui (not signed) 0.9 mile (1.5km) west of Bab Ftouh and follow it 0.75 mile (1.2km) through the Bab Jedid and along the course of the Oued Fès, now in a culvert, to the heart of the medina where (with luck) you can park. This is the favourite entry for most coach tours.

Balek! Most of the goods sold in the medina, from crates of Coca-Cola to raw sheepskins, are delivered on the backs of donkeys. The load occasionally fills the alleys, touching the walls each side and forcing people into doorways. As these donkeys never stop for you to move aside, listen for the shout of "Balek!" ("Look out!")

Via Bab Bou Jeloud.

Bab Bou Jeloud is an impressive gateway, with blue and gold tiles on the outer face and Islamic green and gold on the inner, but it was built in 1913. Immediately inside the bab you have a choice of routes: left is an alley leading to the Rue Talaa Kebira; right, with a dogleg, the Rue Talaa

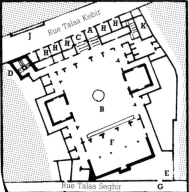

BOU INANIA MEDERSA, FES

KEY

A 'Barefoot Doorway'
B Courtyard
C Main doorway
D Minaret
E Mosque of the Dead
F Prayer chamber
G Rear entrance
H Shops
J Water clock
K Water closet

Seghira. And if you're looking for cheap hotels or restaurants; or street entertainers in the evening, look no further.

Talaa Kebira. The Rue Talaa Kebira or Great Hill Street plunges you straight into the mystic world of the Arab medina, with the first of the thousands of tiny shops you'll see on your exploration.

Medersa Bou Inania. This is one of two buildings in Old Fès that you should not miss seeing, as it is licensed for Friday prayers and is therefore technically a mosque, the only significant Islamic building in the country which non-Moslems may enter — for a fee of 3DH (standard hours, closed to non-Moslems on Friday and during any other prayers).

Built between 1351 and 1357 by Abu Inan, and almost completely filling his reign as sultan, this Koranic school is an architectural and a craftsman's masterpiece, with main doors sheeted in bronze, with onyx and other beautiful stone used in the decoration, with wood carving second to nothing in Morocco, and giving an overall impression of being on the set for some cinema epic.

Barefoot Doorway. The doors are set amid a row of shops; on the right, the main entrance, and on the left the door for pious moslems, the *va-nu-pieds* or 'go barefoot,' with a channel of running water in the threshold for the necessary ablutions.

The inner courtyard is as impressive as the exterior, with marble, carved wood, and ornate plasterwork decorating all surfaces, and another waterway separating it from the prayer hall, which is out of bounds to all but the Faithful. As the prayer hall of the Medersa Bou Inania is licensed, it gives the establishment the status of a Friday Mosque — we might look upon it as a parish church — with the right to hold prayers, and unless you've come in perilously near a midweek prayer-meeting, this is your best chance in all of Morocco to see what a working prayer-hall is like: empty, except for the mats covering the floor. If you want to explore a mosque in its entirety, including the prayer-hall, go to Jerusalem or Turkey.

Minaret. Because of its status as a mosque, the medersa has a minaret. Built in the north-west corner, the tower is open to visitors and gives a splendid view over the neighbourhood.

On the first floor (closed at the time of writing but due to reopen) are the students' rooms, with letter-box openings beside each door for the receipt of the daily bread, the only food provided on the premises.

The Medersa's Role. A medersa was a school for the informal study of the Koran and allied subjects, but the syllabus was more restricted than that of the early universities of Islam, such as the one at Fès. Students, always male, came from the wealthier families, who usually provided some financial support while the youths prepared for careers in religion, the legal profession based on the Koranic law, or government. Other support came from donations or from trusts set up by the medersas' founders who were, of necessity, men of great wealth and influence.

The principle of a Koranic school began in Persia and spread across the Islamic world, reaching Morocco in the 13th cent and enduring until the introduction of Western-style schools under the Protectorate.

Water Clock. Opposite the medersa at first floor level is a dilapidated water clock with 13 windows, seven of which each has a small brass bell beneath it: the other six bells are missing. The clock, built in 1357, worked by dropping a weight from each window into its bell and so marking the hours — but why 13 hours? Time has stood still here for several centuries though restoration is planned, when somebody decides how the original mechanism worked. One legend claims a magician built the clock, and another that a magician stopped it, but the building beneath was owned by a rabbi who was believed to have occult powers.

Ibn Khaldoun's House. Another 180 metres take you past a Marinite prison that was later a fondouk and is now a honey-merchants' souk. Another 100m along the Talaa Kebir a slightly wider alley leads off right to the House of Ibn Khaldoun (90 metres, on left), the venerated Arab historian (1332-1406). There are plans to convert the house into a Khaldoun Museum.

Back on the Talaa Kebir your steps pass (left) the entrance to a former fondouk, now the fellmongers' souk. A fellmonger? Your nose will tell you he prepares animal skins for the tanner. A kink in the route, and the oldest hammam in Fès (left), mark the spot where Rue Talaa Kebir becomes Rue ech Cherabliyyin and leads to the **Cherabliyyin Mosque** (120m, right). Built by Abu el Hassan in the mid-14th cent the minaret is original but the main mosque is much restored.

You will find much more interest in the men making *cherabliyyin* — Arab slippers with turned-up toes and straight out of *Aladdin* — and in the nearby **Souk Aïn Allou,** where leatherworkers sell their goods by auction, every day except Friday.

Souk el Attarin. Rue Ben Safi, an extension of Rue Talaa Seghira, meets Rue ech Cherabliyyin by an archway which marks the beginning of the Souk el Attarin, the Spicers' Souk. These rich perfumes, so different from the stench of the tanneries, warn you that you are approaching the heart of the medina and the great mosque, where only the sweetest of smells are tolerated.

But first there is the **Souk du Henné,** the henna market, on a parallel alley to the right. Henna dye is made from the crushed leaves of the *lawsonia inermis* shrub. Soaked in water, henna turns hair red and skin yellow, and is a popular cosmetic with many Berber women who colour their palms and soles; they use the shrub's flowers for a powerful perfume. The souk also does a good trade in kohl, a black paste used to enhance female eyelashes and brows.

Nejjarin Fountain. The henna souk leads south to Place en Nejjarin, 'Carpenters' Square,' and the Nejjarin Fountain, a piped outlet for water set in an ornate throne-like surround covered in mosaics and under a green-tiled roof. It reminds one of well-dressing in England, but this is permanent.

The Bastion de l'Ange in El Jadida's 'Cité Portugaise'

Nejjarin Fondouk. The nearby 18th-cent fondouk is in a poor state of repair. It was last used as a student hostel and may be restored to serve as a craft centre. And an equal distance further south are the **Guerniz tanneries,** established by Moulay Idriss II and surprisingly close to the great mosque. You may later argue that the main tannery is no further away, but it has the distinct advantage of being set on the bank of the Oued Fès.

If you've made it to the Guerniz tanneries without a guide and without losing your directions, you've done well. Back now to the Place Nejjarin and turn east into the alley called Bab Moulay Ismail for 50m, passing shops selling offertory candles, to the Zaouia of Moulay Idriss.

Zaouia of Moulay Idriss. The zaouia is one of the holiest places in Morocco as it holds the tomb of Fès's founder and patron saint, the second Idrissid sultan. When the dynasty collapsed in 923 the original Chorfa Mosque was left to decay, and it was only the discovery of human remains that prompted the 1437 rebuilding and the subsequent veneration of the site. It had been assumed that Idriss II was buried at Volubilis beside his father, and there's no proof that the bones lying here are his. The zaouia was restored again in the 18th cent and the minaret built in the 19th.

Wooden barriers were erected across every street leading to the zaouia, forcing the Faithful to bow their heads as they approached, and keeping away all beasts of burden, Jews and Christians. With the Protectorate, the last two categories have been allowed to pass the barrier into the *horm*, the sanctified area, although they are still forbidden to enter the building itself — but if you go to the women's entrance (follow the women, who form a large part of the supplicants) you may catch a glimpse of the courtyard and the room which holds the founder-saint's tomb. You might also see the women touching a copper plaque to receive the saint's blessing as they enter the zaouia.

Idriss's tomb is mounted on a catafalque and draped in expensive materials which are renewed each year by the city's guild of silk-weavers. There is an impressive display of offertory candles and, surprisingly, a collection of clocks made as individual offerings in the 19th cent. Most of them are European and many were made in Manchester.

Kaysaria. The Kaysaria, Qaysariya or Kissaria is the covered market beside the zaouia. This unusual name comes from the original Kaysaria in Antioch, built by the Romans and so called a Caesarion. The Kaysaria in Fès is a collection of stalls specialising in textiles and lacking character, having been rebuilt after a major fire in 1960.

Attarin Medersa. Onto the Souk el Attarin again and backtrack 25 metres to the **Dar Saada,** a 19th cent 'palace' converted to a carpet shop and restaurant. Forward again to the main crossroads of the medina, with the Kairouan Mosque just visible through the crush of humanity ahead and to the right, and the Attarin Medersa dead ahead.

This medersa was built between 1323 and 1325 by Sultan Abu Saïd and is therefore one of the oldest in the city and, according to Moroccan taste, the most beautiful. (Standard hours except Friday morning) The bronze-plated door leads into a small courtyard whose tall columns carry the eye upwards, creating the illusion of space. Follow your gaze and climb to the first-floor terrace for a view across the city and down into the courtyard of the Kairouan Mosque.

In the Islamic world a few religious buildings are deliberately kept austere while others have lavish decoration. The Attarin Medersa is in the latter class and has some of the best examples in Morocco of *zellig* work. Zellig — or zellij — is a highly-detailed form of mosaic using small pieces of ceramic fired in a variety of geometric shapes and arranged in intricate patterns. The craftsmen laid out the zellig design face-down and then pressed it onto soft plaster, keeping it almost exclusively for floors and the lower parts of walls.

Misbahiya Medersa. The Misbahiya Medersa, alongside, is in ruins with a promise of resoration. Much of its timberwork is in the **Dar Batha Museum** but its marble basin, brought over from Algeciras by the Saadians, is in place. This basin has led to the alternative name of Medersa er Rokkam, the 'Marble College.' It was built in 1346 by Abu el Hassan.

Tetouani Fondouk. If we fight our way through the crowds around the Great Mosque we come, at the next bend, to the Tetouani Fondouk, built in the 14th cent for merchants from that city whose reputation for dishonesty made them unwelcome in other fondouks. It's now a carpet store and for a dirham or two you might be shown the large lock which fastened the original door. Beside the fondouk is the former **Palais de Fès**, now also in the carpet trade. A few more dirhams allow you to the roof for another peep into the Kairouan courtyard.

Place es Seffarin. The alley narrows before opening onto the Place es Seffarin, a surprising sight in the midst of an ancient medina. Here, at the south-east corner of the Kairouan Mosque, is an open space shaded by large fig trees and resounding to the din of metalworkers hammering patterns onto brass and copper plates. This is where to come if you want to buy a cauldron big enough to boil a couple of whole sheep.

There's a legend that the fleur-de-lys patterns on the square's fountain were the work of French slaves.

Kairouan Library. The Kairouan Library has its simple entrance from the square, but only the followers of the Prophet are allowed through. Established in the 9th cent, it was enlarged in the 14th and absorbed the great library of Córdoba, making it among the most important in the Islamic world. Fès's 17th cent decline saw the collection dispersed, but it is now together again and totals 30,000 volumes, including a 9th cent hand-written and illuminated Koran and a manuscript presented by Ibn Khaldoun.

Medersa ech Cherratin. Turn west (right), continuing the circumnavigation of the Kairouan Mosque and in 70 metres you reach the Medersa ech Cherratin (standard hours including Friday morning), built in 1670 by Moulay er Rachid, founder of the Alaouite dynasty, to hold around 250 students. It's a much simpler place than the other medersas though it has an unusual knocker carved from the main wood of the door, and it was used as a medersa until a few years ago.

KAIROUAN MOSQUE. You will now have walked around the Kairouan Mosque and doubtless looked in several of its doorways. If you came on a Friday you would have noticed, and perhaps joined in, the undignified press of tourists at the portals as the Fassi men came in to pray. Only the followers of Mahomet may set foot through any of the doors but you can nonetheless see, as our cover picture shows, the ritual ablutions at the central fountain before the men go to the prayer-chamber.

It's a pity the Nazranis may not enter, for the Kairouan is the largest mosque in the Maghreb and the centre of Morocco's religious life, as well as being the seat of the world's first university from an indeterminate year in the mid-10th cent. By contrast, Salamanca University in Spain was established in 1230 and Cambridge's oldest college, Peterhouse, dates from 1281.

Fatma. Fatma, daughter of Mohammed el Feheri of Kairouan in Tunisia, has the unusual distinction in a male-dominated Moslem land of being the founder of the Kairouan Mosque. That original mosque, built in 857, was quite small; it was enlarged and given greater religious significance in 933 and had its minaret in 956, slightly more slender than the customary height-width ratio of 5:1. Abd er Rahman, the Sultan of Córdoba, added to the building but the Almoravide Sultan Ali ben Yusef gave it its final dimensions between 1135 and 1144, making it big enough to hold 20,000 people, but whether they're standing or doing obeisance isn't clear.

Hidden Glories. We may not glimpse the two pavilions, built in the 16th cent by the Saadian Abdallah ech Sheikh to the design used in the Court of the Lions at the Alhambra in Granada, Spain, nor may we see the heavily-decorated 12th-cent minbah, similar to a Christian pulpit. Not for us the water-clock made in 1317, part of an astronomer's set. Ah, well... But we can imagine the vast prayer-chamber of 16 naves and 21 traverses, and we can count the ten doors which are all opened to give access to the mosque on Fridays.

North to the Palais Jamai. From just inside the arch leading into the Souk el Attarin, take the most promising alley north. Assuming you don't lose your way you'll pass the **Joutier,** the souk for salt where the Jews were first settled in the city. As *mellah* is the Arabic for 'salt,' this is the word which has come to apply to Jewish ghettos throughout Morocco and it's by chance that the Fès mellah also has another name. There is a memorable but incorrect story which claims the Jews were settled by this particular salt market as they had the grim task of cleaning out and salting the heads of decapitated rebels before they were put on display at the city gates.

The alley then passes the fountain at the **Sagha Fondouk** by the jewellers' souk, and goes through the **Souk el Ghezel** where multicoloured wool is sold.

The path climbs steeply to **Fondouk el Ihoud** or Fondouk Guissa, the 'Jews' Fondouk,' which was the Jewish quarter until their mass migration to the Mellah in Fès el Jedid.

Six hundred metres from where you started (but it seems much longer), you should come upon another surprise — a five star hotel, the Palais Jamai, with 120 rooms and 20 suites, a bar, night-club and excellent Moroccan-style restaurant, all in a converted *menzeh* — playboys' hideaway — built in 1879 by the brothers Jamai, viziers (ministers of state) to Moulay Hassan.

The brothers were in effect the power behind the throne but when Moulay Abd el Aziz became sultan in 1894 their corruption was exposed and they tumbled from grace and were thrown into a dungeon in Tetouan. One of them died, still shackled to his brother, and the survivor was released in 1908, crippled, near-blind, and destitute.

The menzeh was converted in 1930 and the resulting Palais Jamai Hotel is set amid a beautiful garden laid out in Andalous style with oleanders, palms and pomegranates, and tinkling fountains.

Escape. The Fondouk el Ihoud is by the Bab Guissa, built in 1204, and the Palais Jamai Hotel is close to the Bab Ferdaous, where you can *catch a bus to Fès el Jedid or a petit taxi to anywhere, including the starting-place, Bab Bou Jeloud.*

SORTIES FROM PLACE ES SEFFARIN. Or, going back to the Place es Seffarin, you can use this landmark a base for making short sorties into other parts of the medina. First, down the alley opposite the library for 20 metres to an insignifant door on your left which opens onto the **Medersa es Seffarin,** built in 1280 by Abu Yusef. The oldest of all the koranic schools in Fès, it had an extensive library which went to the Kairouan collection centuries ago. The building is now virtually neglected but if you can find anybody with a key, I'm told there's a good view from the roof.

The view should show you the Rue Mechatine — 'Comb-makers' Street' — which leads from the fountain north-east for 180m to the **Quartier des Tanneurs** and probably your most memorable experience in Fès, if not in Morocco. Imagine a honeycomb of individual vats, mostly in the open air. Give each clutch of vats a different colour: white, for the lime in which skins are soaked for a fortnight; then colours, for tanning and dyeing operations together, using crushed date kernels, palm oil, saffron, poppy petals, dried pomegranate peel, indigo, mint and antimony. Add the smells: stale cow urine, an essential ingredient in tanning, and the odour of the oued whose already-polluted waters fill the vats. Now add the hustle and bustle of normal medina life and you're beginning to get the picture.

Thirty metres south of the Place es Seffarin, the alley zigzags to the Oued Fès, a fast-flowing open sewer crossed by the open-air bridge, the Pont Gzam ben Skoum. Ignore the bridge, for immediately in front of you is **Rue des Teinturiers,** Dyers' Street. This is another fantasia of colours and smells, where men labour over concrete vats no wider than an armspan, dyeing wool or sheepskins a variety of colours. If you've managed to get here without the services of a guide, follow the tourists into the main workshop (2DH) and up a rickety staircase to the roof for a splendid view over the cauldrons of hell.

At the far end of the souk the Pont Sidi el Aouad leads over the Oued Fès to the Quartier Andalous, but the hump in the road is your only clue. To the north, shops block off the view of the waterway, and to the south you see only the main **car park** which is built over the oued. *A local bus or a petit taxi from the car park can take you back to your starting place at the Bab Bou Jeloud.*

Ninety metres south of the hump bridge is the **Mosque er Rsif,** built between 1757 and 1790 and with a minaret decorated with Islamic-green tiles.

Back to Bab Bou Jeloud. Return to the arch at the entrance to Souk el Attarin, continue west, and at 80m take the major alley left, Rue Souikat ben Safi. Alternatively, from the Place en Nejjarin, take the climbing, tunnel-like alley to the right of the fountain, go up the steps and at 50 metres turn left into Souikat ben Safi.

About 350 metres along, on the left, is the **Palais Mnebhi,** General Lyautey's official residence from 1912 but now a restaurant. Just beyond the palace and on the right, an alley leads straight — with only one zigzag — to the Talaa Kebir, or you can continue down the Talaa Seghir, facing you, to Bou Jeloud.

via Bab Ftouh: the Andalous Quarter.

The Andalous Quarter is the smaller part of the medina, but you are much more likely to lose your way in it, for lack of any main route.

Come through the ramparts at **Bab Ftouh,** a gate that's been rebuilt several times and now exists in triplicate. Inside, at the Place Tamdert, you find a *bus and petit taxi terminal and space to park a car,* then three roads leading away from the top of the square.

The medina here is much more recent, the streets almost straight, the buildings grubby and nondescript, but the Andalous Quarter has always been the poor relation.

Mystic Saints. The road on the left leads unenticingly into the Bab Hamra cemetery with its memorial to **Sidi Bou Ghaleb,** an Andalous Moor who came to Fès in the 12th cent and is buried at Ksar el Kbir. But people have been coming *here* for centuries to sit by the memorial throughout the night of Tuesday-Wednesday to have their illnesses cured. Some people, not surprisingly perhaps, see the saint in their dreams.

There's a similar phenomenon in the cemetery of Bab Ftouh on the slope *outside* the city walls. Here is the **Koubba of Sidi Harazem** ('koubba' means *cupola,* but in this sense read 'marabout' or tomb, though the body is buried at the village of Sidi Harazem). This mystic who came from the Orient and died in Fès around 1164 had the reputation of being able to communicate with the spirits and, again not surprisingly, he has become the patron saint of the mentally sick. His moussem is celebrated at the end of April.

Andalous Mosque. Back in the Place Tamdert take the Rue Caid Khammar which leads uphill from the right by the cheap Hotel Moulay Idriss, and at 400 metres you cannot fail to find the Andalous Mosque ahead of you. This, too, was the work of a woman — Meriam, the sister of Fatma who founded the Kairouan Mosque — but it began as a simple oratory in the late 9th cent. It was enlarged and improved over the centuries, notably in 956 with a minaret based on that of the Kairouan, in 1203-07 when all else was rebuilt, in 1307, and in 1416 with the addition of a fountain and library.

The great doorway on the north came in the 13th cent rebuilding and still has its woodcarvings and *zellig* mosaics.

In spring the mosque is host to a week-long festival for the election of a Student King for the Kairouan University, coming somewhere between a religious procession and a student rag.

Sahrij Medersa. Twenty metres west of the mosque is the only other building of note in the Andalous Quarter, the Sahrij Medersa, built between 1321 and 1323 by Abu Hassan Ali who became sultan in 1331. It's slowly being restored, hopefully to its former greatness as the third most important medersa in the city.

From the Andalous Mosque the Rue Seftah leads steeply downhill to the Ben el Moudoun, the 'bridge between the cities,' and takes you over the Oued Fès with the Kairouan Mosque to your left and the tanneries to your right. In theory it's an easy route but in practise, with the crush of people and the many distractions, it's ridiculously easy to lose oneself.

Distractions? It was around here that I saw a small souk selling dried animal and bird skins: hedgehog, fox, a vulture's wing, a kid with its head intact, a reminder that people still practise sorcery in Morocco.

FÈS EL JEDID

Fès el Jedid, 'Fès the New,' is not new. It was begun around 1273 by the Marinite Sultan Abu Yusef Yakub, and completed in less than four years, while the dynasty lost control of the last of Moorish Spain to the upstart Emir of Granada, and lost the territory from Melilla almost to Benghazi, to the Hafsid Sultanate.

New Fès was an administrative city by concept, much of its area being taken by the Dar el Makhzen, the Royal Palace, and most of the remainder by buildings supporting the sultanate. There was a sector for Christian mercenaries and slaves, many of whom laboured on building the great mosque which the Jews involuntarily financed from extra taxation. In the mid-14th cent the Jews were moved over from Old Fès to their ghetto beside the palace. And in the 19th cent, when Fès el Jedid became the nation's capital for the last time, the city walls were completed, linking those of the new city with those of the old.

Travel in Fès el Jedid is much easier than in Fès el Bali, but there is much less to see. We'll start our itinerary from the Bab Bou Jeloud again, in the area that was built up last century when the cities' walls joined.

Bab el Mahrouk. Beyond the short-haul bus station in Place du Pacha el Baghdadi is the Bab el Mahrouk, not part of the old city yet built 60 years before the new city. It was originally Bab ech Cheria, the Gate of Justice, for under its arch the Berber chieftain El Obeid was burned at the stake for leading a tribal revolt. Its present name, in Arabic, is 'Gate of Fire,' which still recalls the event.

Castle of Flowers. The high wall which links Bab el Mahrouk and Bab Bou Jeloud hides the Kasbah en Nouar, the 'Castle of Flowers,' built by the Almohade Sultan Mohammed en Nasr, though the walls are 18th-cent. Access is only through the Bab ech Chorfa which opens onto the bus station.

Dar Batha Museum. Around 200m south of Bou Jeloud is the Dar Batha Museum, the Moroccan National Museum and worth a visit even if you're not a lover of static exhibits. It's open daily except Tues (standard hours) for 3DH, and beware being taken in by a 'guide' who may double the price for each of you.

The Andalous-style palace is about 300 feet long and was begun by Moulay el Hassan in 1894, the last year of his reign, and completed in 1909 by Abd el Aziz. It was intended as an impressive reception hall for newly-arrived ambassadors but was put out of business by the

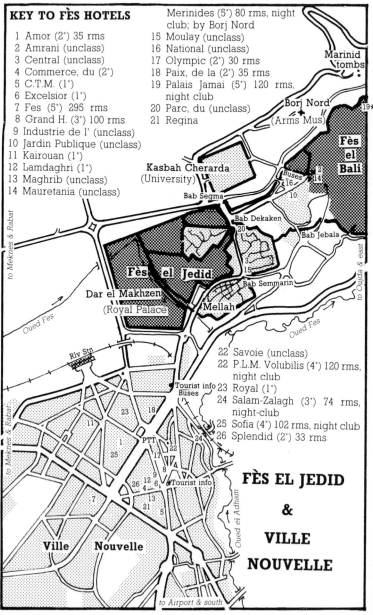

KEY TO FÈS HOTELS

1 Amor (2˚) 35 rms
2 Amrani (unclass)
3 Central (unclass)
4 Commerce, du (2˚)
5 C.T.M. (1˚)
6 Excelsior (1˚)
7 Fes (5˚) 295 rms
8 Grand H. (3˚) 100 rms
9 Industrie de l' (unclass)
10 Jardin Publique (unclass)
11 Kairouan (1˚)
12 Lamdaghri (1˚)
13 Maghrib (unclass)
14 Mauretania (unclass)

Merinides (5˚) 80 rms, night club; by Borj Nord
15 Moulay (unclass)
16 National (unclass)
17 Olympic (2˚) 30 rms
18 Paix, de la (2˚) 35 rms
19 Palais Jamai (5˚) 120 rms, night club
20 Parc, du (unclass)
21 Regina

Marinid tombs

Borj Nord
(Arms Mus)

Fès el Bali

Kasbah Cherarda
(University)

Bab Segma

Buses

Bab Dekaken

Bab Jebala

Fès el Jedid

Dar el Makhzen
(Royal Palace)

Bab Semmarin

Mellah

to Meknes & Rabat

to Oujda & east

Oued Fes

Oued Fes

Rly Stn

Tourist info
Buses

22 Savoie (unclass)
22 P.L.M. Volubilis (4˚) 120 rms, night club
23 Royal (1˚)
24 Salam-Zalagh (3˚) 74 rms, night-club
25 Sofia (4˚) 102 rms, night club
26 Splendid (2˚) 33 rms

PTT

Tourist info

FÈS EL JEDID

&

VILLE

NOUVELLE

Ville   Nouvelle

to Meknes & Rabat

Oued el Adham

to Airport & south

Protectorate; its present role is probably more suitable and the building itself is the museum's largest exhibit.

The first rooms cover **archaeology** from 12th to 18th cents, also featuring some interesting astrolabes and a selection of carpets from the Middle Atlas. One inner chamber displays the art of the blacksmith while another centres on coinage.

The section for **woodcarving** holds parts from the Misbahiya Medersa, an ancient cedarwood door, and the work of a 14th-cent turner. **Sculpted plasterwork** from the same era and later, shows the same craftsmanship that has been lavished on the mosques, but the main exhibit of **Fès pottery** fills several rooms.

But for appreciating the life of the middle-class Moroccan, search out the section showing ancient wedding costumes and a baby's cradle.

Old Mechouar. The Avenue des Français leads from Bou Jeloud into Fès el Jedid passing the Gardens of Bou Jeloud, fed by the Oued Fès before it flows into the old city and becomes incapable of supporting life. Beyond are the walls of New Fès leading you to the Vieux Mechouar, the Old Assembly-ground, a vast open space surrounded by high walls. On the west is the **Makina**, built by Italians around 1886 as an arms factory but now serving as a carpet workshop.

University. To the north, Bab Segma leads out to the main ring road and to the modern buildings of Kairouan University hidden in the foursquare Kasbah des Cherarda, dating from 1670 and built by Moulay er Rachid to keep his Berber troops under supervision.

Waterwheels. And to the south, Bab Dekaken leads to the **Petit Mechouar** on the left and the almost-enclosed Moulay Abdallah area on the right where Abu Yakub Abd el Hak established the Great Mosque in 1276 and where French administrators had their brothels in the days of the Protectorate. The early Marinites built an enormous waterwheel here in 1287 to take irrigation from the Oued Fès, and a much smaller and more recent waterwheel is still rotting away near the back of the Bou Jeloud Gardens.

Bab Dekaken. In 1437 the Portuguese raid on Tanger went wrong and Prince Ferdinão was captured. When his countrymen refused to ransom him he was hanged by his heels from Bab Dekaken, then his corpse was put on show for many years. The Bab was the entrance to the royal palace until 1971 but it now leads only to the Grande Rue de Fès el Jedid which cuts straight through the old medina with a string of textile merchants on its pavements. On the left is the Jemaa el Hamra, the Red Mosque, and the Jemaa el Beïda, the White Mosque. And at the end of the Grande Rue, Bab Semmarin, rebuilt in 1924, leads into the Mellah, the Jewish Quarter.

Mellah. The old Jewish Quarter has lost much of its charm along with almost all its Jews. At Moroccan independence in 1956, the new State of Israel had an open-door policy for Jews anywhere in the world, and many migrated from north Africa.

Medieval Spain was among many countries where Jews had been prominent for centuries, but when Ferdinand and Isabella defeated the Emirate of Granada in 1492, the last Islamic stronghold in western Europe, it was seen as God's vindication of Christianity. If Spain were to be cleansed of the infidel Moors, then why not cleanse it of the infidel Jews as well? It was no fault of the Christians that the expelled Jews — between 165,000 and 800,000 of them, according to later estimates — had no homeland to accept them, so they went with the Moors to Morocco where they were grudgingly accepted, but kept firmly in their place.

Royal Palace. Understandably out of bounds, the Dar el Makhzen stands in grounds of around 200 acres (80 hectares) and, following work done between 1969 and '71, now has its main entry onto the Place des Alaouites in the Mellah. The high security walls hold a mosque, the Abu Saïd Otman Medersa founded in 1320, the Dar Ayad el Kebira, an 18th-cent palace built by Sidi Mohammed ben Abdallah, and the Dar el Bahia which housed the Arab Summit in 1981 and '82.

LA VILLE NOUVELLE. La Ville Nouvelle is a smart, clean and well-designed European town that happens to be in Africa, but there is nothing to hold the traveller once the basic necessities of life have been satisfied. It was the administrative sector under the Protectorate and it's now home to law courts, courts of appeal, a cultural centre, the main police and post offices, the railway station, most of the hotels and restaurants, car hire agencies, and the two tourist offices.

HOTELS: see map of Fès el Bali and the Ville Nouvelle. Other hotel: Les Merinides (5*) by Borj Nord, 80 rooms and a stupendous view over the medina, but you pay for it.

There are budget hotels clustering around the Bab Bou Jeloud and the Bab F'touh in Fès el Bali, and at each end of the Grande Rue in Fès el Jedid; and there's a **youth hostel** (auberge de la jeunesse) on Ave Hoummani Fetouaki. The unsavoury campsite in the Moulay Slimane park has closed.

RESTAURANTS: the Hotel Fès is claimed to have the best French restaurant in Morocco, and the Hotel Palais Jamai the best Moroccan restaurant in Fès, but after that the city does little to earn a reputation for excellent cuisine.

The Dar Tajine is in a converted mansion in the old medina and offers a good bill of fare, but you will almost certainly need a guide to get you there. Other places with atmosphere as well as food include the Palais de Fès, facing the Kairouan Mosque, the Palais M'Nebhi on the Talaa Seghir and the Dar Saada on the Souk el Attarin.

For straightforward unpretentious eating shop around at the Bab Bou Jeloud or along the Blv Mohammed V and its sidestreets in the Ville Nouvelle. Du Centre at 105 (not to be confused with the nearby Hotel Central), and La Chope at 55, do French cuisine.

Alcohol is almost non-existent in the medinas (the Palais Jamai has a good bar) but comes to light along Blv Mohammed V; try Roi de la Bière at 59.

NIGHTLIFE: except for Ramadan, nightlife is usually limited to the night clubs in the top-rated hotels. During the Islamic holy month you can find semi-spontaneous after-dark street life around the Bab Bou Jeloud.

BUSES: inter-city bus depots are by Bab Mahrouk, Fès el Bali, and on Blv Mohammed V (southern end) in the Ville Nouvelle. A lesser station

Agadir's splendid beach and its matchstick bathers

serving the Rif and Oujda is *outside* Bab Ftouh. Town buses operate from Dar Batha, Bab Ferdaous, *inside* Bab Ftouh, and the car park by the Dyers' Souk (all in Fès el Bali); plus the Place de la Résistance, Place des Alaouites (outside the Royal Palace main gate), and the railway station.

TAXIS: petit taxis operate from all the bus stops, or within sight of them, plus Dar Batha and the PTT in Ville Nouvelle.

RAIL: the railway station is on Ave des Almohades to the north of Ville Nouvelle. Eastbound trains for Oujda; westbound for Meknès, then Tanger or Casablanca and the south.

AIRPORT: see Chapter 4.

FESTIVALS: Moussem of Sidi Harazem in April; of Sidi Ahmed and Moulay Idriss in September.

TOURIST INFO: S.I. in Banque Marocain du Credit, Pl Mohammed V, Ville Nouvelle, and so keeps bank hours, here 0815-1345. ONMT, Place de la Résistance.

FÈS ENVIRONS

The easiest way to see the places of interest along the Route du Tour de Fès is by car; if not your own then one hired for the day. Failing this, try the tourist offices for suggestions of local excursions, or take a petit taxi to the furthest point and walk back.

Borj Nord. Starting at Bab Bou Jeloud again, in a hypothetical car, drive out through Bab Mahrouk and keep *straight on* for 300 metres for the outer section of the ring road, passing the walls of the Kasbah Cherarda on your left. Turn right, and in 300m you have a slip-road right for Borj Nord which, with its brother on the other side of the medina, was built during the reign of the Saadian Sultan Ahmed el Mansour (1578-1609).

Neither place was built to defend the Fassi against outside attack, but to force them into submission if they developed ideas above their station — and both forts used Christian slave labour.

Arms Museum. Since 1964, Borj Nord has held the Arms Museum (open daily except Tuesday, standard hours; guide available). Most types of portable weapons are on display here, from prehistoric axes to automatic small arms, including several samples of the latter from Birmingham, but the dominant exhibit is of rifles seized during the Rif revolt of 1958.

Marinite Tombs. The route passes the five-star Hotel des Mérinides and offers an excellent view of Fès el Bali, before another slip road leads to the Marinite Tombs. The tombs are uninspiring and have been badly damaged in their 600 years, but this is a perfect spot for a picnic or to rest tired feet...if it were not for the press of would-be guides.

If you are on foot, walk a mile around the hairpin bend to Bab Ferdaous and take a petit taxi to Bab Ftouh for the *Quartier des Potiers*, the Potters' Quarter.

Potters' Quarter. The potters, who were moved out of town to this hillside site, carry on a traditional craft that has been practised in Fès almost since the city's beginnings. You can watch in relative comfort most stages of the craft of making pots and tiles, from moulding the clay to the firing of the glaze; the comfort is relative to the press of tourist excursions and if you choose your time carefully you might get a worthwhile souvenir at bargain price.

The Bab Ftouh cemetery covers the hillslope, both inside and outside the city walls, and if you can walk to the top you might find the mausoleum of Sebatou Rijal, the 'Seven Men,' saints of unknown identity who are venerated throughout Morocco. From the Bab Ftouh another petit taxi, or your hypothetical car, will take you back into town.

Excursions around Fès.

Sidi Harazem. Ten miles (16km) east of Fès is the bustling village of Sidi Harazem, whose name is on the label of Morocco's most popular mineral water. Unfortunately the bottling plant now dominates the village, and what's left belongs to the hotels.

Léon l'Africain, a historian born in Granada in 1483 as Hassan ibn Mohammed el Fassi, wrote of Sidi Harazem that its waters were good for the liver and kidneys. He spoke of an ancient pool which is still in existence, though the new pool gets all the custom. Yet he called the village Hammam Khaoulan, although it has been associated with the holy man Sidi Harazem for generations, and Harazem's tomb here is the setting for a moussem in late April.

The village has the small three-star **Hotel** Sidi Harazem and a holiday village run by Maroc-Tourist for people taking the waters. **Buses** run from Ville Nouvelle and Bab Ftouh.

Sebou Gorge. You need your own transport to begin to appreciate the Sebou Gorge, but to see it at its best there is no better way than to walk along its bed. At Birtam-Tam, 23 miles (37km) east of Fès on the P1, turn right onto S326 for 15 miles (25km) to El Menzel. Just at the town's

The 'Paysage d'Ito' near Azrou: corn in spring, searing heat in summer

Souk des Teinturiers, the dyers' vats in Fès medina

The tiny beach at Al Hoceima is crowded in high summer

Volubilis: ruins on the south slope

approaches turn left onto 4618, a poor-grade road leading 8 miles (14km) to Aïn Timedrine, the 'Source du Sebou.' The village is in a well-cultivated and terraced landscape, and the most accessible part of the gorge is to the north, where the water has cut through the rust-red rocks.

From El Menzel your transport and the 4610 take you in 20 miles (32km) to Sefrou, a town that's even older than Fès-the-Old.

Sefrou. Sefrou sits at the foot of the Middle Atlas amid an oasis devoted to the production, not of dates, but of cherries and strawberries; its 'Fête des Cerises' in June is a high point in the local festive calendar. It's a pleasant town of 47,000 people in a picturesque location, flanked to the south by barren foothills yet having the Oued Aggai run through the middle of the medina. Several mountain streams, plus the Oued el Yhoudi, join the Aggai nearby.

The name 'Yhoudi' hints at Sefrou's strange history. It was colonised by Jews who converted the Berber tribe Ahel Sefrou to Judaism before the coming of Islam. Moulay Idriss II persuaded most Berbers they should heed Mahomet, but the sons of David held onto their beliefs and for several centuries outnumbered the Moslem Berbers in the town. The Jews remained a major force here until Israel shocked the Arab World with the triumph of the 1967 Six-day War, when prudence dictated an immediate mass migration to Israel. The Mellah still occupies the centre of the old medina, but its inhabitants are now all Berber.

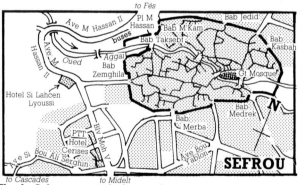

Floods. Sefrou grew as the last staging post before the mountains on the caravan route to the south, and had its walled medina before Fès was built. Its location didn't encourage growth and its present walls were rebuilt in the late 18th cent — but look at the Jemaa el Kebir, literally the 'Great Mosque,' on the north bank of the river by the main bridge. In this town which sees floods most years, a plaque marks the level of the 1950 waters which killed 30 people.

The Ave Sidi Bou Ali Serghin, beside the post office, degenerates to a footpath on the way to the **Cascades d'Aggai,** damaged in the spring floods of 1977. One of the caves nearby is the Kef el Yhoudi, unusual in that it's sacred to both Jews and Moslems as the place where the prophet Daniel died.

Madness. You'll need to ask directions for the Koubba of Sidi Bou Ali Serghin a mile or so away and use this to find the 'miraculous' spring of Lalla Rekia, the female Saint Rekia. Until early this century this was the setting for the annual sacrifice of a white chicken and a white billy-goat whose blood, dropped into the young stream and then drunk, would cure madness. If you don't believe it, at least console yourself with the view.

The two-star **Hotel** Sidi Lahcen Lyoussi and the unclassified Hotel des Cerises are on Blv Mohammed V (see map). The Bou Ali Serghin is near the koubba. **Buses** to and from Fès stop at the Place Moulay Hassan.

Moulay Ismail's Mausoleum at Meknes – ONMT

12: MEKNES

And Moulay Idriss

MEKNES IS THE MOST RECENT OF THE IMPERIAL CITIES, but its origins are by far the bloodiest. The Berber tribe of the Meknassa established a cluster of tiny settlements here along the banks of the Oued Boufekrane, growing fruit and vegetables in the lush soil.

Abd el Moumen, the second Almohade sultan, seized Fès in 1145, then added the infant Meknassa before going on to take Marrakech two years later. He razed Meknassa and rebuilt it to his own design, with the hint of a grid-plan for the street layout. But the townspeople lacked confidence in the future and faded away.

Medersa Bou Inania. The Marinites, who built Fès el Jedid and its celebrated Medersa Bou Inania, built a less spectacular Medersa Bou Inania in Meknès. But still Meknès lacked the spark of life.

Moulay Ismail. In 1672 the second Alaouite sultan, Moulay Ismail, transferred his capital to the ailing city and tried to give it that vital spark.

Death. Instead, he brought grim death. A reporter who survived ten years as captive in Meknès claimed Moulay Ismail's prisons held 25,000 Christians and 30,000 criminals: it's reassuring to note there was a distinction. His stables had 30,000 slaves and his harem 500 wives of all nationalities and races.

The sultan, claimed this reporter, had great strength and courage, an overpowering charisma, and yet he dressed cheaply in wool and ate plain food while living in luxurious palaces.

Sadist. In an age of cruelty, Moulay Ismail was among the most sadistic rulers of his time. He crushed skulls, cut off heads and impaled stomachs with no provocation at all, and he is reputed to have killed 36,000 men with as much sympathy as anybody else might swat flies.

Within a few years he had destroyed the Marinite kasbah and replaced it with kasbahs for his own negro bodyguards, plus palaces, a harem — he fathered 800 children — mosques, stables, granaries and gardens. His new city had 20 gateways, and walls that stretched for 15 miles (25km).

But Moulay Ismail was frustrated in one desire. After signing a treaty with Louis XIV of France in 1682 he demanded, time after time, that Marie-Anne de Bourbon, daughter of the Sun-King, should join the other ladies of his harem.

Decline. When Moulay Ismail died in 1727 there was nobody else of such stern character able to hold the terrorised Meknès together. It's not surprising that the population hurried away and the city fell into decay, its decline enhanced by the transfer of sovereign authority once more to Fès and to Marrakech.

Meknès: the Medina and Ville Imperiale.

The basic building material for the medina was a mixture of earth and lime, yet as you enter up the one-way Rue des Moulins from the Ville Nouvelle, you have an impression of a granite-grey city. The road kinks left, left again, and right into Rue Dar Semen, with the PTT at one end, a cluster of cheapish hotels nearby, a bus station in the middle, and the Place el Hedim at the far end.

Place el Hedim. The long *place*, the 'Square of Destruction,' was cleared in Moulay Ismail's era to give a grand approach to the impressive Bab Mansour and the Dar Kebira, the 'Great Palace,' beyond its arches. Not so long ago it was home to snake charmers and acrobats but the *place* now has a row of stalls down one side, offering fruit and some good quality pottery; as it's not a tourist trap you can pick up a decent souvenir here.

Bab Mansour. The Bab Mansour is the largest gateway in Meknès and among the most impressive in Morocco, particularly as it can be appreciated from a distance. Work on the gate began shortly before Moulay Ismail's death and was completed under his son, Sultan Moulay Abdallah, whose respect for human life matched that of his father. The

MEKNES MEDINA
KEY TO STREETS
(both maps)

1 Dar Semen, R
2 Fes, Ave de
3 F.A.R, Ave des
4 Haboul, Blv
5 Hassan II, Ave
6 Idriss II, Ave
7 Moulins, R des
8 Rouamazin, R

KEY TO HOTELS

A Continental (1*), 42 rms
B Excelsior (1*), 37 rms
C Majestic (2*), 42 rms
D Maroc (unclass) medina
E Moderne (1*), 30 rms
F Nice, de (2*), 33 rms
G Palace (2*), 32 rms

H Panorama (2*), 23 rms
J Regina (unclass) medina
K Rif (4*), 120 rms, night club
L Touring (1*), 39 rms
M Transatlantique (5*), 120 rms, gardens
N Volubilis (1*), 33 rms

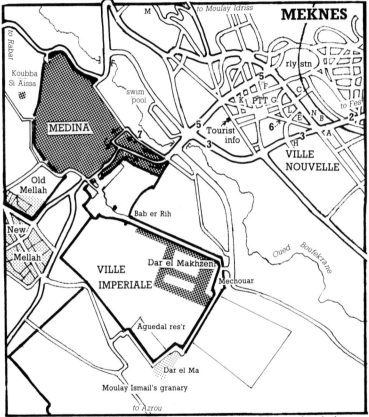

gate's architect was a Christian who converted to Islam and took the name of Mansour el Aleuj, and when he admitted to the sultan that his next commission could be an improvement on this, he was immediately executed.

The design on the side facing the *place* features *entrelac* work, the intricate twisting and interweaving of a single ribbon prominent in Islamic patterns — and in Celtic ones, as well.

Through the gate lies the well-kept but unimpressive garden of the

101

Place Lalla Aouda fronting the blank façade of the Dar Kebira, the complex built in 1697 to hold Moulay Ismail's Great Palace.

The Imperial City. Turn right at the blank façade — or follow the crowds — into another square, un-named and still surrounded by high walls. On the right of the wall facing you is the Koubba el Khiyatin, originally the palace where the sultans greeted arriving ambassadors but, when Meknès fell from glory, where tailors ('khiyatin') worked on military uniforms.

Granary — or Slaves' Quarters? Beside the koubba a stairway leads down into a vast network of vaulted cellars, popularly known as the living quarters for the many Christian slaves engaged in building the Imperial City. They were more likely to be used for storing grain, for even the slaves had to be fed. Yet there is a story which claims these passages to be Cara's Prison, taking the name of a Portuguese captive whom Moulay Ismail promised to release in exchange for the plan of a Christian prison holding 40,000 Moslems.

Moulay Ismail's Mausoleum. Turn left from the koubba and another high wall faces you, broken by two gates. That on the right would let you into the Royal Golf Gardens past the Palace Guard if you had the available written authority (see 'sport' at end of chapter); on the left the Bab Moulay Ismail leads to a canyonlike passage between more high walls. On the left again is a magnificent doorway leading to Moulay Ismail's Mausoleum, almost a sanctuary in Moslem eyes and yet open to visitors of all faiths, provided they are appropriately dressed.

The mausoleum was built during the sultan's reign and has remained a place of veneration and pilgrimage ever since, despite Moulay Ismail's bloodthirsty career. Even to non-Moslems it has an air of reverence, with a series of high-ceiling rooms, fountains in the courtyard — and a display of clocks which Louis XIV of France presented instead of his daughter, Princess Marie-Anne de Bourbon, whom Moulay Ismail requested. Non-Moslems may go no further than this annexe.

Dar Kebira. A near-contemporary report said the Dar Kebira, beyond the mausoleum, had at least 20 mini-palaces surrounded by high square towers and protected by two massive walls. Other reports say that Moulay Ismail was creating a rival to the Palace of Versailles, probably for his anticipated French bride, but the two projects were not running at exactly the same time. Regardless of intention, the complex is now near-abandoned and crumbling.

Gate of the Winds. The high walls come closer as you approach the Bab Er Ruah, the Gate of the Winds, an apt name in the half-mile-long (0.75km) man-made canyon that leads away from town, with the vast modern Dar el Makhzen, the Royal Palace, out of sight on your right. A mechouar — assembly-ground — gives access to the ordinary world by the palace gate, or you can continue in this canyon for a further 2km, circling the Royal Palace and coming back to the New Mellah.

Viewpoint. You pass the 100-acre grounds of the Dar el Beïda horticultural school (open to the public) on the way to the Dar el Ma, the Water Palace, part of the complex known as the Heri es Souani. The large block of masonry called the Dar el Ma is open to the public (standard museum hours) and from its rooftop terrace you can see into the royal park, particularly the 10-acre, 120-foot (40m) deep Aguedal, Moulay Ismail's regal reservoir which is now also a palatial boating lake. The view also takes in the horticultural school, and the Dar el Beïda itself, the 'White Palace' to the south, built in the 18th cent and now a military academy.

Heri es Souani. Once again you are called underground, but if you thought the Dar el Ma was large then the Heri es Souani is an excavation of mammoth proportions, originally lit through openings in the vaulted roof 40 feet (12m) overhead, but now open to the skies. If this were a cathedral, there would be 23 naves each flanked by stone columns, but the word *heri* is the clue: this is yet another granary, built to allow Moulay Ismail's Meknès to withstand a siege of indeterminate length.

The granary has several wells of around 120 feet (40m) deep with animal-powered bucket-chains for raising the water, one of which has been restored to its original condition. Thinking of water, as you stand here you're 30 feet below the surface of the Aguedal, across the road.

Heri el Mansour. Some tourist guides of the two-legged kind call the Heri es Souani the sultan's stables, but that title belongs to the Heri el Mansour, 500 yards beyond the Dar el Beïda. If you thought the first heri was colossal then take a deep breath, for this undertaking dwarfs the Heri es Souani into insignificance. The two are of similar design but the Mansour granary is built on the surface rather than being excavated, and its first floor was a palace covering two acres (0.8ha).

The entire structure is now in advanced stages of decay but the best opinion available claims that these were indeed Moulay Ismail's stables, capable of sheltering 12,000 horses and storing their fodder.

The Stable Mosque, built in 1790 by Sidi Mohammed ben Abdallah and heavily restored, stands conveniently close to the Heri el Mansour to lend some credence to the story.

Dar Jamai. Back at the Place el Hedim, the unimposing building at the north end, furthest from Bab Mansour, is the Dar Jamai. Translated into English it becomes the Palace Jamai and, yes, it was built in the 19th cent by that same family which created the Palais Jamai in Fès el Bali. Since 1926 it has been a two-storey museum of Moroccan art (standard hours, closed Tuesday and random other days), specialising in the crafts of the Meknès area and including woodcarving, leatherwork, ironwork and jewellery, but with emphasis on ceramics and weaving.

The old kitchens have been converted into a smithy for the fine wrought-iron artefacts on display elsewhere, and several tableaux show the Berber way of life of the 19th cent.

Souks. The alley to the left of the Dar Jamai leads to the souks; left, the Souk en Nejjarin with the mosque of the same name; right, the Souk es Sebbat and the Medersa Bou Inania.

The Souk en Nejjarin, the Carpenters' Souk, also has a wealth of cloth merchants, but if you come on a Friday and see the streets empty and all the shops shut, you will notice how little character there is in this medina: the main alleys have few twists and the shop shutters look as if they were mass-produced to one design.

Mellah. At the end of Souk en Nejjarin and to the left, Bab Berrima leads to the 18th-cent Mosque of Bab Berrima and the Old Mellah, the original Jewish town. Moulay Ismail, the sultan who ordered one of his wives to be tortured to death while he watched, had a touch of compassion after all. When a Jew managed to cure the sultan's favourite daughter he was offered a parcel of land to build this ghetto for his people, while all around them men were being slaughtered for the fun of it. No matter that the mellah was entirely surrounded by a high wall and had only three gates, all lockable, and that the sultan could therefore starve its occupants into submission or death: no matter — it was home. But the Jews have now left, most to Israel and the remaining few to the New Mellah, and the old ghetto is crumbling, with storks nesting on the rotting masonry.

Medersa Bou Inania. The Souk es Sebbat takes you to the Medersa Bou Inania started, like its Fès namesake, by Sultan Abu el Hassan and completed in 1358 by Abu Inan, who gave it his name (standard hours). It is highly decorated as all medersas and mosques are in Morocco, but it is not in the same class as Abu Inan's other monument. Probably the most impressive feature is the immense folding doors, covered with hammered bronze brought from the Dar el Ma and protected by a cupola stretching over the roadway.

The medersa held 100 students whose cells still retain their carved cedar screens. And from the roof there is a view into the courtyard of the 12th-cent Great Mosque nearby.

Follow the main souk through the kaysaria to a prominent T-junction where you have another choice: right, left, and right brings you to the PTT on Rue Dar Semen; or left up the Rue Karmouni takes you through a not very inspiring district past the Palais El Mansour, a 19th-cent mansion converted into a bazaar.

Koubba of Moulay Ahmed. The fourth opening on the right leads to a tomb built for a man who died in 1933 having achieved fame for surviving his first, and accidental, burial in 1917. Although Moulay Ahmed el Ouazzani was a cripple he managed to escape from the original tomb and thereafter chose to live out of doors.

Saddlers' Gate. The route ends in the long and narrow Place Berdaine and Moulay Ismail's enormous Bab Berdaine, the Saddlers' Gate, which marks the spot where pack saddles were sold.

Bloodbath. North of Bab Berdaine and the city walls, the road circles a walled cemetery which is off-limits to non-Moslems. You'll therefore not see the Koubba of Sidi Aïssa, a contemporary of Moulay Ismail and who had a similar love of the macabre.

Sidi Aïssa stood at his door and told the amazed crowd that the Prophet had ordered him to sacrifice his most faithful followers. The first volunteer entered; there came a scream and a surge of blood under the door. The second man followed to meet the same fate and by the time the 40th stepped forward the crowd had vanished. Then Sidi Aïssa led a procession through the medina of the 40 bloodstained, sacrificed, dead men — but who were obviously still alive.

The townspeople accepted Aïssa as a man of supernatural powers, though a few suspected there were 40 less sheep in the fields, and so began the cult of the Aïssaouas, men who could swallow poison or living scorpions, eat glass or impale their tongues with daggers...or who could fool others into believing the evidence of their eyes. The Aïssaouas thrived until put down by the French Protectorate.

Ville Nouvelle. Meknès had 486,600 inhabitants in the 1981 census but the combined city, new and old, appears much smaller than the triple city of Fès. The Ville Nouvelle is a pleasant extension of the old but has no sights worth seeing. Here are the smarter hotels — which usually hang out the *complet* (full) sign in high summer — and the tourist offices, the railway stations, the main PTT, and life as Europeans know it. Meknès sees fewer tourists than Fès or Marrakech and as a consequence there is less harassment: in fact, nobody at all offered to be my guide to the medina!

HOTELS: see maps. Also: Zaki (4*), Rte d'El Hajeb. Several unclassified and basic hotels are on the medina's Rue Dar Semen near the PTT, of which the Regina is the most interesting. Built on the old caravanserai design, it overlooks a courtyard. Has character, and parking by the door, but overpriced.
　　YOUTH HOSTEL: north of Hotel Transatlantique.
　　CAMPING: Agdal, 10 acres (4ha), near Heri as Souani (Moulay Ismail's Granary).
　　RESTAURANTS: poor scope. Top-ranking is L'Hacienda on Route de Fès, also a night club. Ave Hassan II in Ville Nouvelle has La Coupole and a few others.
　　NIGHTLIFE. Nightlife? Try the night clubs at L'Hacienda or the Hotel Rif.
　　BUSES: the new depot is by Place Abd el Aziz ben Idriss in the Ville Nouvelle; a secondary one is by the river (see map); the old CTM depot in Rue Dar Semen still operates. **Grands taxis** run from Place el Hedim and Place Abd el Aziz.
　　RAIL: two stations on the same loop of line; trains stop at both.
　　FESTIVAL: Fantasia in September is the most impressive in Morocco. Details from tourist offices.
　　SPORT: fancy playing golf in the palace grounds? I'm told you can ring 307.53 for a fixture.
　　TOURIST INFO: ONMT, Place Administrative; SI, Esplanade de la Foire.

MOULAY IDRISS

The town of Moulay Idriss presents challenge, excitement, and disappointment. The good news is that this is a truly Moroccan town with no European building permitted, even during the Protectorate; indeed, no non-Moslem had been tolerated near the village until 1912.

This community of 10,000 people, 14 miles (22km) north of Meknès and standing dramatically on a hilltop surrounded by higher mountains, is Morocco's holy city and holds the tomb of Moulay Idriss ibn Abdallah ben Hassan ben Ali, otherwise known as Moulay Idriss el Akbar ('the Great;' recall the chant *Allah u-akbar*, 'God is great'?) Moulay Idriss the man, a direct descendant of the Prophet's daughter Fatima and her husband Ali, hence the 'ben Ali' in his name, fled from Damascus around 778 after the Umayyad victory divided Islam into the Sunnis and the Shias. Arriving at Volubilis, he converted the Berber tribe of the Aouraba to Islam, and was appointed their sultan in return.

He chose this hilltop as the better-defendable site for his new capital, but a year later decided that Fès was preferable. In 792 the Umayyad sultans contrived to poison him and he was buried here in the town which henceforth was to bear his name.

L'accès n'est pas permis aux non-Musulmans. The bad news is that all the religious relics have always been — and still are — closed to non-Moslems, with bars across the streets banning Christians, Jews and beasts of burden. Religious fervour is still so intense that it forbids non-Moslems from staying in the town after dark, hence there are no hotels for non-believers. And the worse news is that, despite there being little to see, the pressure from self-appointed tourist guides is intense.

Tourists arrive in excursion coaches, in public buses or grands taxis from Bab Mansour in Meknès, on foot from the junction at the base of the hill or, as I did, by car. There is adequate parking space by a sharp left bend as you climb into the town, with guides and *guardiens de voiture* equally anxious for your custom; the latter leave no doubt that their modest fee is protection money.

At the top of the next steep bend the road levels and holds a moderate souk and open-air market. There's a good view down over the roofs of the lower town and the cultivated valley, while above you is the Khibier quarter where your guide (you're not still guideless?) will point out a medersa, and the zaouia which holds Moulay Idriss's tomb.

VOLUBILIS

Volubilis is one of the two most important ancient sites in Morocco, but it's not easy to get there unless you're in an organised excursion. The only public transport is via the private bus operating from the Bab Mansour at Meknès, or you might find a taxi to take you there from Moulay Idriss. In your own transport, at the foot of the narrow road from Moulay Idriss, turn right, and right again at an unsignposted Y-fork onto a minor road.

The site is two miles ahead, 19 miles (31km) north of Meknès, with a large and mainly empty car park. Opening hours vary year by year but on my last visit were listed as 0800-1600 daily, with entry costing an adult 5DH and a child 2DH. There is a small refreshment block by the ticket office — and a toilet.

Neolithic. Stone Age man was here, leaving a few artefacts as evidence, and the Carthaginians found this gently-sloping hillside to be an important defensive post. The Berber chieftain Juba II (25BC to around 24AD) chose this location for one of his chief towns and was strong enough not only to defy Roman occupation but also to take Cleopatra's daughter Selena as his wife.

Roman. Eventually the Romans were strong enough to occupy this hillside fortress which they called Volubilis. They built a road from Tingis (Tanger) to here and made Volubilis the capital of their province of Mauritania Tingitana. But they never progressed further south; the tribesmen of the western Atlas defeated conquest although the Berbers of Tunisia succumbed.

Age of Glory. The 2nd and 3rd cents were Volubilis's age of glory. With the city walls in place, Commodus (180-192) added the monuments, Caracalla (later known as Marcus Aurelius Antonius, 211-

217) gave the city its triumphal arch, one of the three Gordians rebuilt the procurator's palace, and Macrinus (217-218) built the Capitol. The city was a major collecting station for the produce of Mauritania, ranging from corn to wild animals for the Roman arenas, and undoubtedly led to the extinction of the lion and the elephant in north Africa.

Decadence. Shortly after Emperor Probus died in 282, Volubilis was abandoned and its garrison sent to quell troubles closer to home. Christianised Berbers stayed on until Moulay Idriss converted them to Islam, but they quit with the building of Fès.

English Discovery. An Englishman, John Windus, found the place in 1721 and at great risk to life and liberty watched its destruction as Moulay Ismaïl carried away its masonry to built Meknès. The earthquake of 1755 which destroyed Lisbon, 350 miles away, shattered Volubilis — now known to the Arab world as Oualila — and it stayed derelict until excavations began in 1887.

Mosaics. The most impressive feature at Volubilis is the high-quality mosaics, still in place where the Romans laid them. The **House of Orpheus** has nine dolphins in the private rooms, while the **House of the Desultor** shows an athlete whose skill is jumping from a chariot or horse and remounting, at full gallop. This event was in the original Olympics and has, understandably, been dropped from the modern games.

Bacchus finds Ariane asleep on the beach of Naxos in the **Cavalier's**

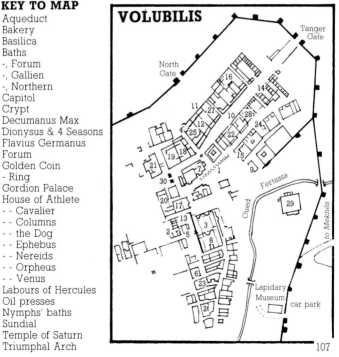

KEY TO MAP

1 Aqueduct
2 Bakery
3 Basilica
4 Baths
5 -, Forum
6 -, Gallien
7 -, Northern
8 Capitol
9 Crypt
10 Decumanus Max
11 Dionysus & 4 Seasons
12 Flavius Germanus
13 Forum
14 Golden Coin
15 - Ring
16 Gordion Palace
17 House of Athlete
18 - - Cavalier
19 - - Columns
20 - - the Dog
21 - - Ephebus
22 - - Nereids
23 - - Orpheus
24 - - Venus
25 Labours of Hercules
26 Oil presses
27 Nymphs' baths
28 Sundial
29 Temple of Saturn
30 Triumphal Arch

The minaret of the Koutoubia Mosque in Marrakesh is 252 feet (77m) tall and was completed by 1189

House, and in the **House of the Labours of Hercules** ten of his twelve tasks are preserved in mosaics. The **House of Ephebus** shows a Nereid, one of the 50 daughters of the sea-god Poseidon, mounting a sea-animal, and elsewhere Bacchus riding in a chariot. The god of wine appears again in the **House of Bacchus and the Four Seasons** which, with the **House of the Nymphs' Bath,** invites investigation. The **House of the Nereids** is aptly named, but the most elaborate mosaics are to be found in the **House of Venus's Cortège** where they originally decorated eight rooms and seven passages. I use the past tense because the mosaic showing the Voyage of Venus is in the Antiquities Museum, Tanger.

Ruined City. Volubilis's industrial quarter was at the foot of the slope where olive oil was pressed in great quantity, and the commercial area was at the top, lining the main street, Decumanus Maximus, where merchants had their mansions behind their shops.

The city centre held the **triumphal arch,** once endowed with a bronze chariot, and the **capitol and basilica,** whose re-erected columns now form the focal point of the ruins.

13: MARRAKECH

Capital of the South

MARRAKECH IS MOROCCO IN MINIATURE, and has given its name to the country. A rust-red city, half as old as time (to modify the description of Petra), Marrakech is now an up-to-date metropolis with 548,700 people at the 1981 census. It stands in a slight depression surrounded by an oasis of date palms, and controls the access to the passes over the High Atlas to the south. Although it's at 1,500 feet (450m), Marrakech can be very hot in summer, which is why people prefer to come here in winter, when the snow-covered High Atlas look their most alluring.

Travelling south from the city, your road takes you through the most impressive mountain scenery in north Africa — the Tizi n'Test route often taken by the excursion coaches from Agadir — but the road west to Essaouria goes through semi-desert flatlands devoid of any detail.

Marrakech: a potted history

Marrakech was, and still is, a Berber rather than an Arab town, but its origins are obscure. The most favoured account claims that Abu Bekr, a chief of the Almoravide people, established a market — or was it just a camp? — here in 1070. He was following it with a stone castle, literally the Ksar el Hajar (its foundations have been found north of the Koutoubia Mosque), when he was recalled to the south to quell an uprising.

Abu Bekr left his wife and his troops in the care of his cousin Yusef ibn Taxfin (Youssef ben Tachfin in French spelling), who relocated the camp amid some boulders from which he could persuade other travellers of the folly of dallying: "On your way, at the double," as we might put it today, sounded like 'Marroukech' in the Berber of the time.

Unfaithful Cousin. Yusef built a mosque of which nothing remains, then recruited Christian troops from Spain (the Christians ruled north of the Oporto—Barcelona axis) and 2,000 blacks who had already been brought from the deep south. By the time Abu Bekr returned in 1072 or '73 to reclaim his kingdom, Yusef was too powerful to be dethroned. He was able to say 'Marroukech' to his cousin and assume the undisputed role of Sultan of Marrakech, the effective founder of the Almoravide (Murabit) dynasty.

When the Emir of Islamic Seville appealed to him for help, against advice, Yusef responded briskly and seized the Iberian territories so that his empire stretched from Zaragoza to the edge of the Sahara (see *Discover Gibraltar* in this series), and with Fès already established, Yusef chose that city as his capital.

Moroccan Bound. At his death in 1106, his son, Ali ben Yusef, continued to build Marrakech and succeeded in establishing it as the country's major leather producer. The city has been so successful in this field that it has given us 'Moroccan bound' as the accolade of perfect leather bookbinding, as Córdoba in Spain gave us the word 'cordwainer' for a maker of leather shoes. There is a strong connection, as craftsmen from Córdoba helped in the building of Ali ben Yusef's city.

Disaster. The Almohades, also known as the Muwahids or Unitarians, were creating the next dynasty in their stronghold at Tin-Mal in the Atlas and in 1121, under Ibn Toumert and his lieutenant Abd el Moumen, they attacked Marrakech.

In 1145 Abd el Moumen seized Fès, followed in June 1146 by the beginning of the siege of Marrakech. The city fell on 23 March, 1147, and after allowing it to be plundered for the traditional three days — often the only payment the common soldier received — Abd el Moumen installed himself in Ali ben Yusef's palace and Marrakech was once more the chief city.

Koutoubia. He built the Koutoubia mosque but as soon as it was finished in 1157 he built another beside it, completing it except for the minaret within the year 1158, and then he demolished the first one. He added gardens and underground reservoirs, his successor Abu Yakub Yusef added the Agdal and extended the city's walls...and then came Yakub el Mansour.

'The Victorious.' Yakub el Mansour, dubbed 'the Victorious' after winning the Battle of the Three Kings by proxy, added the Koutoubia minaret as part of a major building programme that spanned the 15 years of his reign to 1199. He created the Kasbah with its dozen palaces and many other buildings, then moved to the coast to turn crumbling Rabat into Rbat el Fath, 'Ribat of the Victory,' while simultaneously overseeing the building of the great mosque in Seville, Spain, whose minaret is now the celebrated Giralda.

Divided We Fall. The Marinite dynasty chose Fès as its capital in 1269, sending Marrakech into a decline which its rulers found intolerable. By 1374 the city was the seat of vice-regal government which inevitably led to the country being divided, with Fès and Marrakech each ruling its own territory. Ahmed el Araj, a prince of the Saadian dynasty, occupied the city in 1521 and ignoring its run-down appearance he made it his capital; when his brother Mohammed ech Sheikh, ruler of Fès, decided to join him in Marrakech in 1554 the country was again united — and took the name of its chief city.

United We Conquer. Yakub el Mansour conquered Timbuktoo in 1591 and brought the wealth of that mystic city to Morocco, earning himself the accolade ed Dehbi, 'the Golden,' to go with 'the Victorious.' Marrakech now found further wealth by acting as middleman between Black Africa and Europe; some of the marble for building was paid for, weight by weight, in cane sugar.

But the Golden Sultan died, from poison or from the plague, and his empire sank into anarchy. It was rescued by Moulay Ismail, the bloodthirsty builder of Meknès, the latest of the imperial cities. Marrakech paid a heavy price for its fall from power, including the destruction of all Mansour's works except the Saadian Tombs.

Latest Glory. At the end of the 19th cent, Moulay Hassan brought Marrakech its latest glories, including the Dar el Beïda and the Dar Si Said. And in 1912 the city had its latest thrust for power when El Hiba, the 'Blue Sultan,' led a revolt from Tiznit against the coming of the French.

Sidi Thami el Glaoui, the pasha (governor) of Marrakech from 1908 to 1956, was tired of the years of unrest and helped the French to pacify his city. But in 1953 the same man led the protest against the French occupation and ultimately brought about the return of the exiled Mohammed V as King-in-waiting.

MARRAKECH MEDINA

The Koutoubia Mosque. Abd el Moumen's second Koutoubia Mosque, built in 1158, is among the largest in western Islam, around 300 feet by 200 (90m by 60m), plus a small extension on the south side. The name, meaning 'bookseller,' comes from the 100 or so scribes and manuscript sellers who set up stalls around it in its early years.

Minaret. For people accustomed to high-rise buildings, the minaret could be dismissed as yet another square tower, but consider its marvels. It was built eight centuries ago by Abd el Moumen's grandson, Yakub el Mansour (1184-'89) and has survived wind, weather and earthquake. Each of its four limestone walls, 42 feet (12.8m) wide, rises to 226 feet (69m) and each has a different design, including much delicate interlacing. The merlons — castellations or battlements — in tapering square-block style are typical Almohade and Marinie design which we shall see again.

A legend claims that the three spheres of gilded copper which rise from the tiny dome to 253 feet (77m), were worked from gifts to Yakub el Mansour's principal wife which she had to forfeit as a penalty for breaking the Ramadan fast, and that the spirit world has been summoned to place a curse upon any mortal who even considers stealing them.

Access. You can reach the Koutoubia — though, as with all mosques in Morocco, non-Moslems are not allowed inside — through Bab Doukkala from the bus station, through Bab Nkob (Bab Potterne) from the Ville Nouvelle, or through Bab Jedid from the direction of the airport.

Place Jemaa el Fna. From the eastern side of the Koutoubia a wide road, carrying taxis, lorries, buses and horse-drawn calèches, leads to Place Jemaa el Fna, the centre of interest in the medina if not its geographic centre, and the easiest way in to the warren of alleys. The name means 'meeting-place of sinners' and recalls the hundreds of convicted or suspected criminals who were executed here in byegone centuries, their severed heads serving as a warning to others.

Nowadays the square is altogether a livelier place and on an evening in Ramadan probably the liveliest in all Morocco. In the morning it is a vast market for virtually anything portable, except livestock: you can buy fruit and veg, cure-all medicines, tourist souvenirs, herbs, trinkets. You can engage a scribe to write for you in Arabic, and you can even have your teeth pulled out. In the afternoon the *jemaa* — meeting-place

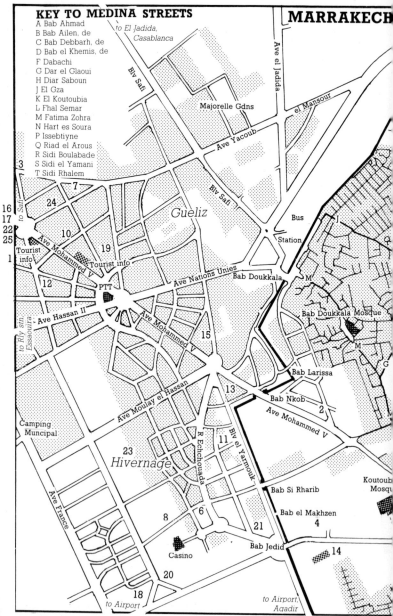

KEY TO MEDINA STREETS

A Bab Ahmad
B Bab Ailen, de
C Bab Debbarh, de
D Bab el Khemis, de
F Dabachi
G Dar el Glaoui
H Diar Saboun
J El Gza
K El Koutoubia
L Fhal Semar
M Fatima Zohra
N Hart es Soura
P Issebtiyne
Q Riad el Arous
R Sidi Boulabade
S Sidi el Yamani
T Sidi Rhalem

MARRAKECH

to El Jadida,
Casablanca

Majorelle Gdns

Ave el Jadida

el Mansour

Ave Yacoub

Blv Safi

Gueliz

Bus

Station

Blv Safi

to Safi

Tourist
info

Ave Mohammed V

Tourist info

PTT

Ave Nations Unies   Bab Doukkala

Bab Doukkala Mosque

Ave Hassan II

Ave Mohammed V

Bab Larissa

to Rly stn.
Essaouira

Ave Moulay el Hassan

Bab Nkob

Ave Mohammed V

Camping
Muncipal

Hivernage

R Echchouada

Blv el Yarmouk

Bab Si Rharib

Koutoub
Mosqu

Bab el Makhzen

Ave France

Casino

Bab Jedid

to Airport

to Airport,
Aqadir

112

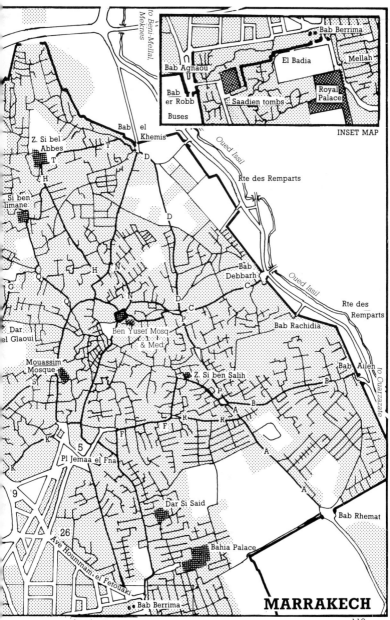

INSET MAP

to Beni-Mellal, Meknes

Oued Issil

Rte des Remparts

Bab el Khemis

Z. Si bel Abbes

Si ben Slimane

Dar el Glaoui

Bab Debbarh

Oued Issil

Rte des Remparts

Bab Rachidia

Ben Yuset Mosq & Med

Mouassim Mosque

Z. Si ben Salih

Bab Aïleh

to Ouarzazate

Pl Jemaa el Fna

Dar Si Said

Bab Rhemat

Bahia Palace

Ave Hoummam el Fetouaki

Bab Berrima

MARRAKECH

(see inset map)

Inset map labels

Bab Berrima

Bab Agnaou

El Badia

Mellah

Bab er Robb

Buses

Saadien tombs

Royal Palace

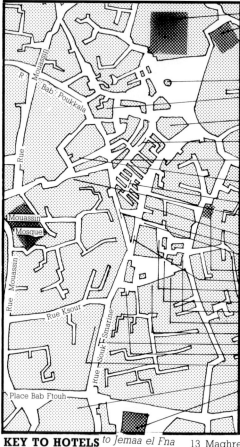

MARRAKECH SOUKS

- Ben Yusef Mosque
- Ben Yusef Medersa
- Koubba
- Haddadine Souk (ironwork)
- Cherratine Souk (leather)
- Souk Babouches (slippers)
- Souk du Cuivre (copper)
- Souk Chouari (palm-weaving)
- Kissaria (tiny stalls)
- Souk aux Teinturiers (dyeing)
- Jewellers' Souk
- Souk Attarine (spices)
- Souk Fagharine
- Sidi Ishak Mosque
- Souk el Kebir ('great')
- Criée Berbère (carpets)
- Slave Market
- Vegetable Market
- Black Magic Stalls
- Souk Btana (sheepskins)
- Souk Smarine (textiles)
- Souk Larzal (wool)
- Kissaria
- Spices
- Kessabine Mosque

0   scale: 100

metres

to Jemaa el Fna

KEY TO HOTELS

1 Agdal (3˚), 133 rms
2 Almoravides (3˚), 100 rms
3 Ambassadeurs, des (2˚), 23 rms
4 Chems (3˚), 138 rms
5 C.T.M. (1˚), 16 rms
6 Es Saadi (5˚), 200 rms
7 Excelsior (2˚), 45 rms
8 Farah Safir (5˚, ex-Hotel Sofitel), 300 rms
9 Foulcauld (1˚), 32 rms
10 Franco-Belge (unclass), 21 rms (by Voyageurs)
11 Imilchil (3˚), 95 rms
12 Koutoubia (2˚), 60 rms

13 Maghreb, El (2˚), 80 rms
14 Mamounia, La (5˚), 196 rms
15 Marrakech (4˚), 367 rms
16 Mouatamid, Al (2˚), 45 rms
17 Oasis (1˚), 33 rms
18 Palais el Badia (5˚), 300 rms
19 Palmerai, de la (1˚)
20 P.L.M. N'Fis (4˚), 290 rms
21 P.L.M. Toubkal (4˚), 60 rms
22 Renaissance de la (2˚), 45 rms
23 Siaha-Safir (4˚), c250 rms
24 Sun (2˚), 40 rms
25 Tachfin (3˚), 50 rms
26 Tazi, Grand Hotel de (2˚), 60 rms
10 Voyageurs (unclass), 26 rms

— has its water-sellers, snake-charmers, musicians, story-tellers and acrobats, the like of whom have been coming here for centuries but nowadays the major part of their income is from posing for tourists' photographs. Regrettably there's another type of entrepreneur who lives off the tourists: the pickpocket.

The square has no architectural interest but is a handy place for cheap hotels at the centre of activity — and there's even a Club Méditerranée here, 85 miles (136km) from the nearest sea.

SOUKS. Marrakech's souks are more concentrated, more animated, more varied and more interesting than in any other city in the country, and the best way in to them is from Jemaa el Fna.

From the north end of the *place* bear left, beside the Kessabine Mosque then follow the **Potters' Souk** to the bottom end of the **Souk Smarine,** the cloth-merchants' alley. This souk took its name came from the rushes, *smar,* which shaded the shops until fire struck in the 1960s.

Slave Market. Around 150 metres along on the right is **Souk Larzal,** the small wool market active only in the early morning. It leads you into the **Rahba Kedima,** formerly the market for grain but now a tatty vegetable market. On the north of the square is a small alley known as **La Criée Berbère** from the shouts of auctioneers selling slaves here at sunset three days a week until the French put a stop to it in 1912, 105 years after Britain abolished the slave trade (see *Discover The Gambia*). The victims had been stolen in Black Africa and brought across the Sahara in camel caravans. The 'Berber Cry' can still be heard here, but now the voices are selling carpets.

On the south side of the Rahba Kedima is the **Souk el Btana,** devoted to complete sheepskins and smelling as pungent as any tannery. Almost imperceptibly the sheepskins give way to a more grisly display best described as 'ear of bat, wing of owl,' and you can imagine yourself back in the Middle Ages, buying the basic ingredients for magic spells. There is some concession to modernity in that the souk also sells the raw materials for female cosmetics.

The main alley now divides into two; on the right the **Souk el Kebir** takes you through the **Souk des Bijoutiers** (Jewellers' Souk) to the **Kaysaria,** a mini-market enclosed in its own lockable gates where you can buy the results of European and Far Eastern mass production.

The Great Souk has the inevitable leather merchants, some of them speaking excellent English and accepting a range of credit cards, and then you find yourself at the **Souk Cherratin,** almost exclusively devoted to leather goods in a wide range of products.

Had you not turned right into the Souk el Kebir you would have gone into the **Souk Attarine,** the Perfumers' Market, from where a left turn would take you to the **Souk Chouari,** where men weave donkey-panniers from shredded palm-leaves — *chouari* means 'donkey' — and the parallel **Souk des Teinturiers,** the dyers' souk and the most colourful and odorous of all the alleys of any medina.

The north side of the Kaysaria holds the **Souk des Babouches,** home of the slipper-makers and, behind it, the smaller souks of the coppersmiths and blacksmiths, the latter noisily engaged in fashioning delicate wrought-iron products.

MOSQUES and MEDERSAS. The original **Ben Yusef Mosque,** its green-tiled roof visible across the open square, was built by the Almoravides (1062-1147) on a site which, for reasons soon to be explained, must have included much of the open space to the south. It was rebuilt in the 16th and again in the early 19th cent, so nothing of the original remains.

Koubba el Ba'adiyn. Or does it? The small two-storey building that seems to have slid down to its dome in a hole in the middle of the open space, is the Koubba el Ba'adiyn, the only Almoravide building in Morocco to have survived more than eight centuries untouched, and then only because it was buried intact when the area was levelled.

It was discovered in 1948 and is now open to view provided you can find anybody to let you in, but the only object of interest is an original ablutions basin that served the first Ben Yusef Mosque. The exterior, however, is unique, and if you are interested in Almohade art and architecture, this is your source material.

Ben Yusef Medersa. This Koranic school, a hundred yards from the koubba, is among the most interesting buildings in Marrakech. Open daily (except Friday morning and certain religious holidays) at standard hours — knock hard on the door if it's locked — the 14th-cent medersa built by the Marinite Sultan Abu el Hassan was rebuilt in 1564-65 by Moulay Abdallah who wanted to create the most important religious school in the Maghreb.

The building was restored in 1960 but still shows most of what Moulay Abdallah achieved for his 900 students: the entrance corridor adorned with mosaics leads to an ablutions chamber where the most eyecatching object is a basin bearing a heraldic gryphon with eagle's wings, carved in Córdoba in the 10th cent. Islam doesn't tolerate the representation of any creature, man or beast, as this might detract from praying to Allah, the creator of all — so how did a gryphon survive first in the mosque and now in the medersa?

A decorated marble basin stands in the centre of the main court, surrounded by covered balconies from which the luckier students could look down; the less-favoured had views of tiny, cramped courts.

Sidi bel Abbès. North of the Ben Yusef Mosque you are off the tourist track, but our map of the medina should be easy enough to lead you along Rue Diar Saboun and through the Bab Taghzout, which marks the city limits in Almoravide times, to the Sidi bel Abbès quarter, where the zaouia of this 12th-cent patron saint, one of the city's seven guardians, is surrounded by small buildings of religious importance.

The block is out of bounds to non-Moslems as it does considerable charitable work for the local blind, commemorating Sidi bel Abbès's reputation as a miracle-worker.

Sidi ben Sliman. South-west from Bab Taghzout, lesser alleys lead to the Zaouia of Sidi ben Sliman el Jazouli, another of the sacred seven and a 14th-cent descendant of Mahomet prominent in the campaigns to drive the Portuguese from the Barbary coast. Once again, don't go too close.

Dar el Glaoui. Your return route to the koubba can take in the Dar el Glaoui, but before you risk losing yourself in the back alleys, check with the tourist office to see if the Glaoui's house has yet been opened to the public. Sidi Thami el Glaoui, who was born at Telouet in the High Atlas, welcomed the French in 1912 and campaigned for their withdrawal until his death in 1956 — which happened to be the year the French withdrew — was the last of the southern pashas and in this reputedly sumptuous house, hidden behind high walls, he entertained lavishly.

From the Dar el Glaoui you can turn west, leave the medina by the Bab Doukkala and walk straight into the main bus station, passing the 16th-cent Mosque of Bab Doukkala, built by Moulay Ahmed el Mansour's mother, Lalla Messaouada. In byegone centuries the city's lepers lived outside this gate, probably on the site of the bus station itself.

Tanners' Gate. Or you can turn east and walk back to the Dyers' Souk and so to Jemaa el Fna. Another variation is to go east from the Ben Yusef Medersa for 1,000 yards (1km) to the Bab ed Debbagh, the Tanners' Gate. This gate, much rebuilt from its Almoravide origins, conceals a stairway to the ramparts from where there's an excellent view across open country, medina, and the tanneries: but you may have difficulty in finding the guardian with the key.

The tanneries have been here for centuries, exiled to the edge of the city because of their stench, though they also need the water from the capricious Oued Issil.

THE PALACES. Fes el Jedid is acceptably different from Fes el Bali because it was created outside the walls of the old medina. Marrakesh has no separate towns for the 'bali' and the 'jedid' districts and as both are within the medina walls, the contrast between the north with its maze of narrow alleys, and the south with its straight roads and sense of space, is startling.

Bab Agnaou. Using the Koutoubia Mosque as a starting place, the Rue du Bab Agnaou leads south to a recess in the city walls, with Bab er Robb in front (it leads to a cemetery and minor bus station) and Bab Agnaou on the right. *Er Robb* is the juice of the grape, the raw material for wine and alcohol, and Yakub el Mansour ruled that all grape juice entering the medina must do so through this gate, where it could be controlled. *Agnau* is a hornless ram — compare it with the French *agneau*, 'lamb' — which is what the Bab Agnaou resembles now it has lost its original twin turrets. The 'lamb' gate has always been purely for show, with the 'grape juice' gate being the true barricade.

Bab Agnaou leads directly to the Mansour Mosque, also known as the Kasbah Mosque, built by Yakub el Mansour around 1185-90 and restored by Moulay Abdallah in the late 16th cent, with the highly-decorated minaret being authentically restored again in the 1960s.

As you won't be allowed in, here are some statistics about the mosque: its frontage stretches for 260 feet (80m), it has 11 naves (clear passages between supporting columns), one main court and four smaller ones.

Saadian Tombs. But behind the mosque is the underground entrance to the necropolis which the Marinite Sultan Abu el Hassan dug for himself and his successors. He died in 1351 but the first body to be laid here was of Mohammed ech Sheikh in 1557, of the Saadian dynasty. His successor was buried here in 1574, followed in 1591 by Lalla Messaouada, founder of the Bab Doukkla Mosque and mother of Moulay el Mansour, who extended the mausoleum before being laid to rest here in 1603.

Moulay Ismail had this outside entrance covered, leaving access only from inside the mosque, so that the last sultan to be buried here, 'Mad' Moulay el Yazid in 1792, was interred via the mosque itself, an unusual feature in the Islamic world which believes interment should be in the cemetery, not in the building where people pray.

A French civil servant working for the Ministry of Fine Arts located the external entrance in 1917 and so led to non-Moslems being permitted to view the tombs of several of Morocco's sultans.

Entry is at standard hours, except Friday morning and Aïd el Kebir (currently in July), for 3DH, but go early or late to avoid the crowds and don't tag onto a guided tour or you might be asked to pay 10DH to get out. Guides were originally obligatory but you're now allowed to wander alone.

The twin mausoleums are highly decorated, and look more like a mosque interior than any other building a non-Moslem will be allowed to enter. Both are designed to have three rooms, with Moulay el Mansour's mausoleum, the first one you enter, being by far the better equipped. Here you will be able to inspect the beautifully-presented *mihrab*, the prayer-niche which shows the faithful where to face when prostrating themselves towards Mecca; normally this is in the prayer-chamber deep in the confines of the mosque and far from the gaze of infidels.

Yusef bin Taxfin. Outside are the tombs of many lesser dignitaries of the Saadian dynasty. And 400 yards away, on the left of Rue Sidi Mimoun, is the modest mausoleum of Marrakech's founder, Yusef bin Taxfin. The building is austere because, as tradition claims, the shadow of the long-dead sultan demolishes all attempts at ornamentation.

El Badia. To reach the Badia Palace from the Saadian Tombs you need to backtrack half way to Yusef's mausoleum and then take the road which leads almost due east to the Place des Ferblantiers. From here the Bab Berrima gives access to the Palace of El Badia, the 'Incomparable,' one of the 99 names for Allah.

Soon after Moulay Ahmed el Mansour emerged victorious from the Battle of the Three Kings, on 4 August 1578, he decided he would create the most lavish reception palace in Occidental Islam. Work began that same year and continued until his death in 1603, and his short journey to interment in the Saadian Tombs. The Incomparable Palace, according to contemporary reports, lived up to its name; El Mansour engaged an architect from Andalous and bought the finest marble from Italy — 50 carved columns, said one chronicler, paid for in sugar.

At the state opening, with ambassadors from many European countries as guests of honour, El Mansour asked the court jester his opinion of the palace and was told: "When it's demolished it will make a big heap of stones."

Prophetic words, perhaps, for Moulay Ismail deemed it too extravagant and setting a standard which he and his architects could not surpass. Starting in 1696 he began dismantling El Badia, using its stones for his fantasies in Meknès — and needing to rebuild the Bab Berrima to allow his wagons to pass.

El Badia is now the palace that was, joining the Hanging Gardens of Babylon and other wonders about which we can only guess. Even the big heap of stones has gone, but we are left with a pleasant open space with flowering shrubs growing by ornamental lakes, and storks nesting atop the taller ruins. Opening hours are close to standard for museums, and there's an entrance fee.

Folklore Festival. The annual Moroccan Folklore Festival, held each evening for a fortnight in early June, and one of the most important such celebrations in the country, is staged in El Badia.

Mellah. Place des Ferblantiers, which was the original Place du Mellah, leads east directly into the walled mellah, set up in 1557 for the city's Jews. Throughout Morocco it was imperial policy to establish the Jewish quarter as close to the royal palace as possible, and here they are only yards apart. One theory is that the sultan could keep an eye on them so much easier, another that they would act as buffer between him and any rebelling Berbers, but I favour the idea that they formed a convenient and discreet source of immediate finance, either by borrowing or taxation.

Jews have at best been tolerated in the Arab world and seldom permitted to own land. They've therefore been forced into the role of merchant, craftsman, and banker, and in Saadian Marrakech they controlled the sugar trade which financed El Badia. There were 16,000 Jews here as recently as the 1930s but the vast majority left in 1956 and only one or two synagogues are still in use.

La Bahia Palace. There is one letter difference in the names, so don't confuse El Badia with La Bahia which is 300 yards away to the north-east.

La Bahia was the private palace of Sidi Ahmed ben Moussa, a negro slave who rose to prominence at the court of Moulay el Hassan and his successor Abd el Aziz through intrigue and corruption. Sidi Ahmed, better known as Bou Ahmed, became Grand Vizier (chief minister) in 1894 at the accession of the young Abd el Aziz amid the scandal of the downfall of the previous viziers, the Jamai brothers, who built the Jamai Palace in Fès.

Bou Ahmed did the same in Marrakech, and La Bahia is his Jamai Palace, begun in 1894 and completed seven years later, just before his death. A Frenchman named Erckmann acting as overseer, commanded the architect to "Take your time," giving rise to the Arabic expression *Qarahat al Bahia,* 'the Bahia is finished,' for a job which takes forever.

As *bahia* also means 'incomparable, brilliant, magnificent,' but this time describing the palace, the expression took on a double meaning when Bou Ahmed died and his servants, slaves and wives fought, sometimes to the death, for their share of the jewels and lavish furnishings. Within days the lace was empty — 'the magnificence is finished' — which is how you find the interior today. The palace is open at standard times and is very popular with organised excursions; an independent traveller must negotiate his entrance fee at the beginning otherwise he'll be charged an extortionate amount to get out: I was quoted 10DH or "We'll talk about it later."

The interior is extremely garish and on your guided tour you see only a part of the 20-acre gardens, part of the harem, and some of the reception rooms, usually including one that measures 150 feet by 25.

Calèches carry tourists in Marrakech

Gharnata Palace. The nearby Gharnata, Riad, and Riad el *(sic)* Bahia palaces are smart restaurants.

Dar Si Saïd. The Rue Riad es Zitoun el Jedid leads north through a smart residental district. Take the first opening on the right under an arch, then turn left to the Dar Si Saïd, the mansion of Moulay el Hassan's chamberlain, and brother to Bou Ahmed.

The palace is now a **Museum of Moroccan Art** and in this guise well worth a visit (standard hours, probably closed Tuesday, guided tour). Exhibits on three floors include metalwork, small arms and sidearms, Berber jewellery and carpets, and an unusual display of doors and other woodcarving from the Saadian dynasty.

Gardens. Marrakech is surprisingly well-endowed with gardens for a city so close to the Sahara, and the Marrakchi have two of the best in the country. The largest and most impressive is the **Agdal** or Aguedal Garden south of the Royal Palace, 1.8 miles long by up to 0.9 of a mile wide (3km by 1.5km) and covering 920 acres (372ha). Access on foot is preferable from either the Saadian Tombs (continue down the Route de la Kasbah) or from the Places des Ferblantiers (enter the Mellah and turn right into Rue Berrima). Both routes go around the palace and meet at the Bab Agdal (Porte de l'Aguedal) from where you can go through another gate into the garden. By car, follow the Route des Remparts clockwise to its finish at Bab Ahmar then walk past the palace to Bab Agdal.

The mid-19th cent garden was the dream of Moulay Abd er Rahman who used irrigation canals and conduits that had existed since the early days of the city. The grounds now hold a sample of most of the fruiting trees of the region, including olives, on rectangular plots. Pass the Dar el Beïda, the 'white house,' a 19th-cent royal palace, to the pools at the far end of the grounds. Climb onto the terrace of the ruined pavilion, and you have a good view over the city and back to the Atlas Mountains.

The **Menara Garden** is the work of Sidi Mohammed ben Abd er Rahman, son of the sultan who created the Agdal Garden. It is a little less formal in design and specialises in olive trees, but is shady nonetheless. Statistics? The plot is 4,000 feet by 2,600 (1,200m by 800) and the central pool is 200 feet by 150. How to get there? Leave Bab Jedid for the Avenue de la Menara which runs dead straight for 1.5 miles (2.4km) and ends by the poolside pavilion.

Yves Saint-Laurent owned, and may still own, the **Jardin Majorelle** north of the main bus station. The work of the French artist and furniture-maker Louis Majorelle in his last years — he died in 1926 — this garden has a much better selection to offer but on a smaller scale.

Stay at La **Mamounia Hotel** just inside the Bab Jedid and you can share the delights of its splendid garden, laid out in the 18th cent. Or just wander the streets of the Ville Nouvelle and admire the corner plots and the hedges where jasmine, jacaranda, hibiscus, oleander, bougainvillea and other exotic flowers grow as if wild. But don't try eating the miniature oranges; they're bitter.

Ville Nouvelle. The French-inspired 'new town,' known as the **Gueliz,** is smart, clean, well-designed and very much a garden city, but it is in the mould of all the villes nouvelles: there is nothing in particular to look at.

Route des Remparts. By car, by cycle, by calèche, or even on foot in the cooler months, a journey down the Route des Remparts reveals the medina's eastern gates. In addition to those mentioned, the **Bab el Khemis,** formerly Bab Fès, had doors that were brought over from Moorish Spain. The present name comes from the livestock market originally held here on the fifth day, *el khemis,* of the Islamic week but now almost a daily event. **Bab Ailen** is named from a Berber tribe and marks the spot where the Almohades were defeated in 1128.

Route de la Palmerai. A few miles out of town on the way to Fès, signs point prominently to the Route de la Palmerai, a 14.5 mile (22.5km) circuit of Morocco's most northerly palm grove, where 100,000 trees grow on 32,000 acres (13,000ha). The road is surfaced throughout but is narrow and twisting, a reasonable evening excursion by hired cycle or calèche. The trees are of poor quality and have no comparison with the oases of Tunisia.

HOTELS. For an experience of a lifetime, particularly when funds are unlimited, try La Mamounia, a 5* hotel inside Bab Jedid and standing in its own elegant grounds. This was Winston Churchill's favourite for many years, and the 1986 restoration has preserved the Churchill suite. The Mamounia runs one of the two casinos in Morocco, on Ave Pres. Kennedy in the Hivernage garden district, and it has a night club, sauna, and hammam, as well as 196 rooms.

See map for hotels. Others, not on maps: Amine (3*), 146 rms, 1 mile on Rte Casablanca; Andalous, el (4*), 195 rms, Ave Kennedy; Ibn Batouta (3*), 52 rms, Ave Yakub el Marini; Kenza (4*), 93 rms, Ave Yakub el

Mansour; Menara (3*), 100 rms, Rte des Remparts; Pacha, du (2*), 39 rms, Blv de la Liberté; Sahara Inn (4*), 167 rms, 3 miles on Rte Casa; Semiramis-Salam (4*), 186 rms, 3 miles on Rte Casa; Smara (3*), 49 rms, Blv Moh Zerktouni; Tafilalet (4*), 84 rms, 2 miles on Rte Casa; Tichka (4*), 140 rms, on Rte Casa. Several small 1* or unclassified hotels are in the streets east of Ave Mohammed V, and budget hotels cluster in the alleys around the Jemaa el Fna.

HOLIDAY CLUBS: Club Médterranée, 400 beds (sports in palm grove), Place Jemaa el Fna; Palais de Congres, 1,500 beds, Ave de France.

YOUTH HOSTEL: near the **Camping Municipal;** see main map.

RESTAURANTS: Marrakech has a good selection, particularly in the top class, including Gharnata Palace and Riad *el* Bahia, both near *La* Bahia; and others along the Route de Casablanca, including Sun Set Boulevard, El Bordj which serves in caïd-style military tents and has a folklore show, and others: all serve Moroccan dishes.

Cheaper restaurants are around the Place Jemaa el Fna, and French-style food is along Ave Mohammed V.

NIGHTLIFE: try the casino or the night clubs in the smart hotels. Genuine local nightlife centres around Jemaa el Fna.

BUSES: main bus station is by Bab Doukkala where is also a large **car park** with guardiens. Some long-distance departures are very early. Buses for Ourika Valley and Oukaimeden leave from Bab er Rob.

TAXIS: grand and petit from Bab Doukkala on shuttle service. Also from Bab er Robb and Jemaa el Fna.

CALÈCHES: several hundred horse carriages operate in the city; useful for leisurely drive around Route des Palmerai. Best pick-ups, Ave Mohammed V and by Koutoubia.

RAIL: terminus at Ave Hassan II 1.2km west of main PTT; through trains to Casablanca, change for other destinations.

FESTIVALS: National Folklore Festival at El Badia, first two weeks in June; same time or early July, fantasia spectacle at Bab Jedid.

TOURIST INFO: ONMT at Place Abd el Moumen ben Ali (Ave Mohammed V); S.I, 500 metres to east on Ave Mohammed V junction with Rue Sourya. Afternoon openings restricted, closed Sunday.

MARRAKECH EXCURSION

Ourika Valley and Oukaimeden. Leave Marrakech from Dar er Robb, either by public transport or your own car, for a step back in history in the Ourika Valley. After 21 miles (34km) you reach the Atlas Mountains near Dar Caïd Ouriki, a village with a mosque, a zaouia and a busy Monday market, but set back from the road.

At **Arhbalou** the road forks; left for the Ourika and right for Oukaimeden. The village, at 3,360 ft (1,025m) has basic accommodation for tourists, mostly mountain trekkers. Forking left into the narrowing valley, we enter wild and rugged country broken by innumerable signs of habitation; an occasional tiny village, orchards, tiny terraced fields, and irrigation canals taking water from the permanent stream.

Prehistoric Paintings. It's possible to hire mules and a guide in Annameure for serious trekking to **Jebel Yagour** at 8,944ft (2,726m), near where some 2,000 cave and cliff paintings have been found, showing swords, spears and even boomerangs, yet believed to be more than 2,000 years old. These mountains hold several collections of early art; to the south are deer and elephants, showing the fauna that formerly lived here, and near Azibs n'Lisk is a painting of a cow 15 feet (5m) tall. You will, of course, need special equipment and a skilled guide before setting out on the trail of primitive art.

Further up the valley, tiny villages cling to the mountain slopes with mule tracks their only means of access, and you soon see evidence of the flash flood which struck in 1987: this is life reduced to the basic struggle for survival and a world away from the relative affluence of Marrakech.

The road, and the bus service, end a little short of **Zaouia Setti Fatma** and its tiny neighbour, Zaouia Mohammed. Here you are overwhelmed by the High Atlas all around, rugged, red, and almost devoid of vegetation, yet the village has lush pastures, chestnut trees, and permanent water: the mountains are high enough to generate their own rain at any time of the year.

Accommodation is basic with camping the main option, or you might find rooms in a private house.

Oukaimeden. At Arhbalou, 15 miles (24km) down valley, the right fork puts you on a well-maintained road that climbs the much steeper Lekak Valley past cork oaks and evergreen oaks to Oukaimeden, at 8,700ft (2,650m) one of the highest villages in Africa north of the Sahara. The Berber name means 'crossroad of the winds,' an apt description as the village sits on a steep slope with a splendid view down the Lekak.

Ask at the *Refuge de la Jeunesse et des Sports* for locations of the prehistoric paintings in the neighbourhood, as some of them are only a short walk away.

A marked track of 1.5 miles climbs to the top of Jebel Tizerag (8,990ft, 2,740m) north of the village, now crowned with a TV transmitter. On a clear day you feel you can reach out and touch Marrakech, 28 miles (45km) away.

Ski Resort. Oukaimeden is Morocco's main ski resort, with a season roughly from Christmas to mid-April although the snow can be erratic. See 'Sports.'

ACCOMMODATION: there is a reasonable choice: Hotel Imil (3*), 34 rms and night-club (après-ski is a long way short of Alpine standards); Auberge Chez Juju (1*), 16 rms and chalets for longer hire; Refuge de la Jeunesse et des Sports, 70 beds; Club Alpin 50 beds.

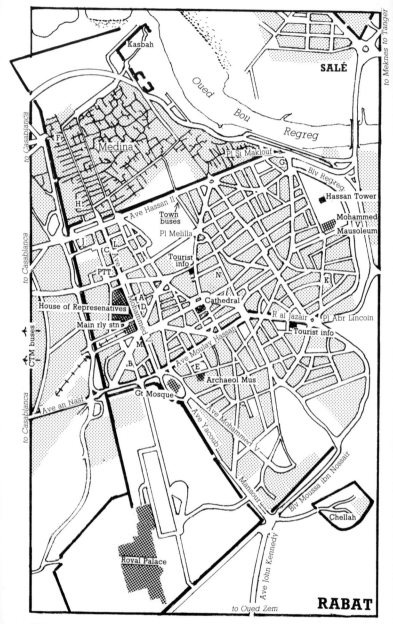

RABAT

14: RABAT and SALÉ

The modern capital

RABAT IS AN IMPERIAL CITY that was never quite accepted as capital of the Moorish empire, but it has been the capital of modern Morocco since 1956.

Chellah. Eight centuries before Christ, the Berber tribe of the Chellah lived on these coastal plains, and tangible 3rd cent BC evidence of their settlement has been found. The Phoenicians and the Carthaginians later made use of the site, hidden around the first bend of the waterway now known as the Oued Bou Regreg, the 'Father of Reflection.'

Sala. By the time the Romans arrived the name had been corrupted to Sala, as Ptolemy recorded it. Sala was, like Volubilis, at the end of its own road from Tingis and was the southernmost point of effective Roman power on the Atlantic seaboard. Trajan, who ruled from 98 to 117, gave it the status of a colony, but when the centurions were forced to pull back towards Rome, Sala Colonia sank into decline and its estuary began silting.

Berghuata. By the time Islam swept across north Africa, Sala was nothing more than a ruin on the site of the present Chellah and its few inhabitants made no objection to accepting the new faith; there is a fanciful but impossible story which claims that Mahomet himself came here to pray. A few decades later the Berghuata tribe of Berbers, who had accepted hardcore Islamic beliefs, moved onto the coastal plains and caused the more orthodox Moslems to follow, lest the Kharijite ideas were to gain ground.

The orthodox followers built a ribat in the late 9th cent, siting it on the south bank of the oued at its mouth, where the Kasbah des Oudaias stands today, and from here their *mujahadin* (holy warriors) began their *jihad* (holy war) against the Berghuata, but with little success.

Meanwhile, the Beni Ifren tribe, whom the Almoravides had defeated in 1058, moved in to the north bank of the oued and built their own walled medina. As they were orthodox Moslems they joined in the

---

KEY TO HOTELS

A Balima (2˚) 69 rms
B Belère (4˚), 90 rms, night club
C Capitol (2˚) 40 rms
D Central, (1˚) 34 rms
E Chellah (4˚), 100 rms
F Darna (1˚), 40 rms
G Farah Sofitel (5˚), 200 rms

H France, de (unclass)
J Majestic (1˚), 36 rms
   Paix, de la (1˚, see Splendid)
K Sheherezade (3˚), 36 rms
L Splendid (1˚), 41 rms
M Terminus (3˚), 72 rms
N Tour Hassan, H de la (5˚), 249 rms, night club

campaign against the Kharijites, a struggle which jogged along until the Almohade Sultan Abd el Moumen seized the region around 1146 and defeated the Berghuata, who faded from history.

Kasbah. Abd el Moumen extended the single-fort ribat into a kasbah, a fortified community, including a small palace for himself. From here, he decreed, the jihad would continue, but its target was now the Christians who had already reconquered half of Iberia and were steadily encroaching on al-Andalus.

His grandson Yakub el Mansour had great plans to make Sala — Sla in Arabic — this town on the *south* bank of the Oued Bou Regreg, his imperial capital. He built the Oudaia Gate on the south of the kasbah, then threw a vast retaining wall from there to the ocean, inland almost to the old Chellah, then back to the oued and the kasbah: these are the city walls which still stand today, plus some that have gone. This sultan who had already built the minaret at the Koutoubia Mosque in Marrakech now started the great Mosque of Hassan in Sala, beginning with the minaret, a near-duplicate of the Koutoubia tower. He died before building the mosque at its base and so the minaret stands alone. Known as the Tower of Hassan, it is the city's main landmark.

Ribat el Fath. Yakub had designs on creating a second Alexandria on the Atlantic coast and he called this new city Ribat el Fath, 'Ribat the Victorious,' but accounts differ on whether Mansour was marking his first victory, the seizure of the sultanate after the Battle of the Three Kings, or his later triumph at Alarcos in Spain. Certainly he vowed that the jihad would continue — and yet, among his wives, were the daughters of the kings of Navarra and León, freely given in marriage!

But the name Ribat el Fath never stuck. The city became Sla el Jedid, 'Salé the New,' which made that other medina across the Bou Regreg where the Beni Ifren people had settled, Sla el Bali, 'Salé the Old.' Old Salé eventually became the present Salé and New Salé became Rabat, so for convenience we'll use those names henceforth, not forgetting they're still Sla and ar Ribat to their inhabitants.

El Mansour died in 1199 and with him went the spark that had glowed in Rabat. The city, which had come no nearer to filling its ambitious ramparts than it had to fulfilling its creator's dreams, went into decline. The Almohades gave way to the Marinites, whose Sultan Abu Yusef Yakub built a zaouia and a mausoleum in the tiny and still separate walled city of Chellah, but there was no respite for Rabat.

Spanish Attack. At the feast of Aïd es Seghir, marking the end of Ramadan in 1260, the fleet of Alfonso X of Spain sailed into the Bou Regreg and sacked Salé and Rabat. The Moors rebuilt both cities, and now gave Salé a mosque and a medersa, and the aqueduct which ran in through the Bab Mrisa. But Rabat continued to collapse so that three centuries later the historian Léon the African could comment that it was down to 100 habitable houses.

Andalous Eviction. By now Spain had discovered the New World and regained all its territory lost to the Moors in 711, two events which were to have great significance at Rabat and Salé. For in 1609, with Catholicism becoming an intolerant church, Felipe III exiled from his land anybody who was obviously of Moorish origin. Thousands of the so-called Andalous, known in Spain as Moriscos and many of whom were unable to speak Arabic or who had even become Christian, fled across the strait to Morocco.

Rempart des Andalous. Less at ease in Morocco than they had been in Spain, they crowded into the medina at Rabat, squeezed up behind the kasbah, and built a wall to shut off the open space to the south; now known as the Rempart des Andalous, it separates the Arab-style medina from the new city along the route of Ave Hassan II.

Republic of Bou Regreg. These new citizens owed nothing to Morocco and even less to Spain, and by 1627 they had set up their own state in miniature, the Republic of Bou Regreg, with its capital in the Oudaia Kasbah. Using funds salvaged from their exodus they created a pirate fleet and sailed off to harass Spanish ships bringing home treasures from the New World.

Sallee Rovers. Some of the Andalous in Salé joined them, while others began trading with the Europeans, selling them leather and ivory, cloth and wool, honey and beeswax, in return for guns and ammunition which they or their fellows promptly used against other Europeans. The Barbary Coast in the north was notorious for its pirates, but they were ineffective compared with the Sallee Rovers who terrorised the Christians' merchant shipping and even raided European ports, often with renegade Christians among the crews.

Meanwhile, the French merchant Pierre Mazet, based in Rabat, developed a useful business as negotiator for the ransoming of prisoners and slaves, brought abruptly to a halt in 1666 when Moulay er Rachid seized the Republic of Bou Regreg. Now its pirates were working for the sultan!

Moulay Rachid and later sultans rebuilt the kasbah and for a while, when the political climate in the Imperial Cities was uncomfortable, Rabat became the temporary seat of government. Work began on a royal palace, the embryo of the present Dar el Makhzen.

Around 1700 Moulay Ismail made Salé a satellite of Rabat and brought in the Oudaia tribesmen to monitor the twin cities, but piracy continued as a way of life until 1829 when the last ship was seized, a vessel sailing under the Austro-Hungarian flag.

Capital. From the mid-19th cent Morocco began to weaken, and in 1845-46 the sultanate opened discussions with the French in Rabat, which eventually led to the establishment of the Protectorate in 1912. France's first resident-general, Lyautey, trying to demoralise the country still further, moved its capital from Fès to Rabat, followed by the puppet sultan, Moulay Yusef, who thus endorsed Lyautey's choice. From independence in 1956 Rabat, with its satellite of Salé, has been the capital of the entire nation, but even with a combined population of 841,800 at the 1981 census it's still not the largest city: that distinction goes to Casablanca.

Rabat Today. The capital of Morocco is a relatively quiet place with much of its European-inspired new town within the ancient walled city. Indeed, all the tourist attractions are inside Yakub el Mansour's ramparts: the Chambre des Représentatives, the one-chamber Parliament; the Tour Hassan and the Mausoleum of Mohammed V; the museums; the Andalous gardens and wall; the medina, kasbah and mellah; the town bus and main rail stations; and in their respective walls, Chellah's and Salé's souks. Only the main bus stations are out of town.

Understandably, Rabat shows a much stronger European influence than any other walled city in Morocco, but it has yet to suffer the congestion of European cities. Despite the maze of one-way-streets there's no problem in finding parking space — without the services of a *guardien de voiture.*

RABAT

The Medina. The European influence shows even in the heart of the old Arab city, because the Spanish sacked it at the end of Ramadan in 1260 and it was not rebuilt until the Moriscos came over from Spain in 1609-10, bringing a Europeanised concept of straight streets. Crooked streets had been favoured in the days of hand-to-hand fighting when each house-corner could be defended, but firearms and artillery were now the weapons of war.

The refugees from al-Andalous built the Andalous Wall, 1,400 yards long and well-preserved to this day. Within its defences the medina prospered, the **Souk el Ghezel,** the wool market by the kasbah, continuing its established trade in selling Christian slaves. This is where many of the Sallee Rovers' captives began their new lives in the Arab world, while those who were seen as enemies of the state, be they Arab or Christian, had their severed heads displayed at the Bab el Had, a custom which extended into the 19th cent.

Medieval timber-and-plaster houses stand beside stone buildings in the covered **Souk es Sebat** and the **Rue Souika,** forming the business core of the old city and where you will find an array of mini-restaurants and general shops. When foreign residents were once again tolerated in any number, they were compelled to live in the Souk es Sebat or its neighbouring alley, Rue des Consuls, now the home of carpet sellers. The Jews were forcibly moved in 1808 to their mellah in the eastern corner of the medina, but other nationals were still confined to quarters until 1912.

Rue Souika starts at the **Bab el Had,** the Sunday Market Gate rebuilt in 1814, but the food market nearby is an everyday affair. The rue passes the **Moulay Sliman Mosque,** begun in 1812 by the sultan of that name. Further along, the first Great Mosque was rebuilt in 1882 with the minaret added in 1939; it has recently been outranked by the former As Sounina Mosque near Bab er Rouah.

Between Rue des Consuls and the river, now too silted to be of commercial use, stand the small **Musée Nationale de l'Artisanat** (National Crafts Museum, open office hours), the craft centre and, closer to the main bridge, the Borj Lalla Kadiya and its neighbouring sanctuary, where pilgrims returning from Mecca traditionally spent their first night in the city.

Kasbah des Oudaias. Yakub el Mansour revitalised the Kasbah des Oudaias and built the elaborate Bab Oudaia, though the names came later as the Oudaia tribe had not yet appeared at Rabat. Mansour, who wanted the kasbah to be his capital but who stayed with Marrakech, created in the **Bab Oudaia** more a work of art than a practical defence. Its warm red stonework is highly decorated on both sides and is a prime example of Almohade art. The attractive, chubby symbols of the Kufic script, originally from Kufa in Iraq, are so unlike the harsher cursives of later times, seen in such profusion in the Haghia Sophia Mosque in Istanbul.

Moulay er Rachid, who seized the Republic of Bou Regreg, began a palace which his successor Moulay Ismail completed; it's now the **Museum of the Oudaias** (standard hours except Tuesdays; restricted hours in Ramadan) or, more properly, another Museum of Moroccan Art. Its exhibits include ceramics and tapestries as well as many artefacts from the life of the common Berber in many parts of the country. You can see costumes worn by the blue men of the south, wedding dresses from Berbers in many areas, and even a display of beds. The building itself, despite some of its rooms being closed, is also a major exhibit: note the hammam.

Oudaia. The Arab tribe of the Oudaia came west in the 13th cent but were uneasy settlers in the Sahara and in Fès, so Moulay Ismail, the builder of Meknès, allowed them to settle around the kasbah as auxiliaries to his army, in return for checking the pirates paid their dues and for keeping another tribe, the Zaer, at bay.

The raised area around the palace-museum holds the **Andalous Garden** which, despite its name, was built by the French during the First World War. A path leads from the garden to the **Café Maure,** which isn't all that Moorish but is a well-known meeting-spot for drinking a glass of mint tea while admiring the view over the estuary.

Another good viewpoint is at the **Pirates' Tower,** 160 metres away, built in the 17th cent for reasons too obvious to mention. At the northern tip of the kasbah is the **Semaphore platform,** with another good view and an equally obvious use. An 18th-cent warehouse on the platform now holds the School of Carpetmaking (standard hours, closed at weekends) which gives a good insight into the craft. Did you know that Rabat carpets have 150,000 hand-tied knots to the square metre?

From any of the viewpoints you can't miss seeing the minaret of the **Atika Mosque,** Rabat's oldest, built around 1150 and restored many times, on the last occasion around 1770 by Ahmed el Inglizi, an Englishmen who joined the Sallee Rovers.

Tour Hassan. South of the Andalous Wall the most distinctive landmark is Yakub el Mansour's minaret, the Hassan Tower, which was to have crowned the second largest mosque in the world, giving place only to the Friday Mosque of Samarra, in Iraq's Mesopotamia. Mansour began the project in 1195 and managed to create a minaret 53 feet (16.2m) square and rising to 145 feet (44m). When he died in 1199 the tower was unfinished, but work ceased. There was little work done on the main mosque which would have covered 6 acres (2.5ha) and held around 50,000 people in a prayer hall where 400 columns supported the vast roof.

But no Sultan el Mansour meant no mosque. The townspeople gradually began using the dressed stones for their own use, and the earthquake of 1755 levelled what little remained. Since the site has never been consecrated the only restriction on non-Moslems climbing the internal ramp to the top, has been the recent restoration work.

Mohammed V Mausoleum. On the south side of the plot which should have held Mansour's Hassan Mosque, there is now the Mausoleum of King Mohammed V, the first sovereign of post-Protectorate Morocco and the first to call himself 'king' rather than 'sultan.' The mausoleum was built in 1971 in traditional style but on a modern concrete skeleton: did its Vietnamese architect remember this is an earthquake zone?

Although this is almost a holy site, non-Moslems are allowed in (daily, 0800-2100) to see the king's tomb of white onyx from Pakistan permanently watched over by a contingent from the Royal Guard. The associated mosque was begun in 1961 and dedicated in 1967, and is open only to Moslems.

Royal Palace. Surprisingly, parts of the grounds of the Royal Palace, the Dar el Makhzen, are also open to visitors (standard hours). The original palace was 18th-cent, built into the bottom corner of the 12th-cent Almohade walls as if they were designed for the purpose. The present palace was begun in 1864 by Sidi Mohammed ben Abd er Rahman and extended for Mohammed V and Hassan II.

The remainder of the Ville Nouvelle offers a selection of new buildings and an old gateway; among the new are the Cathedral of St Pierre, General Lyautey's mausoleum (his ashes lie here in the ministerial quarter of town yet he has a tomb in Les Invalides, Paris), and the surprisingly small Chamber of Representatives, closed to visitors. The old gateway of note is the **Bab er Rouah,** the Gate of the Winds, which is almost as impressive as the Bab Oudaia and was presumably conceived as a monumental entrance even though there was nothing beyond the walls in Almohade times.

Bab el Mrisa leads into the old Jewish Quarter of Salé; a canal originally flowed through this gate

The PTT, commanding a view down the tree-lined gardens in the centre of Ave Mohammed V, has a small **Postal Museum** open during business hours, while the Archaeological Museum, smaller than one would expect, is in a purpose-built home near the new Great Mosque.

Archaeological Museum. Open standard hours except Tuesdays, this is Morocco's main archaeological collection with a number of displays worth seeing, regardless of whether you have Volubilis, Lixus and Cotta on your itinerary. Exhibits cover the history of human occupation of this corner of Africa from prehistoric to early Islamic times, understandably with Volubilis contributing many of the discoveries.

Chellah. Or perhaps you prefer your archaeology still on site? In that case, come to Chellah, the original city in its own self-contained walls 300 metres east of Bab Zaer, the 12th-cent gate restored in the 18th cent.

The entire city, surrounded by walls just 1,100 metres long, is known as the Necropolis and its most interesting feature is probably its main gate built — with the walls — by Abu el Hassan (1331-48), the 'Black Sultan.' Critics have called the gate 'Roman art faced with Gothic,' but the kufic inscription leaves no doubt about its Arab origins: 'begun during the reign of Abu Saïd and finished by Abu el Hassan in 1339' (Gregorian calendar).

The oldest relics here are **Roman** in the north corner and with a little imagination you can accept them as foundations of a triumphal arch and the capitol, and picture the toga-wearing crowds on the flagstones of the Decumanus Maximus and its side streets. There is more excavation to be done, then the curators must use their own imagination in explaining the ruins.

Curators? There are none. The site is open from around 0830 to sunset, there's neither fee to get in nor out, the only guides are of the inevitable self-appointed type, and nobody has lived here since 1154; you can't count the genies whom Moulay Yakub ordered to guard the place in perpetuity.

Sanctuary. Abu el Hassan's sanctuary is the main ruin in Chellah and incorporates Abu Yusef Yakub's mosque, built before 1286 and destroyed by the earthquake of 1755. The quake also helped bring down Yakub's minaret and seriously damage the main building.

You enter through Yusef Yakub's mosque and see the chancel holding the tomb of Hassan ahead and to the right. The tombstone of his Christian-born wife Chams ed Douha is on the left. Chams was also known as the 'Morning Sun' and the 'Lady (Lalla) of Chellah,' but as the mother of Abu Inan, builder of the Bou Inania medersas, she had an unhappy end to her life, for her son was responsible for her husband's death.

Hassan's zaouia on the far left is in a better state of repair and gives a rare opportunity to inspect the interior of an Islamic holy building, studying its toilet, the purification cells, and finally the oratory and the mihrab. It's difficult to appreciate why non-Moslems are forbidden entry to mosques since Moslems don't believe that God — Allah — graces them with his presence; the prayers go out in search of the divinity.

Dinosaur. A complete dinosaur skeleton 50 feet long and 15 feet tall

(15m by 4.5m) is on display in the **Musée des Sciences de la Terre** on the ground floor of the Ministry of Energy in the Agdal district. When the skeleton was found in the High Atlas 1979 it was the world's best example of a dinosaur and was dated at 165,000,000 years old.

The Energy Ministry is 400m east of Pl Moh Zerktouni near the Jardins d'Essai, and the museum is open at office hours (restricted during Ramadan). The **Jardins d'Essai** — trial grounds — have an excellent collection of cacti among other specimens and are almost a last vestige of the Imperial Gardens of the Agdal which covered hundreds of acres west of the medina until the Ville Nouvelle moved in.

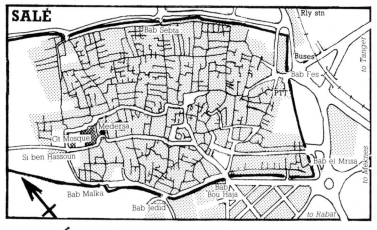

SALÉ

Salé has slumbered on since independence, originally the more important of these twin medinas but totally overshadowed since Rabat became the seat of government. Even the *ville nouvelle* is small but, by contrast, the Moslem cemeteries north and west of the town are now half the size of the inhabited medina.

Bab Fès is the main gate but **Bab Mrisa,** 'Gate of the Little Port,' is more impressive. It was the work of Yakub el Mansour after Alfonso X's attack in 1260, and allowed a channel to come into town bringing water from the Oued Bou Regreg. Reports also point out that the unusually high arch of Bab Mrisa permitted ships to enter the city with masts stepped. History supports the story: the name of the gate, and the ten years' work prompted by the 1260 raid — but what a major undertaking it must have been! And as navigation locks weren't in existence in the 13th cent the canal must have left the river a considerable way upstream.

The souks cluster in the centre of town, radiating from the kaysaria, with Souk el Ghezel, the wool souk, usually the most colourful — and with a few pungent smells, which is why it's an early-morning market. Elsewhere, prayer mat weavers have their own souk amid the other craftsmen.

Sidi Abdallah ben Hassoun. Rue de la Grande Mosquée leads past a fondouk to Yusef Yakub's Great Mosque and its neighbour, the Medersa of Abu el Hassan, the 'Black Sultan.' Just beyond the mosque is the Marabout of Sidi Abdallah ben Hassoun, Salé's patron saint, who is the subject of a colourful annual procession through the streets late in the afternoon of the day before Mahomet's birthday.

Towards dusk the townspeople gather at the marabout, the men dressed as the Turks who originated the event, and accompanied by children playing flutes and rattling tambourines, and with everybody carrying long candles carved with religious symbols. The night which welcomes in Mouloud is spent in prayer inside the marabout, and on Achoura, the sixth day of the Islamic New Year (a date fixed by the phases of the moon and with no relation to Mouloud), the remains of the candles are returned to the marabout and kept until the next year's procession.

Slaoui (people of Salé) planning a long journey used to lay coloured wooden sticks on Sidi Abdallah's tomb on the day before departure. If the sticks were rearranged during the night, the journey would be successful. No rearrangement boded badly.

Sidi ben Achir. Great Mosque Street ends at the Marabout of Sidi ben Achir, a 14th-cent Morisco who could call foreign merchant ships onto the rocks and calm storms: a useful character for the Salle Rovers and who is now busy curing mental illness from beyond the grave. Non-Moslems shouldn't approach too closely.

Wheat is still threshed by hand in the Rif mountains

HOTELS: see map of Rabat. Others, not marked: Dahir (2*), 129 rms, disco, Ave Hassan II, 600m NW Pl Moh Zerktouni & buses; d'Orsay (2*), 30 rms, 11 Ave Moulay Yusef near rail stn; Oudaias, les (3*), 35 rms, 4 Rue Tobrouk, Pl Moulay Hassan. The Rabat Hilton has closed. There are a few cheap hotels in the medina but the one-star places in the Ville Nouvelle are no dearer in high summer.

The only hotel in Salé is the unclassified Saadiens by the bus station.

RESTAURANTS: are rather sparse. The Casabella and the Koutoubia serve French and Moroccan menus respectively, along Ave Moulay Hassan north of the Archaeological Museum. Otherwise try around the rail station or Ave Moulay Yusef, towards Bab Rouah. **Nightlife** is confined to hotels with entertainment, or discos around Place Melilya (Melilla) south of Bab Mellah.

BUSES: for long-distances *southbound* leave from Pl Mohammed Zerktouni, 1 mile (1.6km) from Bab Rouah along Ave an Nasr, or on no 30 bus from *local* bus station on middle of Ave Hassan II (by Andalous Wall). The bus station by Bab el Had no longer operates. For long-distances *northbound* take a 6 or 12 from the town depot to the bus station outside Bab Fès, Salé.

TAXIS: grands taxis duplicating the bus routes leave from the same places; petits taxis from the *town* bus station.

RAIL: both cities have rail stations; Rabat's Gare Agdal is by the Pl road in the new town; its Gare Centrale is on Ave Mohammed V by the Parliament building; and Salé's station is just north of Bab Fès and the bus station. The line runs through all three stations in sequence, and passes under Rabat city centre.

AIRPORTS: Casablanca is the main international airport; special bus from Ave Mohammed V, Rabat, for 45DH but it's cheaper to take service bus to Casablanca then line 6.

FERRY: from near the end of the Andalous Wall to Salé beach.

FESTIVALS: Salé's Abdallah ben Hassoun parade is on the day before Mouloud; the associated Candle Festival (Fête des Cires) is in April, mixing Islamic and Christian calendars.

TOURIST INFO: ONMT, 22 Ave Al Jazair; S.I, Rue Patrice Lumumba, Rabat. 0800-1200, Mon-Sat, occasionally open afternoons.

Evening in Tanger, with Spain on the horizon across the Strait of Gibraltar

15: CASABLANCA

And the Coastal Plain

CASABLANCA IS A EUROPEAN CITY WITH LITTLE CONCESSION to African or to Arab culture. A metropolis of wide, straight avenues, of bustling traffic that also experiences the worst congestion in Morocco, Casablanca is superficially less Moroccan than is Agadir. Few women wear the veil, alcohol is freely available, and even the city's popular name is European.

Yet beneath the surface, Casablanca *is* Morocco, since it holds one-seventh of the population, half the heavy industry (omitting phosphate mining), it is the heart of the financial market, the food, metal and chemical industries, and it has most of the university places.

Casablanca has no showpiece for the tourist, nothing specific to look at, unless you consider the city itself to be its own showcase. For most foreigners it is a place to go *through* rather than *to:* either via the airport or driving along the coast road.

Ancient Anfa. Stone Age Man was here, as proved by discoveries made in 1955. The Phoenicians came, then the Berbers, but none left any great mark. It was the Berghouata tribe, with their hardcore Kharijite interpretation of Islam which troubled the people of Chella (Rabat), who first settled two miles west of the Old Medina, calling their town Anfa.

Pirates. Abd el Moumen seized the community in the 12th cent and Anfa almost crumbled away, but in the early 14th cent the few remaining inhabitants discovered piracy as a way of life, long before the Sallee Rovers put to sea. They attacked Cádiz and southern Portugal with such ferocity that in 1468 King Ferdiñão of Portugal led a 50-strong armada which sacked the town.

The Portuguese had to repeat the lesson in 1515, then in 1575 they sailed out yet again, this time from their base at Mazagan (El Jadida), seized Anfa and destroyed it. Their new town, now the basis of the Old Medina, had a touch of European influence in its limewashed buildings, so they called it *Casa Branca,* 'White House.'

Earthquake. The Portuguese pulled out of Casa Branca in 1755 when a major earthquake destroyed Lisbon and severely damaged this African settlement. The town was abandoned until Sidi Mohammed ben Abdallah (Mohammed III) resettled it in 1770 and called it, for lack of any other name, Dar el Beïda, Arabic for 'White House.'

Dar el Beïda. Under Mohammed III, Dar el Beïda began growing, although slowly. He built the Great Mosque and the Borj Sidi el Kairouani, and in the late 18th cent his successors allowed Spanish merchants to settle and trade in the city. The Arabs continued to call the place Dar el Beïda, as they do to this day, but for the Europeans it became known as White House in Spanish — Casablanca.

The original Casablanca had no harbour at all, sailors relying purely on the slight shelter from the headland of Ras el Hank. With Rabat's Oued Bou Regreg silting up and no other harbour available, the creation of the first breakwater at Casablanca stimulated trade. Soon the city was exporting wheat and cotton to Europe, with phosphates, sugar and vegetables later to be added. The first foreign consulate, the British, opened in 1857, with the French coming in '61 and the Spanish in '65.

Population explosion. The result was a population explosion on a phenomenal scale, which is still going on. In 1830 the town had 600 people; in 1860, 8,000; in 1907, 20,000, and the medina was no longer able to hold them. In 1912 the population had reached 60,000; in 1936, 263,000; in 1952, 682,000; in 1961 it passed the million mark; the 1981 census recorded 2,408,600, and by now there are many more than 3,000,000.

Casablanca has managed to cope with this unprecedented growth probably because of European help; the French took over the port in 1906 and after riots in '07, brought in troops to help keep order. The French influence was strong during the Protectorate and Casablanca managed to avoid urban sprawl, though it had its shanty towns filled with landless tribesmen who scratched a living on the edge of prosperity; some of those *bidonvilles* remain, but they are unobtrusive and not as much a problem here as in Black Africa.

The port of Casablanca is now the fourth busiest on this continent (trade leaders are Port Harcourt, Durban, and Arzew in Algeria) moving 17,300,240 tons of cargo in and out during 1983 (11,500,000 of it being phosphates for export), and more than 20,000,000 tons in 1984. More statistics? The commercial quay can store 70,000 tons of cereals, the main breakwater is now 10,433 feet long, and more than 70,000 passengers use the port each year, including people on cruise liners. And while the country continues its population boom and industrial expansion, Casablanca's city and port will grow at the same rate.

Sightseeing. For once, the **Old Medina** has no specific attraction, not

KEY TO HOTELS

1 Almohades, les (4*), 138 rms
2 Astoria (3*), 30 rms
3 Balmoral (2*), 34 rms
4 Bon Rêve (unclass)
5 Cernay (2*), 60 rms
6 Excelsior (2*), 60 rms
7 Foucauld, de (1*) 22 rms
8 Gallia (unclass)
9 Georges V (2*), 35 rms
10 Hyatt Regency (5*), 300 rms, night club
11 Lincoln (1*), 53 rms
12 Louvre, du (1*), 32 rms
13 Majestic (1*), 88 rms
14 Mansour, el (5*), 250 rms
15 Marhaba (4*), 135 rms
16 Metropole (3*) 57 rms
17 Negotiants, les (unclass)
18 Noailles, de (3*), 53 rms
19 Oumnia, el (4*), 53 rms, night club
20 Plaza (3*), 27 rms
21 Périgord, du (unclass)
22 Rialto (1*), 21 rms
23 Safir Palace (5*), 350 rms, night club
24 Sully (2*), 49 rms
25 Toubkal (3*), 64 rms, night club
26 Touring (1*) 32 rms
27 Transatlantique (4*), 60 rms
28 Trocadero (2*), 30 rms
29 Washington (3*), 84 rms
30 Windsor (2*), 32 rms

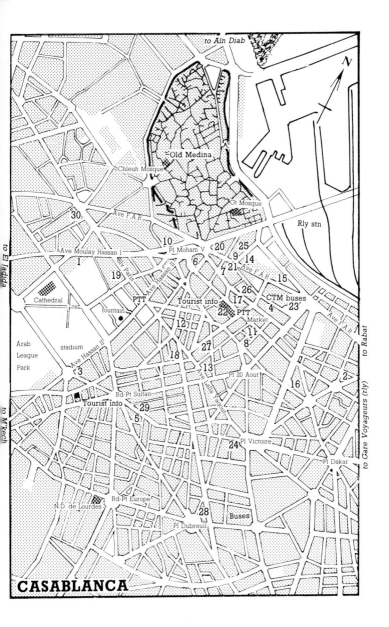

CASABLANCA

to Aïn Diab

N

Old Medina

Chleuh Mosque

Gt Mosque

Rly stn

Ave FAR

30

Ave Moulay Hassan I

10

Pl Moham V

20   25

9   14

1

19

6

7   21

Ave FAR

15

PTT

Tourist info

26

17

CTM buses

4   23

Cathedral

fountain

22   PTT

Market

Arab

League

Park

stadium

Ave Hassan II

12

11

8

3

18

27

Rd-Pt Sultan

13

Pl 20 Aout

16

2

Tourist info

29

5

24   Pl Victoire

Pl Dakar

N D de Lourdes

Rd-Pt Europe

28

Buses

Pl Dubreuil

to El Jadida

to M'Kech

to Gare Voyageurs (rly)

to Rabat

137

even the Borj Sidi el Kairouani, now a sanctuary for the city's patron saint. There's a hint of squalour in the air but the medina still retains something of the Arab character and is worth a stroll. The **New Medina** or the Habbous Quarter, just off the bottom of our map, was begun in 1923 beyond the then city limits to take in the population influx, and is a district of short straight souks circling a *place* like the strands of a cobweb.

The large open square of the **Place des Nations Unies** offers a variation of *son et lumière* with coloured floodlights on the fountain and public buildings, and European-style classical music in the background.

Five hundred yards west, the beautiful **Cathedral of the Sacred Heart** (Sacré Coeur) in the Arab League Park, is now a school, but the newest church, Nôtre Dame de Lourdes by the Rond Pont d'Europe (Europe Roundabout) is a massive concrete-and-glass edifice. And it was built by a Frenchman named Dangleterre.

Aïn Diab and the Beach. Casablanca's only concession towards being a resort is the development at Aïn Diab, a rocky headland 3.7 miles (6km) west of the medina. The beach at the base of the cliffs has good sand but the possibility of strong currents; however, the attraction here is in the smart and classy hotels and beach clubs, offering light sports and pool swimming, but at a price. Several of the hotels have night clubs — for which read 'discos' — which double the city's capacity.

HOTELS: in city, see map; on Blv de la Corniche, Aïn Diab: Anfa Plage (3*), 126 rms, night club; Bellerive (3*), 35 rms; Corniche, de la, (3*), 53 rms; Karam (3*), 96 rms, night club; Riad Salam (5*), 93 rms & 50 chalets; Suisse (4*), 192 rms, night club; Tarik (3*), 58 rms, night club; Tropicana (3*) 66 rms.

Don't bother with medina hotels; the one-star places in the city are no more expensive and offer better quality.

RESTAURANTS: Casablanca has the best selection of restaurants in Morocco — but so it should. If you're dining out rather than just eating, consider Al Mounia (95, Rue Prince Moulay Abdallah, near Hotel du Louvre) or Étoile de Marrakech (126, Blv Mohammed V, near Hotel Lincoln) for Moroccan dishes; locate the hotels on the map as a guide.

For French menus at easy-to-find restaurants, consider Maxim's at 144 Blv Moh V or Le Petit Poucet at 86-90 Blv Moh V, with a cheaper snack-bar beside it. For basic eating, look around Blv Reitzer and the S.I. office, or in the Old Medina.

NIGHTLIFE: head for Aïn Diab for the night-clubs called Bahra, Balcon 33, Calypso, Le Tube, Zoom Zoom, Wichita, and others, plus the clubs in the smart hotels, but be prepared for several to be no more than bright-lights discos.

BUSES: CTM buses for all long-haul destinations, including European connections, leave from Rue Léon l'Africain off the Ave des F.A.R; other buses use the depot on Blv de la Résistance, east of Place Lemaigre Dubreuil. For airport buses see chapter 4.

On a normal working day this CTM depot receives 13 buses from Rabat, 8 from Meknès, 7 from Fès, 6 from Safi, 5 from El Jadida, 4 each from Tanger and Beni Mellal; 3 each from Marrakech and Tetouan, 2 each from Essaouira, Agadir and Tiznit, and 1 each from Azrou, Nador, Taza, Errachidia, Chaouen — and even Ceuta.

RAIL: Gare Voyageurs is at the east end of Blv Mohammed V, off the map; Gare du Port is near the CTM bus station. Many trains call at both stations.

TOURIST INFO: ONMT, 55 Rue Omar Slaoui and airport; S.I, 98, Blv Mohammed V, by PTT.

THE COASTAL PLAIN. Inland from Casablanca lies the country's breadbasket, one of the few areas in Morocco where the ground is flat enough to take combine harvesters and tractors. Irrigation is essential for consistent yields, with much of the water coming from the Oued Oum er Rbia, a year-round river. As it enters the plain the oued brings an average 1,400 cubic feet of water a second (40 cu.m/sec), which seldom drops below 1,000 cu.ft/sec even in August, and during the spring thaw can reach 35,000 cu.ft/sec (1,000 cu.m/sec).

The soil produces tomatoes and melons, potatoes and carrots, wheat and millet, with large areas still down to cotton — and what is not used on the home market is exported to Europe through Casablanca.

Plateau des Phosphates. Deeper inland, beyond the reach of irrigation, Khouribga and Oued Zem are industrial towns in the Plateau des Phosphates which make their living by digging up the very rock on which they stand. Khouribga was created solely for mining and had a population of 229,600 at the 1981 census; Oued Zem, at the end of a railway from Casablanca, has its own mines and quarries as well as factories to convert the minerals into superphosphates and other chemicals.

The reserves here are vast, with three seams each covering up to 1,500 square miles (4,000 sq.km); only the top seam is being worked, but in places it is 120 feet (40m) thick. The first truckloads were shipped in 1921 and the annual production is now around 15,000,000 tons, but nobody in Khouribga is worried about needing another job in the foreseeable future.

This gorge is in the Monts des Beni-Snassen — and the stream was crowded with frogs

16: THE RIF MOUNTAINS

Land of the kif

THE MOUNTAINS OF AR-RIF, reaching from the jagged tear at the Strait of Gibraltar to the Oued Moulouya south of Nador, include some of the most lawless regions of the country. While driving along this tortuous road I quickly lost count of the number of boys and young men — and several older men as well — who stood by the verge offering kif, kef, hemp, hash, hashish, marijuana, cannabis, or who would simply yell "Smoke!"

Drug-pushers. The road is an unending series of hairpin bends combined with steep climbs and dips, set amid some of the most spine-chilling and awesome scenery in Morocco. It's seldom possible to maintain 50mph (80kph) for more than a few seconds and where the tarmac has been damaged motorists are reduced to a crawl: the hash merchants know these places and frequently trot beside their victims' cars shouting offers, which may change to curses as the prospect of trade recedes.

European passengers disembarking from buses along this route are pestered by hash sellers almost as persistent as the self-appointed guides of Fès, but potentially far more menacing.

Warning. The worldly-wise have no doubt what is on sale but for the innocent traveller this might be his first encounter with the flat plastic envelope two inches (6cm) square, packed with cannabis resin, which

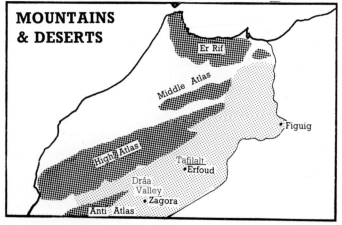

is what customs officers back home are looking for amid the backpack brigade. Hash is available in other forms and in much larger quantities in the Rif but you buy, or even show an interest, at your peril. Remember that this is the Barbary Coast, noted for piracy until historically recent times. Don't forget that slaves were still auctioned in public in Morocco in 1912. Do you then expect a drug pusher to live by the accepted rules of commerce?

Modern-day Pirates. You are not entirely safe inside your own car on this road; there are reports of travellers who have been held up in full daylight and forced to make a purchase, there are other stories of modern-day pirates patrolling the road in fast cars, and I can verify that there are delays caused by accidents — the standard of driving is low and I saw two cars which had crashed head-on at a blind corner; I squeezed past the wrecks with wheels on the edge of a ravine.

You are at even greater risk on foot in any of the Riffian villages; don't accept invitations into private houses or sheds, and above all else don't wander the countryside after dark.

The Law. So if it's illegal to possess, sell, distribute and export the drug, why isn't it illegal to grow or harvest it? Simply because hash has become a part of daily life in the Rif, and the law would be unenforceable. There's very little attempt to enforce the law that *does* exist; police patrols aren't the answer as half the dealers step out onto the road from behind a tree or boulder when a victim comes into view, and the police would need to be a virtual army of occupation to control the problem in Ketama. As it was, I was stopped by a police patrol north of Chaouen — the only such check in the country — and cannabis wasn't even mentioned; the cop just wanted to see my passport.

Verdict. To go or not to go? My advice is to go; the scenery is outstanding. But be careful: if you're driving, cross the region in one day and don't go out of sight of your car; don't even get out of the vehicle unless you're absolutely certain there's nobody about. If you're travelling by bus and forced to make it two days, get in at the **Hotel Tidighine in Ketama** — it's three-star with 68 rooms — and stay inside until it's time to go in the morning. This is probably over-dramatising the situation, but the Rif is a hundred *years* from home.

Historical Background. Spain had agreed to the joint Protectorate of Morocco in 1912 with some reluctance, as its forces had been trying to pacify the Rif tribes since 1909 with little effect. Spain was weak at home and saw no profit from the Rif, whereas wealthier France stood to gain from southern Morocco's phosphates and other riches.

Abd el Krim. Some while into the Protectorate, King Alfonso XIII of Spain overruled his Government and appointed General Silvestre as commander of the troops in Morocco. In July 1921, Silvestre led an army of 20,000 into the Rif Mountains and was soundly defeated by the armed tribesmen led by Mohammed Abd el Krim. The battle was at Annoual, 30 miles (48km) east of Al Hoceima, and the Riffians drove the Spanish almost to Melilla.

This disaster undermined confidence in the Spanish monarchy and the *Cortes,* and led directly to Primo de Rivera's *coup* on 13 September 1923, which put a military dictatorship in control in Madrid and eventually led to the Spanish Civil War of 1936-39.

Rif Republic. Abd el Krim meanwhile set up the Riffian Republic, managing to forge some unity among the Berbers who had developed into family groups, each on permanent lookout against its neighbours. The republic even had its own bank and diplomatic representatives, but Krim made the fatal mistake of invading French Morocco south of the mountains and in 1927 a joint Franco-Spanish force defeated him. He was exiled to Réunion where he died in 1963.

Spanish Civil War. Spanish Morocco continued to have a major influence on affairs in Madrid, with Melilla joining the Civil War on the night of 17-18 July, 1936, within hours of its outbreak. The Tetouan, Larache and Ceuta garrisons opted for the Falangists during the 18th, and it was from Ceuta that General Franco started his journey which ultimately led to his becoming dictator, with Berber tribesmen from the Rif helping him all the way to Madrid.

Years later, Riffian tribes started their own uprising to force Spain out of Morocco, and when on 8 April 1956 the withdrawal took effect (except in Ceuta, Melilla and the offshore islands), the Krim legacy lived on, with revolts directed against Rabat in the continuing demand for independence.

Route de l'Unité. Before independence there were only muletracks along the ridge of the Rif Mountains. The P39 road between Chaouen and Al Hoceima was built to improve economic prospects as well as to allow pacification of the area. The sinuous and awesomely scenic S302 south of Ketama, the Route de l'Unité, was completed in 1963 to improve north-south links; it was the brainchild of Ben Barka, first president of the National Assembly, and King Hassan II is reputed to have worked on it, if only symbolically.

Our exploration of the Rif starts at Tetouan and goes beyond the Oued Moulouya to take in the Beni-Snassen mountains and end by the Algerian border at Oujda, which is certainly not in the Rif — but neither does it belong to the Atlas, the desert or the coast.

TETOUAN

Tetouan is a bustling town that gives a first impression of employing half its population in repairing vehicles, and the other half in driving, parking or watching over them. It's not a touristy place by European standards although it's popular with Moroccans in the summer; they spend the day at Martil and come back to Tetouan to eat and sleep.

Tamuda. The Berber name, *Tit ta Aouin*, means 'springs' — *aïn* in Arabic — referring to the lush valley of the Oued Martil beneath the town. There is no connection with Tamuda, the 1st-cent Roman camp a few miles downstream which was built on a 3rd-cent BC berber village and abandoned in the 3rd cent AD, although you might see a few relics of Tamuda in the Tetouan archaological museum.

Tit ta Aouin was established in 1305 or '07 by the Marinite Sultan Abu Tabit and quickly became a pirates' hideout. Enrique III of Castille (Spain) sacked it in 1339, taking into slavery those he didn't slaughter: the town was in ruins until the beginning of the 16th cent when, ironically, Moors driven out of Spain after the fall of Granada in 1492, settled here, bringing a few Jews with them.

Pirates. The Spanish took possession of Ceuta in 1580 and in an intense wave of puritanism sent thousands more refugees across to Africa in the great Morisco — Andalous — expulsions. Many went no further than Tetouan and like their fellows in Salé, began a life of piracy. The Alaouite Sultan Moulay Ismail, who came to power in 1672, preferred trade to plunder (though he found slave labour very useful in

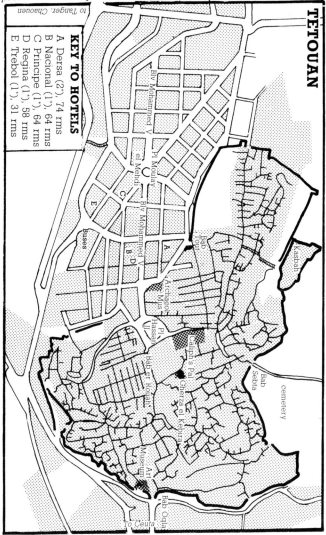

TETOUAN

to Tanger, Chaouen

Blv Mohammed V

Pl Moulay el Mehdi

Blv Mohammed V

E

C

Buses

B D

A

Bab Toot

Kasbah

Archaeol Mus

Pl Hassan II

Bab er Roua

Calip's Pal

Gherza el Kebira

Art Museum

Bab Sebta

cemetery

Bab Okla

To Ceuta

143

Meknès), and so Tetouan was obliged to embark on a career of commerce.

England seized Gibraltar in 1704 and thereby established another influence in the strait. Spain besieged the Rock several times, failing to dislodge the invaders, but in 1860 it captured Tetouan again, intending to add it to its collection of outposts in Morocco. The English weren't keen on the idea and told the Spanish to go. They went in 1862, but were back again in force in 1912 with the Spanish Protectorate, ruling the Rif from Larache to the Moulouya estuary with Tetouan as the capital.

In view of all this influence from across the Strait of Gibraltar it's a surprise to find Tetouan has retained a strong Arab character, although the European new town is larger than the medina; we can't use the expression 'Ville Nouvelle' in the former Spanish Protectorate, but *Ciudad Nueva* doesn't sound right.

Caliph's Palace. From the new town the obvious way in to the medina is through the former market square, Place Hassan II, totally overwhelmed by the Caliph's Palace to the north. The palace was built in Spanish-Moroccan style in the 17th cent under Moulay Ismail and was enlarged early this century when it became another of the royal palaces. It served as the official residence of the sultan's representative during the Protectorate, with major restoration in 1948 and again in 1988-89, leaving little of the original.

Medina. The interesting part of the medina is between Bab Er Rouah (Gate of the Winds) on the east of Place Hassan II, and Bab Sebta in the northern rampart. This route leads through Gherza el Kebira, the textile souk which becomes increasingly a second-hand clothes market as the day progresses. Wander to the north through a miscellany of souks to the Souk el Fouki, once the commercial district and latterly the place to buy bread and home-made biscuits.

Fouki Souk gives access to the Derkaoua Zaouia notable for its heavily-decorated doorway, and to the final few yards to Bab Sebta (Ceuta Gate) and the ancient road to Ceuta, running through a cemetery.

Musée d'Art Marocain. The modern road to Ceuta begins at Bab Oqla on the medina's eastern wall. Bab Oqla's 19th-cent munitions store just inside the gate was converted in 1948 to the The Museum of Moroccan Art, concentrating purely on the former Spanish Morocco and with a strong Andalous influence visible in the exhibits of costume, crafts and furniture (open standard hours except Tuesday).

HOTELS: see map. Others not on the map include: Omaina (2*), 37 rms, Ave du 10 Mai; Safir (4*), 98 rms, night club, Ave Kennedy (Rte de Ceuta). There are several **pensions** in the new town but *refuse all offers from local guides to show you to one or you will never get rid of them.*

BUSES: the underground bus station is on the south rim of the new town; see map. All routes operate from here.

TAXIS: operate from the bus station and from the walls of the medina west of Bab Tout.

TOURIST INFO: ONMT, 30 Blv Mohammed V.

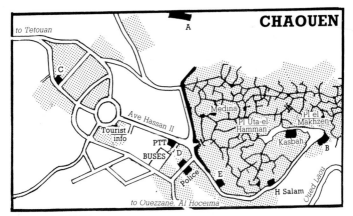

CHAOUEN

Chaouen is an enigma. For a start, it has several names: Chefchaouene, Chechaouen, Shifshawn and Xauen in addition to the one most frequently used, Chaouen, all originating in a Berber word for 'horns,' supposedly describing the mountain above the town. For another, it's very europeanised with a strong Spanish flavour and yet only four Europeans are known to have visited the town before 1920 and escaped with their lives.

Chaouen, now with a population of 27,000, was founded in 1471 by Moulay Ali Ben Rachid as a mountain hideout from which he could attack the Portuguese bases at Ceuta and nearby Ksar es Seghir. The town later received a number of Moriscos expelled from Spain, who understandably hated anything European.

Hostile Town. From that bitter beginning, Chaouen became a focus for Islamic devotion and pilgrimages, as closed to European eyes as was Moulay Idriss. The first Christian European to infiltrate it was the French missionary explorer, Charles de Foucauld who spent one night here in 1883, disguised as a Jew.

Spanish troops entered the town in force in 1920, and found among the descendants of the Moriscos expelled from Spain in the early 17th cent, Jews who still spoke medieval Castillian.

Friendly Town. Chaouen is now one of the friendliest places in Morocco as well as being one of the most picturesque, crowning a small hilltop in the Oued Laou. The medina is small, with steep, cobbled alleys twisting past whitewashed houses from the Bab el Aïn to the Plaza Uta el Hammam. Here, a ruined kasbah stands on the south side of the square with an ancient caravanserai on the north. On Mondays and Thursdays, market days, the caravanseria still fulfils its original role of stabling animals on the ground floor and giving shelter to travellers on the first floor.

Surprises. A hundred yards on, the medina throws another surprise, for in the Place Makhzen (Royal Square) is the smart Hotel Chaouen. And the new town is a mini garden-city — perhaps a garden-village would be more apt — where the locals go on *paseo* each evening just as the Spaniards do. But perhaps the most surprising aspects of Chaouen are that this town which was once so bitterly anti-Christian now has a large church in a prominent position, and there is no harassment at all for European visitors.

World's Deepest Cave? The entrance to the Kef Toghobeit Cave, probably the world's deepest, was discovered in 1959 around 5,600ft (1,700m) on the slope of Jebel Bouhalla, east of Chaouen. The cave has been explored to 2,300ft (700m) down, proving it to be Africa's deepest known hole (the Big Hole at Kimberley is 1,300ft (400m) deep). Cavers have dyed the waters running through the Kef Toghobeit and so established there is a much greater system yet to be explored.

HOTELS: see map. **A** Asmaa (3*), 94 rms; **B** Chaouen (2*), 37 rms, recently refurbished; **C** Ibiza (1*) 12 rms; **D** Magou (2*), 27 rms; **E** Rif (1*), 22 rms. In addition there are several small hotels and pensions in the medina: Pensions Ibn Batuta, Mauritania, Valencia, and Hotels Andaluz, Parador, etc.

I noticed a great difference in the rates: 55DH for a double room at the Ibiza, and 200DH for a double, with obligatory breakfast, at the Rif. Motorists coming over on the ferries often make Chaouen their first overnight stop in Morocco and many of them pay the asking price without shopping around. There is a **camping** site near the Asmaa.

BUSES and TAXIS: from the bus station on Ave Al Khattabi.

FESTIVALS: main Mousseum is for Sidi Allal el Haj, 9 August. Several lesser ones; ask at S.I. for details.

TOURIST INFO: S.I, Rue Tetouan.

OUEZZANE

Ouezzane has certain similarities with Chaouen. Its name is spelled two ways, the other being Wazan, and it was a holy town with non-Moslems banned from certain parts and tolerated in others only for limited periods. Now with a population of 30,000, its smaller new town is 500 yards from the unwalled medina, and the Moroccan Tourist Office doesn't offer any accommodation — though you can find three basic **hotels** by the Place du Marché at the east end of the triangular Place de l'Indépendance.

Moulay Abdallah ben Brahim, a direct descendant of the Prophet and therefore a cherif, established a zaouia here in 1727 on what was the frontier between the lowlands ruled by the sultans, the Bled el Makhzen, and the ungovernable region of the Rif, the Bled es Siba. The zaouia became the focal point for a religious fraternity called the Taïbia and a major centre for Moslem pilgrimages in the 18th and 19th cents. Jews also came here to see their rabbi Amrane, who was reputed to be able to perform miracles, but the Jews had to keep well away from the zaouia and were allowed to lodge in just one fondouk.

In the late 19th cent the pasha of Ouezzane tried to encourage the French to take control of the Rif, but when Morocco was divided into the two protectorates and the Rif went to Spain, Ouezzane fell into the French sector.

Ouezzane Today. From the Place de l'Indépendance and the Place du Marché a zig-zag alley leads in 100 yards to Moulay Abdallah's zaouia, also known now as the Mosque S'Ma and the Mosquée Verte, distinguished by its octagonal minaret decorated with green tiles. Another 100 yards brings you to the Moulay Abdallah Cherif Mosque which, confusingly, is still venerated by pilgrims.

Jebel Bou Hellal. The town is around 1,000 feet (300m) high, but snuggles up the slopes of Jebel Bou Hellal, 1,999ft (609m), which offers a splendid view across the landscape and of the Rif mountains to the north. Don't confuse this mountain with Jebel Bouhalla near Chaouen.

Buses leave from the main road north of Place de l'Indépendance.

KETAMA

Outwardly a reasonably pleasant if sprawling village, Ketama is the centre of the Moroccan drug industry, as already noted. It stands around 5,500 feet high (1,700m) amid spectacular, rust-red scenery which in another country would make it the centre of a thriving tourist region.

From Tleta Ketama, five miles (8km) to the south on the Route de l'Unité, a forest trail suitable only for four-wheel-drive vehicles leads through the mountains and the cedar forest south of **Jebel Tidirhine** and, at Targuist, 23 miles (37km) from Ketama, eventually picks up the *Route des Crêtes,* the ridgeback road to Al Hoceima. There is no track to the top of Jebel Tidirhine, at 8,032ft (2,448m) the highest point in the Rif and — so I'm advised — with a wonderful panoramic view.

BASICS: Ketama has the 3* Hotel Tidighine (sic), popular in winter with French skiers and wild-boar hunters, and serving as the bus-stop on the east-west route. Cheaper hotels are in Tleta Ketama.

Velez de la Gomera. From Targuist a narrow and twisting track plunges down to Torres de Alcalá and Kalah Iris on the Barbary Coast; it's a regular bus route and a good beach awaits you, yet to be 'discovered.' Four miles east of Torres, which still retains its Spanish name, was Badis, the port from where regular caravan trains set out in the Middle Ages for Fès. Badis traded with the European city-states for two centuries until 1508 when the Spanish seized the tiny offshore island of Velez de la Gomera. Badis's trade was so badly hit that in 1522 the townspeople stormed across the tombola beach linking island and mainland.

Two years later, when the Turks were seizing all available islands off the Afrian coast, they snatched this one and used it as a pirates' base for pillaging Spanish ports. Understandably, Felipe II of Spain led a reprisal attack in 1564 but, less understandably, the Spanish have held the Peñon de Velez de la Gomera ever since. *There's no access from Morocco.*

Emirate of Nekor. From Targuist, at the eastern end of the cocaine belt, the road twists interminably to Al Hoceima (Chapter 10) then climbs up the valley of the Oued Nekor which was the unlikely home of the independent Emirate of Nekor for two centuries from its founding in 709. The Fatimites from Kairouan in Tunisia killed the emir in the early 10th cent; Yusef bin Taxfin destroyed the settlement in 1084, and in 1216 a tribe came down from the Rif and established the Marinite dynasty in this parched valley.

From Midar, 64 miles (102km) from Al Hoceima, the road at last becomes civilised for the easy run down to Selouane, where there's a 17th-cent kasbah built by Moulay Ismail. Here you have a choice: left to Nador and Melilla, or right to Oujda and Algeria.

NADOR

Nador is purely industrial, a town of 120,000 people created from a village since the end of the Spanish Protectorate in 1956. It was built by the *Société Nationale de Sidérurgie,* Sonasid, the country's ironfounders, as a snub to the Spanish who continued to hold onto nearby Melilla, where they've been since 1497. The town is very European, designed by someone adept at drawing right-angles and wide approach-roads, and there's nothing at all to attract the tourist. The Sebkha Bou Arg, the almost landlocked lagoon, might look enticing but who wants to go sailing or swimming in the shadow of iron smelters?

Turn right into the first road into town that's labelled *centre ville,* for a selection of reasonable **hotels** such as the Anoual, Khalid, Marrakech and California, or there are the Mansour ed Dahab (3*, 54 rms) at 101 Rue Marrakech and the Rif (3*, 64 rms and disco) at Ave Yusef bin Taxfin. All **buses** and grands taxis leave from the town-centre bus station, including those to the Melilla frontier post at Beni Enzar. The **railway** to Taourirt and Fès is nearing completion.

If you're crossing into Melilla, allow at least an hour for frontier formalities for yourself, plus 30 minutes for your car.

East to Oujda. From Selouane the P27 heads sedately east, the so-called **Pont International** (International Bridge) over the waters of the Oued Moulouya marking not only the end of the Rif but also the end of the former Spanish Protectorate. You're in arid country here, with the mountains of the Beni-Snassen on your right: highest point, 5,027ft (1,532m).

Zegzel Gorge. If you have your own transport the Zegzel Gorge makes a splendidly scenic detour into the Beni-Snassen. Seven miles

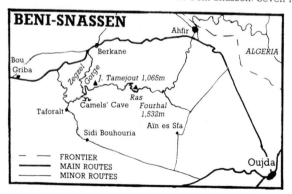

(11km) east of the tiny Bou Griba look for a minor road on the right: there's only one. Within two miles this narrow route takes you into the mountains and presents you with 15% slopes, hairpin bends and broken verges, all rewarded by an excellent view. Your target may well be the caves known as the **Grotte du Chameau** and the **Grotte des Pigeons** deep in the Zegzel.

Camel's Cave. Signposting is abysmal and don't be alarmed if you never find the caves: the Camel Grotto is spoiled by a concrete reservoir in front of it and spray-can graffiti in the entrance, though if you have a torch and clamber deeper inside across the scoured floor you'll be rewarded by a show of stalactites. Why bother? The oleanders and the tinkling stream make the gorge truly picnic-worthy.

From the grottos an even narrower strip of tarmac takes you down to Berkane through more of the Zegzel; if you're relying on taxis, this is your starting-point for the gorge. Or, if driving, you can opt for the hair-raising journey along the crest of the Beni-Snassen.

Ahfir. Ahfir is a small town no more than 500 yards from Algeria: the road sign in the central crossroads proclaims 'Tlemcen' and points to the frontier post which, at the time of research and writing, was once again open to traffic, day and night — but there was very little. If you're planning to go home via one of the Spanish enclaves, grab your yellow exit cards here and avoid problems later.

OUJDA

Oujda lies near the centre of a fertile plain relying totally on irrigation, but its 470,500 inhabitants (1981 census) rely for the most part on the transport and processing of the mines deep in the desert to the south, yielding coal, zinc and lead. It's not a touristy place, nor is it characterless, and as nobody has thought of pestering the poor foreigner you can have a relaxing day or so here.

Founded around 994, Oujda has been in the front line in disputes between what are now Morocco and Algeria. The first people to live here were graziers, but soon the troubles began. The Almoravides took the town in 1070, then came the Almohades in 1206 who built the city walls, then there were the Marinites, the Ziyanites from Tlemcen, the Saadians, the Alaouites, the Turks from Alger, Sultan Moulay Sliman in the early 19th cent, the French in 1844, 1857 and 1907, and finally the French Protectorate in 1912.

The Town. Only three city gates and half the walls remain, of which the Bab Sidi Abd el Wahab (Ouahab) is the most colourful. At the eastern end of the medina, this was where executed criminals' heads were hung for public display.

Watermarket Square. In the centre of the medina is the Place Souk el Ma, where irrigation water was sold in ancient times. No, it wasn't carried away in buckets: this was where the irrigation canals branched off the supplying stream, and farmers bought water in their canals for a specified time, the cost depending upon the season.

HOTELS: see map. **A** Massira-Salam (4*), 108 rms; **B** Oujda (3*), 105 rms; **C** Lutetia (1*), 40 rms; **D** Royal (1*), 52 rms; **E** Terminus (4*), 122 rms;

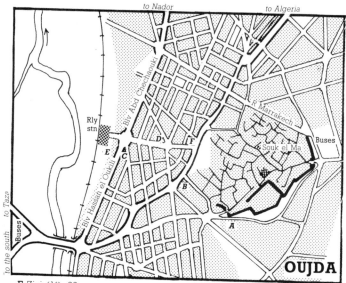

F Ziri (1*), 33 rms.

BUSES: the new bus station is south of town by the road junction and bridge; the old bus depot is to the east of the medina at the end of Rue de Marrakech.

RAIL: daily trains to Fès; weekly to Bouârfa by Figuig.

AIR: Les Angades Airport, see Chapter 4.

A pisé (mudbrick) village in the High Atlas. The earth houses are repaired after every rainy season

17: THE ATLAS MOUNTAINS

Middle, High and Anti

THE THREE RANGES OF MOUNTAINS which cross central Morocco merge to form one massif, but each has its own distinct character. The Moyen or Middle Atlas runs from Beni-Mellal to Taza, with the dissected plateau of the Zaër Zaïane reaching up towards Rabat; its highest point is the Massif du Tichchoukt, 9,174ft (2,796m), 33 miles (50km) due east of Azrou.

The Haut or High Atlas reaches from Agadir to Midelt before sliding back into the desert as a series of jagged hills stretching out their dying fingers towards Figuig. Its highest point is Jebel Toubkal, 13,672ft (4.167m), the highest peak in Africa north of the Sahara.

An ancient volcano, Jebel Siroua, at 10,841ft (3,304m), links the High Atlas to the Anti Atlas, which stretches from Goulimine to the Drâa Valley and then rises to its highest point, Amalou n'Mannsour at 8,898ft (2,712m), before sinking into the desert.

Barrier. Neolithic Man, emerging from east Africa in the pre-dawn of civilization, had thousands of years to go round the mountains, but since the Ice Ages and the formation of the Sahara, the Atlas ranges have been a barrier. They have kept the north Moroccan plains within the Atlantic weather zone and so checked the desert's northward march; they also halted the Roman conquest, and delayed the southern advance of Islam. Abu Bekr reached the Ghana Empire around 1076 but five centuries were to pass before Timbuktoo was conquered.

Life on the northern plains was harsh, but life in these mountains was even harsher, particularly in the habitable parts of the High Atlas; there were few permanent settlements in the Middle Atlas whose western slopes were, and still are, used for summer grazing, and the Anti-Atlas is desert apart from the oases around Tafraoute. There was less chance of being overrun by hostile tribes, but the struggle for daily life amid the near-barren and rugged peaks has produced a hardy strain of Berber, more adept and more versatile than those of the lowlands.

Feudal Caïds. Until the coming of the Protectorate none of the sultans had managed to stamp his authority on the Berbers of the High Atlas, who owed allegiance only to their feudal caïds or lords, such as the Glaoui family who ruled the Tizi n'Test pass and the Goundafi who commanded the Tizi n'Tichka. The system has changed only a little to this day; the Berbers neither give to nor take from Rabat and their local caïds are still the effective local rulers, though they now accept the higher authority of the national government.

Mud-brick Homes. Domestic architecture in the High Atlas is like nothing else in Morocco. Houses are made of ochre-red mud-brick, with flat roofs of ochre-red mud plastered onto a bed of grasses and branches, overhanging the walls to prevent damage by run-off of the winter rains. Even so, many of the roofs must be rebuilt each spring. Most homes are of simple squares with rooms leading off a tiny central courtyard open to the skies.

Villages of a dozen or a score of such houses cling to the ochre-red slopes and are scarcely distinguishable from the bare earth. Their womenfolk tend the tiny fields by day and the men come out at dusk and dawn to irrigate, using canals only inches wide that sometimes cross river beds on rickety aqueducts. Where the modern main roads have twisted over the High Atlas, these communities have access to some of the benefits of civilization, but in the side valleys life has scarcely changed since Columbus landed in the New World.

White-knuckle Experience. The two roads which cross the High Atlas — the Tizi n'Test and the Tizi n'Tichka routes — are well engineered though they have some steep climbs and not one of the bends has the slightest concession of a barrier: wrecked and burned-out cars lie far below as a grim warning. A bus journey over these routes is indeed a white-knuckle experience.

THE MIDDLE ATLAS

BENI-MELLAL

The Middle Atlas range springs from the plains with such abruptness that you can locate the line to within a hundred yards, and on this boundary stands Beni-Mellal, a town of 250,000 people engaged in the growing and selling of olives and oranges, figs and pomegranates, almonds and peaches.

Apart from the important market held each Friday, the only features of interest are the kasbas; the one in town built in 1688 under Moulay Ismail and restored almost out of recognition, and the more photogenic but ruined Kasbah Ras el Aïn in the olive groves.

Cascades d'Ouzoud. Beni-Mellal is a convenient starting-point to explore the Cascades d'Ouzoud, the most spectacular waterfall in Morocco — when the water is actually falling.

In your own car, leave the main P24 Marrakech road at Khemis des Oulad Ayad for the 1811, 29 miles (46km) east of Beni-Mellal. The road crests a rise at 3,216ft (980m) before plunging down into Moulay Aïssa ben Idriss, a tiny village with a green-tiled mosque...and the end of the tarred road. From here a track worn from the bedrock leads over the Oued el Abid and along the rim of a splendid gorge with sides so steep that the bottom is out of sight.

The tarmac resumes shortly before the road ends in a parking area where a dozen excursion coaches may gather at peak season. From here a walk of a few minutes leads to the Cascades d'Ouzoud where the Oued el Abid plunges over the horseshoe-shaped rim of the red rocks into the *Marmite des Géants*, the Giants' Cauldron, 300ft (100m) below, with mist creating a near-permanent rainbow.

A small hotel, several snack-bars and two camp sites offer the basics of life, beside the top of a track which leads down to the base of the falls where you can swim amid the thunder of falling water — but be careful of the broken bottles.

In your car you can backtrack to the main P24 or continue south on a better road to the junction with the east-west S508. If you come by **bus,** the 508 is your only access, from Marrakech or from Beni-Mellal to the nearby village of Azilal. At Azilal you should be able to get a taxi to take you to the cascades.

Bin el Ouidane. The road between Azilal and Beni-Mellal is stunningly scenic, particularly where it passes the reservoir of Bin el Ouidane whose waters cover 14 sq miles (9,300 acres, 3,700ha). A dam 935ft (285m) long has a hydro-electric generating station at its base, capable of producing 500,000,000 kW hours of power a year, before passing the water into a tunnel and so out to irrigate the Tadla plains — which is one reason why the cascades are sometimes down to a trickle.

You may hear more of Lake Bin el Ouidane, as a tourist complex is planned for its northern shore.

Natural Bridge. With your own transport you could consider going on to **Demnate,** an ancient walled town of 10,000 people which is strictly in the High Atlas. Lesser dignitaries of the Glaoui, the Pasha of Marrakech, lived in the kasbah, but your main interest will be the natural bridge of Imi n'Ifri, 4 miles into the mountains. An adjacent cave is the subject of weird legends concerning a seven-headed genie who demanded a young girl each year in sacrifice, but when the caïd saw his daughter chosen he arranged for the genie to be killed. The rotting body, they say, fed millions of maggots which transformed into the crows now living in the cave.

KASBAH-TADLA

Tadla in the local dialect of Berber means 'sheaf,' which indicates that the Tadla plain is a corn-growing area. Moulay Ismail, the man who created Meknès, built the now-crumbling kasbah to house his negro troops brought from the Sudan (*sudan* in Arabic means 'south,' but we can interpret it as west Africa) to pacify the Middle Atlas for the first time in history. The French almost repeated the action in 1913 when they used the town as a base for their incursions into the mountains, bringing European-style order to the region.

There are a few basic **hotels** in town, near the **bus** station.

Boujad. Sixteen miles (25km) north of Kasbah-Tadla on the P13 is the holy city of Boujad, founded in the late 16th cent and now graced with a cluster of small mosques, zaouias, sanctuaries and marabouts — but as these are out of bounds to non-Moslems and the town has a mere 15,000 people, Boujad is worth a call only if you're passing.

El Ksiba. In your own transport you could journey up El Ksiba valley, east of Kasbah-Tadla, purely for the scenery and the orchards, watered by tributaries of the Oum er Rbia.

KHENIFRA

Reds and browns are the predominant colours in the Atlas Mountains, but Khenifra must be the reddest town in the country. It is built of bricks and plaster made from the deep ochre rocks on which it stands, giving a uniformity of colour from the tops of the houses to the bottom of the small

The Oued Oum er Rbia at Khenifra is a rushing stream

gorge through which the Oum er Rbia river rushes. A roundabout on the main road gives access to the poorer end of town over a narrow bridge; another bridge at the other end leads to the souk area which buzzes with activity during the colourful Wednesday and Sunday markets. Towards the end of the 19th cent Sultan Moulay el Hassan created one Moha Bou Hammou as the local caïd; Hammou established the market, the mosque and a fondouk or two, then thought he could manage better without the sultan's authority. He raided caravans, attacked Meknès, then began his own *jihad* against the French. Lyautey's troops stormed the town in November 1914 but withdrew after losing 563 men, and France had to wait until 1921 before it could defeat the ageing Moha Bou Hammou and assert its authority in the region.

Sources of Oum er Rbia. With your own transport and a prayer or two you could shun the P24 to Azrou and take the mountain road to the east, the S530. This is a lonely track (not that the P24 is all that busy) which wanders through splendid mountain scenery and the beginnings of the cedar forests. In summer it is pleasantly cool and very un-Moroccan, but snow may close the road between November and April.

Fifteen miles (24km) from Khenifra is the **Aguelmane Azigza** down a track to the east. This ultramarine lake of deep, crystal-clear waters, fills a cirque in the forest-clad mountains and is a favourite fishing and picnicking spot. The road crosses a near alpine plateau with vast views before dropping into the valley of the Oum er Rbia. Look for a concrete bridge; park here and walk to the so-called **Quarante Sources,** the Forty Springs, where water issues from the rocks in many more than 40 sources, cascading or trickling down to the stream. Many other springs add to the Oum er Rbia in the next few downstream miles, for the true origin of Morocco's longest river lies in a limestone basin to the east, riddled with gulleys and tiny caves.

Barbary Ape. The road crosses strange country where mushroom-shaped rocks stand in isolation amid the cedars and evergreen oaks, and Barbary apes swing wild through the trees. They aren't apes at all, but tailless monkeys, *macaca sylvana,* and directly related to those living on Gibraltar, for when the Rock apes were declining during the war Churchill ordered a replenishment of stock from these mountains.

Ahead, now, lies **Aïn Leuh,** a village accessible by **bus** from Azrou and with a few small cascades on its southern approaches. Moulay Ismail had the kasbah built in the 18th cent but the village's main attraction is its market which attracts the semi-nomadic Beni M'Guild tribe seemingly for most of the week. The Beni M'Guild are graziers and frequently follow their herds of goats, living in Berber-style tents.

Cedar Forest. These nomads and the woodcutters of Aïn Leuh and Azrou were ruining the cedar forest at the start of the century until 1916 when the French introduced one of the first conservation schemes. The forest now covers around 300 sq miles (almost 200,000 acres, 75,000 hectares), mostly with cedars, some of which are immense, even alongside the road. Thuya and evergreen oak are scattered amid the forest, their timber going for cabinetmaking and for railway sleepers respectively.

Cèdre Gouraud. The timber line starts at around 4,500ft (1,500m) altitude, with the best specimens growing above the 6,000ft contour. Stop for a while if you can and wander from the road to breathe in the scented air, and absorb the cathedral-like silence and coolness even on an August day when the plains below are sizzling. To the north-east of the main P21 Azrou—Midelt road one tree in particular is worth seeing; it's signed from the road as the Cèdre Gouraud and marked on the Lascelles map 5 miles (8km) down a track. Col. Gouraud was Gen Lyautey's deputy from 1912 to '14 and his arboreal namesake is an enormous specimen whose trunk has a 30-foot girth at its base.

AZROU

Azrou is at the crossroads at the foot of the mountains yet still 4,000ft (1,200m) above sea level. This is a small market town laid out with plenty of open space and dominated by the *azrou,* the massive volcanic plug a short distance away, ideal country for a hiking holiday.

Moulay Ismail built a kasbah here, too, but there's little of it left. Nearby is the **Co-opérative Artisanale** (0830-1200, 1430-1800 daily) which turns out some of the best tapestry, woodwork and wrought iron work in Morocco — it's such a pity that the town-centre tourist shops sell such junk.

Buses and taxis call at either of two depots in the town centre Place Mohammed V, and for **accommodation** here and at Ifrane, see 'Sports.'

Balcon d'Ito. The road from Azrou to Meknès passes the Balcon d'Ito, a natural platform for viewing the Paysage d'Ito which in summer is a parched yellow-brown landscape reminiscent of the Spanish Meseta.

Ifrane. Eleven miles (17km) north-east is Ifrane, begun by the French

155

in 1929 to match the hill stations that the British had in India. Its chalets and villas now belong to the Moroccan affluent, and there's a royal summer palace tucked away in the trees.

Sefrou and its hinterland are described in the chapter on Fès, which leads us to Taza and the Jebel Tazzeka National Park.

TAZA

For 1,000 years Taza has plugged the gap between the Middle Atlas and the Rif, and on several occasions it has been the capital of a sizeable chunk of territory.

The Meknassa Taza tribe came from Meknès in the 10th cent to build the first fortifications here; they accepted the authority of the Idrissids, then the Fatimites from Kairouan in Tunisia who made one of their chiefs the local caïd. Yusef bin Taxfin seized the fortress in 1074; Abd el Moumen took it in 1132, built the walls and made it his capital until he had snatched Marrakech.

Later in the 12th cent, Taza was snatched back and forth for 30 years as the Almohades tried to consolidate their territories: "Once you've taken Taza you can take Fès," was a cry to arms which was patently true.

In the 13th cent Abu Yakub made Taza a city, with mosques, medersas and strengthened ramparts; Abu el Hassan added his own medersa, Abu Inan built a zaouia and a hospital but put them outside the city walls where later besiegers could destroy them. Léon l'Africain noted in the early 16th cent that Taza was the best-defended place in eastern Morocco — so the Saadians strengthened the fortifications even further.

Capital City. Moulay er Rachid, the first Alaouite sultan, made Taza his capital in 1666 while he prepared to conquer Marrakech, and his successor Moulay Ismail, ensconced in Meknès, held Taza against the Turks invading from Algeria.

Decline. And then in 1902 a local man, Moulay Mohammed bou Hamara, who had been exiled from court for intrigue, proclaimed himself Sultan of Taza and *Rogui*, pretender to the royal throne. He held out for six years until Moulay Hafid's men caged him, then fed him alive to the lions in the Royal Menagerie in Fès. When the lions declined to eat him, Bou Hamara was shot and burned.

During the six-year struggle Taza suffered material damage and had its pride destroyed, then in May 1914 the French marched into town to use it as a base for operations in the Rif and, for the first time in Taza's history, to open the route to Algeria.

Taza Today. Modern Taza is two distinct towns two miles apart. The medina still has its walls, and a street plan that is distinctly European. The Andalous Mosque with its 12th-cent minaret is at the south end, fronted by a long mechouar now serving as the main street. Ask a local boy to take you behind the mosque to show you bou Hamara's house, but don't expect anything spectacular. At the other end of town is the 12th cent Great Mosque, so tucked away that it's difficult to appreciate. Moulay er Rachid's Royal Palace is in ruins.

HOTELS. The Grand Hotel du Dauphiné (2*, 37 rms) on Pl de l'Indépendance has large, airy rooms and asks 104DH for two, with meals. H. de la Poste by the PTT (opposite) is grim, foodless and unclassified, as is H. de la Gare by the **bus** and **rail** stations. Hotel Friouato (3°, 58 rms) between new and old Taza is over-rated, and the 80-place campsite nearby is only partly fenced. On the other hand, my car developed an electrical fault as I arrived at Taza, and the Poste receptionist and two mechanics did a very competent repair. Tourists are few and there's no hassle.

Jebel Tazzeka: Circuit of Taza. The S311 road makes a 66-mile (107-km) loop around the Jebel Tazzeka National Park and so creates the Circuit of Taza, shown graphically on the front of the Hotel Dauphiné. Our route will be clockwise, leaving from Taza's medina, but without your own transport your only option is to pool resources and hire a taxi.

This part of the Middle Atlas is built of limestone, into which the scrub oak and other trees have thrust their roots. Winter's rains penetrate the rocks, creating some of Africa's largest cave systems and an impressive gorge, making this an ideal region for hikers and serious potholers.

The first sights are the **Cascades of Ras el Oued** which flow only in the spring when the Oued Chiker has surplus water. The Pass of Sidi Mejbeur at 3,932ft (1,198m) gives splendid views back across the Rif and the green countryside of the Tazzeka Park.

Soon you see Daïa (Lake) Chiker on your left, its size and depth fluctuating wildly through the year, with nothing left of it by late summer. The lake mops up surplus water from the Oued Chiker which emerges from the **Chiker Caves** nearby, looking like streams popping in and out of the hillside and sliding over travertine terraces of their own making, caused by the deposition of calcium carbonate.

The maze of galleries and sinkholes of the Chiker complex has been explored for 3 miles (5km) underground and may connect with the **Chara Caves,** north Africa's largest labyrinthine maze which is accessible only on foot and is the province of the serious and well-equipped speleologist.

Gouffre de Friouato. Opposite the elusive lake a sign points up a half-mile track to the Gouffre de Friouato, a pothole 100 feet (30m) wide and 600 feet (180m) deep. During the summer a guardian shows visitors down the steps to the richly-encrusted chambers which have been explored for half a mile (750m); bring your own torch.

Jebel Tazzeka. Beyond the pass of Bab Taka (4,788ft, 1,459m, often snowbound between December and April) a track on the right leads 5 miles (9km) to the summit of Jebel Tazzeka at 6,498ft (1,980m), topped by a television relay transmitter and a handy viewing platform. The view is breathtaking, reaching as far as Jebel Tidirhine in the Rif, and Fès, but the ascent is perilous.

The S311 goes down the Zireg Gorge to the P1 Taza—Fès road.

THE HIGH ATLAS

Travelling either of the trans-atlas routes of the Tizi n'Test and the Tizi n'Tichka offers an adventurous if scary way of seeing the High Atlas at first hand, whether you're behind the wheel or in a bus hurtling round the hairpin bends. Both routes are asphalted, both liable to be snowbound in winter, but while the Tichka route is the higher — indeed, the highest road pass in north Africa — the Test route is a real test of nerves as the 22 miles (36km) of carriageway south of the pass is one and a half car-widths across, which brings out the suicidal instinct in some local drivers who wonder why the hell the foreigners are here at all. Bus drivers don't instil confidence in their passengers, particularly when you know that the man who takes the bus out today on perhaps a 14-hour shift, brings it back tomorrow on an equally punishing shift.

If you're driving, make certain your tyres and brakes are in perfect order, carry spare water for the radiator (you can endure thirst for a while) and know how to cure vapour lock in your car. Don't expect to find petrol on the journey.

If you're going by bus be prepared for a very early departure, a very late arrival, or an all-day journey and buy your ticket in advance if possible. Buses stop for half an hour or so by roadside cafés where new-baked bread is delicious but bottled water is twice the Marrakech price. There are no toilets, and a European going behind a rock to answer the call of nature will attract an audience of giggling children.

Tizi n'Test Route. Heading south from Marrakech, at 39 miles (63km) you come to Ourigane, a favourite watering-hole for the French and with two **hotels** to suit their tastes.

Tin-Mal. You're well into the mountains by the time you reach Tin-Mal, noted for its mosque and a bloodcurdling history. The story began with Mohammed ibn Tourmert and his disciple Abd el Moumen wandering the land in the 12th cent and preaching stricter interpretation of Islam. Reaching Tin-Mal, Ibn Tourmert found support among the local tribesmen and decided to proclaim himself the Mahdi, the 'chosen one,' who was to destroy the lax Almoravide rule.

The Mahdi began a rule of terror, slaughtering any individual or tribe refusing to accept his strict interpretation of the Koran and soon he ruled the western High Atlas with Abd el Moumen as his right-hand man. The Almoravide Sultan Ali ben Yusef led an army into the mountains around 1128 but was driven back to Marrakech, which the Mahdi besieged. Ibn Tourmert died soon after, leaving Abd el Moumen the designated commander of the forces of Allah, still waiting at the gates of Marrakech. He backed off, conquering the surrounding countryside bit by bit, before coming back to Marrakech in 1146 and taking it.

Thus Abd el Moumen became the first effective Sultan of the new Almohade dynasty, and Tin-Mal became the Almohade holy city and treasure-house for the royal riches. Abd el Moumen built a near-duplicate of the Koutoubia Mosque here in 1153-54, siting it on a hillock commanding the upper valley of the Oued Nfiss.

Tin-Mal Mosque. The Marinites sacked the walled town of Tin-Mal in 1276, leaving scarcely any trace. The mosque was badly damaged but survived, and today it is not only the best example of Almohade architecture but is also the only true mosque in Morocco (as opposed to medersas with mosque status, such as the Bou Inana Medersa in Fès) which non-Moslems may wander around; it's kept locked, but a guardian will let you in for a negotiable fee.

Despite being open to the skies for centuries, many of the building's finest points have survived in the semi-desert conditions. There are nine naves and five traverses in the main part of the mosque, giving 32 columns to support the roof. Several of the arches still have their *stalactite* decoration, which was the first of its type in Morocco. The main nave faces the mihrab, the most sacred part of any mosque but here open to casual inspection, and you can even climb some way up the truncated minaret.

The road continues another 21 miles (33km) to the 6,890-ft (2,100-m) summit of Tizi n'Test (some French maps give it only 2,092 metres). If you're driving, pause half a mile further on for one of the best panoramas in Morocco, then commit yourself to the steepest prolonged descent in the country, an *average* 1:23 gradient to the P32 main road — and be thankful you're coming down, not up.

Jebel Toubkal. The Jebel Toubkal region of the High Atlas is ideal hiking country in summer, the altitude counteracting the heat, though you will need protection against sunburn and possibly altitude sickness — Toubkal is at 13,672ft (4,167m). The best access is from Asni where there's the three-star Grand **Hotel** du Toubkal (19 rooms, bath, pool, bar) as well as some basic accommodation. A bus connects with Imlil, a meeting-place for hikers and so an ideal spot for swapping news and ideas, or hiring a guide and mule if you're that adventurous. Imlil has a bunkhouse, which is the best type of bed you can expect from hereon, unless you're carrying your alpine tent and sleeping bag.

Large-scale maps of the region are available in the villages on the direct route, but you can buy a 'Jebel Toubkal' map in advance from Edward Stanford, 12-14 Long Acre, London WC2E 9LP for £5.95. The map is at the scale of 1:50,000 and shows contour lines, but it is currently the only one on sale abroad as the Moroccan Government has restricted the export of survey maps.

Tizi n'Tichka Route. The Tizi n'Tichka route is slightly easier on the nerves despite being higher than Tizi n'Test. From Marrakech, the French-engineered road begins to climb at Aït Ourir and doubles back on itself many times before reaching the first col at Tizi n'Aït Imguer at 4,823ft (1,470m), with 22 miles (35km) to go before the Tichka pass at 7,415ft (2,260m).

Kasbah Telouet and the Glaoui. Three miles (4km) further a sinuous but tarred road leads 12 miles (20km) east into the mountains to the isolated hideout of Kasbah Telouet, former capital of the **Glaoua,** the territory ruled by the Glaoui — Alhadj Thami al Glawi (or Glaoui), born 1875 to be a local chief but who was the ruler of southern Morocco when he died in 1956.

During the harsh winter of 1892-3 Sultan Moulay Hassan was unable to lead his 3,000 troops back to Marrakech after a punitive raid in the Tafilalt. He asked for help from the head of the Glaoui tribe, which was almost as tight-knit as a family. Thami al Glaoui realised the best way to achieve power was not to try to seize it by direct confrontation, but to earn it in return for favours, so he gave the sultan hospitality for as long as needed. Knowing that in Morocco things could have gone the other way, Moulay Hassan repaid Thami al Glaoui by allowing him to become caïd of the High Atlas, from Demnate to Zagora to the Ourika, as well as Pasha of Marrakech.

In 1912 the Glaoui knew the French were unstoppable, so he welcomed them, saving some of their troops from an attack by el Hiba, the 'Blue Sultan' from Tiznit. The French wanted to put an end to corruption in Morocco, but bent their rules a little to accommodate the Glaoui who could give them the law and order they wanted while still retaining his direct life-or-death authority over 600,000 people and effectively ruling southern Morocco for the French. The Glaoui, who knew he could never be sultan, was wise enough to settle for second best.

And when French rule was obviously nearing its end, the Glaoui, who had now made a vast fortune from the mining and transport industries, supported Istiqlal, the movement for independence, and campaigned for the return of Sidi Mohammed, the sultan-in-exile. The Glaoui died on 23 January 1956 at Kasbah Telouet, only months before Moroccan independence.

The Kasbah Today. The track from the main road ends quite literally at the door of Dar Glaoui, the pasha's palace. A guide will show you around a very few rooms of this vast and crumbling kasbah, claiming that there's too much decay to venture further, yet the place was built as late as the 19th cent. It's claimed that 300 men spend three years decorating the main rooms of the Dar Glaoui, but when its owner died all the furnishings were confiscated by the state according to custom, leaving this enormous, empty shell which would make a good film set for a spook movie.

There is a very basic **hotel** at Telouet, but no bus service; you might be able to share a taxi from **Igherm n'Ougdal,** 7 miles (12km) along the main road, a fortified village with its own kasbah that's worth a look, if only for the atmosphere. On the downhill side of Igherm is an *agadir,* a fortified communal granary which tourists in the know might ask to see.

Ouarzazate. The southern flanks of the High Atlas are dry and barren, showing the beginnings of the Saharan influence, with Ouarzazate an oasis town commanding not only the southern access to the Tizn n'Tichka but also the northern access to the Drâa Valley and the east-west route between the High and the Anti Atlas. Ouarzazate was built in 1928 as a garrison town for the French and therefore has little Moroccan character, though its main buildings are plastered or painted with the sandy-red of the mountains. The town is smart and neat, with a tiny CTM and a separate private **bus** depot, the PTT, and 'délégation du tourisme' within two minutes' walk.

Kasbah Taourirt. Apart from the scenery the only focus of interest is the Kasbah Taourirt, east of town beyond the airport. The kasbah, a vast structure now in serious decay, was the southern stronghold of the Glaoui family until independence, serving as a dormitory for itinerant craftsmen on the edge of the French military garrison, and if you visit it (standard hours, loosely interpreted) you'll be allowed into only a fraction of the original. With tourism in mind there are plans to restore the kasbah complex and increase the 'soirées folkloriques.'

HOTELS: For a town of 65,000 people, Ouarzazate has an excellent range of hotels: Azghor (4*, 105 rms); la Gazelle (1*, 30 rms, pool), on Agadir road; Karam-Palace (48, 150 rms, night club, large pool, riding); Riad-Salam (5*, 70 rms, riding); Tichka-Salam (4*, 110 rms, beside Riad-Salam); and le Zat (4*, 60 rms). And there is the Club Med **holiday village** (120 beds) on the shore of El Mansour ed Dahbi reservoir on the edge of town and **camping** on the municipal site beyond the kasbah.

Basic hotels are the Atlas, Es Salam, and the Royal, all in the town centre.

Aït Benhaddou. Half a dozen crumbling kasbahs lurk in the southern approaches to the Tichka pass, all of them overtaken by history and bypassed by the newish motor road, and you'll need your own transport to reach the kasbah at Aït Benhaddou, 14 miles (22km) back towards Tizi n'Tichka but along a poor track, optionally accessible from the main road along a more direct 7-mile (11-km) track. This is one of the more picturesque and better-preserved mudbrick forts in the desert fringe, justifiably used as location shots in several films, with part of the rabbit-warren village being rebuilt for *Jesus of Nazareth.*

Tiffoultoute. The kasbah at Tiffoultoute, closer to Ouarzazate, was built for a sheikh, used by the Glaoui caliphs, then 'modernised' in the 1960s as the annexe to a hotel which has since closed. Various folklore spectaculars are held here for package tourists seeing what they may think is the true sub-Atlas culture.

Route of the Kasbahs. The Dadès Valley east of Ouarzazate is often called the Route of the Kasbahs for obvious reasons. There are about 25 to Tinerhir, the same number as there are down the Drâa Valley to Zagora, all built of *pisé* and all close to the basic design of a square with towers at each corner. The towers taper in true Berber fashion, probably because the mudbricks can't carry much weight.

Most of the kasbahs are late 19th or early 20th cent: the winter rains are their ultimate despoilers, although a tribal war in 1893 and French repression during the Protectorate have destroyed several and damaged others. Only a few are inhabited, and then usually by the peasant community.

The **Amerhidil** kasbah, the first on the left, is the favourite for exploration, on the approaches to **Skoura,** a town which produces rose-water from acres of highly-perfumed *rosa damascena.* More statistics? One acre yields 2,200lb (1,000kg) of bloom which gives around 10oz (300gm) of attar of roses.

Skoura also has several kasbah, notably the **Dar Aït Sidi el Mati**, the ex-Glaoui **Dar Toundout** and the fortified granary of Sidi Mbarek, a reminder of how tenuous life can be in these parts: the Oued Dadès provides the only source of life along this barren but scenic valley.

El Kelaa des Mgouna. The fortified village of El Kelaa des Mgouna is a complete surprise. Built to defend the Dadès gap, it now devotes itself entirely to roses: growing them, extracting their oil, celebrating in the late-May Rose Moussem, and catering for well-heeled tourists in the four-star **Hotel** les Roses du Dadès (102 rms) built on a clifftop offering a splendid view. The hotel looks beyond rose-growing to arrange hikes and truck excursions.

Boumalne. The small garrison town of Boumalne marks the beginning of the Dadès Gorge; the town has the inevitable kasbah, the four-star **Hotel** Madayeq (38 rooms, restaurant, pool), and Land-Rover transport up the gorge, the only kind of vehicle which will reach the upper villages and go over the mountains to Imilchil and Kasbah Tadla.

The Dadès Gorge. The touristy part of the gorge is around 40 miles (60km) long, with the track getting progressively worse. The bridge at Aït Oudinar is as far as you should venture in a saloon car; above here the gorge is for hikers.

Beyond the Glaoui kasbah which once guarded the approaches, the Dadès is narrow and sinuous, and becomes even narrower; forcing the kasbahs of Aït Arbi to cling to the cliffside as if there's no room on the floor. Tamnalt has a cheap hotel, and there's an auberge near the bridge at Aït Oudinar. If you're planning to walk from here up the gorge, particularly in early spring or autumn, check the weather. It may sound strange advice, but consider that the upper canyon has vertical sides several hundred feet tall, plunging the river bed into permanent shade. Here, with the sky out of sight and the river gravels your only way in and out, your greatest worry is a heavy rain in the mountains which could cause a flash flood 30 feet (10m) deep, bringing down boulders as big as buses.

To the Plateau of the Lakes. With appropriate transport — your own four-wheel-drive truck or scramble-type motor-cycle — and in late summer only, you could consider driving over the High Atlas to **Imilchil,** an administrative town which comes alive in the second half of September when the nomadic Berbers drift in to barter livestock and cereals, and the young women choose their husbands at the Moussem of Aït Haddidou, which doubles as the Foire des Fiancés.

Apart from the Land-Rovers loaded with package tourists seeing culture at first hand you could be back in the 18th cent, and here in the loneliest high-altitude part of the country, the Plateau of the Lakes, you find a weird landscape which is part sub-alpine and part desert bot totally barren, relieved only by its two small brackish and landlocked lakes.

There is no regular public transport to Imilchil; you must rely on whatever is moving, and allow stopovers of a day or more between lifts. But there is organised tourist accommodation! Book an excursion to Imilchil at any hotel in the Salam chain, such as those in Ouarzazate, and your 'room' will be in a Berber tent. On the other hand, you'd probably get the same accommodation for less money merely by turning up in town.

Tinerhir. Tinerhir (or Tineghir), 33 miles (53km) east of Boumalne, is a small town built around the now-crumbling Glaoui kasbah which guarded the entrance to the Todra (or Todgha) Gorge. The town's other attraction is its oasis, one of the largest in Morocco, divided into individual plots and seeming to accomplish the impossible by cultivating vegetables directly under pomegranate and orange trees which are growing under 50-foot (15m) date palms. Until the French exerted their influence the oasis was ruled by hostile families each in its own kasbah; the blood feuds have gone but the kasbahs remain.

Once again there is a four-star **hotel**, the Sargho (65 rms, pool, bar). Cheaper rooms are at the Todgha (1*, 38 rms) and the unclassified Oasis and Salam.

The isle of Peñon de Alhucemas is Spanish territory in the Bay of Al Hoceima: no access from Morocco

Todra Gorge. The Todra Gorge is shorter and wider than the Dadès but no less spectacular, beginning with a forest of date palms. The road is of acceptable standard but once again the most dramatic part of the gorge, where the cliffs rise to 1,000ft (300m), is accessible only on foot — and beware the risk of flash flood.

Where road and canyon part, seven miles (11km) upstream, are two springs; the one on the right feeds a small pool known as the *Source Imarighen,* or the 'Spring of the Sacred Fish;' the one on the left is said to make sterile women fertile. Around here, too, are the **hotels,** the basic Mansour and, at the head of the good road, the Yasmina and des Roches.

Errachidia. Almost at the eastern end of the highest of the High Atlas, Errachidia is another administrative and garrison town developed by the French, but based on the ancient Ksar es Souk: the 19th-cent ksar is still there to the east of town and the souks are on Sundays, Tuesdays and Thursdays.

It's another crossroads community now swollen to 67,000 inhabitants, where the east-west route meets the trans-atlas road to Meknès and the entry to the Tafilalt (see Chapter 18).

There are enough **hotels** to suit all tastes: Rissani (3*, 60 rms), Rte d'Erfoud; Oasis (2*, 46 rms), Rue Abu Abdallah; Meski (1*, 25 rms) Ave Moulay Ali Cherif; and the unclassified Marhaba and Renaissance. And there are two **campings;** one mile east of town, the other at the Source Bleue de Meski, 14 miles (22km) east. **Buses** and taxis operate from opposite sides of the main street, and the **tourist office** is handy, beside the Chambre de Commerce. Don't forget the **airport** here: see Chapter 4.

Ziz Gorge. North of Errachidia the road passes the earth dam which holds back 360,000,000 cu metres of water in the Hassan Addakhil reservoir, built between 1968 and '71 to irrigate the Tafilalt and generate electricity. Beyond the head of the reservoir the road plunges into the Ziz Gorge through an avenue of date palms; the deep-red limestone contrasts markedly with the emerald blue-green waters, particularly when the sun is low in the sky.

The Roman general Paulinus came through this gorge in 41AD (he was later to be Governor of Britain and the man who defeated Boadicea) and it has been a caravan route for centuries, but the modern motor road was built in the 1930s when the French were imposing their rule on the area; the Foreign Legion did most of the work, which is why the road tunnel at the head of the gorge is known as the *Tunnel du Légionnaire*.

Midelt. Ninety-three miles (150km) north of Er Rachidia on the northern rim of the High Atlas lies Midelt, a lonely outpost of 16,000 people in a half-European, half-Arab town at the base of the Jebel Ayachi which towers an impressive 12,227ft (3,737m), overshadowing the 7,383ft (2,250m) ridge in the foreground. Apart from the sense of isolation you find in such places, Midelt's only attraction is the carpet factory of the Fransiscan Sisters which also sells Berber weaving from the region.

The smartest **hotel** is the Ayachi (3*, 28 rms) on Rte d'Agadir, with the unstarred El Aghouar and Occidentale. **Buses** leave from the centre of town.

Cirque de Jaffar. A bonejarring track leads south-west to the Cirque de Jaffar, a natural amphitheatre gouged from the mountains; tackle it only in dry weather with a really robust vehicle.

THE ANTI ATLAS

The Anti Atlas range is dry and barren, sheltered from the rain-bearing winds by the High Atlas yet lying exposed to the full force of the Saharan oven-blasts. It is a harsh yet beautiful landscape whose only appreciable water supply is around Tafraoute, although a number of oases cling to oueds and salt pans along its southern fringe, nourished by freak storms which in these regions can range from a shower to a cloudburst.

Its attractions are listed elsewhere: see the index for Goulimine, Ouarzazate, Tafraoute, Taroudannt and Tiznit, and the next chapter for the Drâa Valley.

Tanger new town, and the old medina (right) as seen from the Club Méditerranée beach

18: THE DESERTS

Drâa, Tafilalt, Figuig and the Deep South

MOST PEOPLE IMAGINE THE SAHARA to be an endless sea of sand dunes, crossed by camel caravans navigating by some ancestral instinct from one palm-fringed oasis to the next. Forget it — or go to Tunisia or Egypt. Morocco's part of the Sahara is mostly bare rock, the sand being carried eastward to help form those great ergs which occupy most of Algeria, Libya, Egypt and northern Sudan.

You will only see loose sand in Morocco in small patches: the Erg Chebbi in the Tafilalt is the country's largest dune, around 16 miles (25km) long; there is some sand between Taza and **Taourirt**, a caravan town with walls dating from 1295; there are drifts along the coast south of Essaouira; there are several-acre deserts around the Drâa; but you need to go south of Tan-Tan to begin to appreciate the picture-book image of the Sahara.

By the way, it's wrong to talk of the Sahara *Desert*, as *sahra* in Arabic means 'desert.'

THE DRÂA VALLEY. The Oued Drâa is the child of the oueds Ouarzazate and Dadès and flows south-east from El Mansour ed Dahbi reservoir to form Morocco's longest river, though its flow is nothing to match the oueds Oum er Rbia, Bou Regreg or Moulouya; usually it wastes away into the vast salt pans south of M'hamid near the disputed border with Algeria, and reaches the sea by Tan-Tan once in a generation.

The only practical way into the valley is from Ouarzazate, but a rough track grinds over the rock desert to the Tafilalt. If you're travelling by CTM bus, you leave this town around 1340 and arrive at M'Hamid, the end of the road, around 2000 with stops at Agdz and Zagora. By car you'll find it a relatively easy drive over adequate surfaces, despite a stretch of narrow carriageway around the Tizi n'Tinififft which crosses a spur of the Anti Atlas at 5,447ft (1,660m); at this point the river is several miles away.

Agdz. Road and river meet for the first time at Agdz, where the palm groves begin, making the Drâa the longest oasis in Morocco — around 65 miles (100km). Agdz, pronounced Agga-dess, is a small desert outpost of a town built to administer the Mezguita tribe, but one might guess it earns most of its income from the tourist trade since the central square, graced with a smart fountain, is surrounded by restaurants, carpet stores, and the self-styled 'Boutique des Hommes Bleus, Chop (sic) of Arts.' The unclassified **Hotel** des Palmiers is here, charging 40DH for a single, 60DH a double, with no food.

Immediately outside the town you enter the oasis, though for the most part the road stays on the higher and unproductive land. The Drâa is a wide valley, unlike any of the gorges, but at its rim the ground shelves steeply upwards to the pink and russet heat-hazed ragged cliffs which rim the Anti Atlas plateaux on each side.

In less-settled times the Mezguita tribe built the Ksar Tamenougalt, tucked in the palms between road and river and easily accessible. This ksar was formerly the home base of the rulers of the Drâa who had their own mini-republic, answerable only to the Glaoui of the High Atlas, and is one of the 25 ksour which line the valley between here and Zagora.

Having brought your camel train over the Tizi n'Tichka, the Drâa is the obvious route south into the sandy desert and the riches that once lay on its southern 'sahel' (shore); no wonder that the 80,000 people who now live here are a mixture of Berber and Arab, with a touch of Touareg from the Ahaggar Mountains, and of negroes from beyond the desert, and even with a few Jews still around.

Zagora. The good road ends at Zagora, a small town which exerts a great pull on travellers but which offers little to those who arrive: but wait — there is a cinema! All activity is centred on the long and wide main street, including the F.A.R. barracks, banks and petrol stations, **bus** office, and the **hotels** des Amis (unclassified) and Vallée du Drâa (1*, 14 rms). At the end of the street is H. de la Palmerai (1*, 21 rms) with its restaurant in a Berber tent. H. Club Reda is beyond the town limits and H. la Tinsouline (3*, 90 rms) is in the oasis, where you will also find two **camping** sites — C. Sinbad and C. de la Montagne de Zagora. Sinbad charges 20DH per person to sleep in mud huts while des Amis charges 35DH for a double room — but in midsummer a hotel room is like a baker's oven at the end of a long shift. The town's electricity shuts down at night, cutting off water supplies as well.

Going to Timbuctoo? An alluring sign at the end of Zagora's main street, promises in French and Arabic '52 days to Timbuctoo' by camel.

Jebel Zagora. On the edge of town the salmon-pink Jebel Zagora stands like a smaller Table Mountain, its flat top at 3,197ft (974m) offering a complete panorama that's particularly colourful near dawn or dusk. The Almoravides built a small fortress up here, of which a few stubby walls remain.

Tamegrout. The Hotel Tinsouline organises tours to Amazraou and its ancient Jewish Kasbah, and on to Tamegroute (11 miles, 18km) for its dunes and its 17th-cent library. The library, and the nearby zaouia, were founded by Abu Abdallah Bou Nacer, who collected religious literature from all the Arab lands; his 13th-cent illuminated Koran is occasionally on public view.

M'hamid. The daily CTM bus runs down the poor tarmac road to M'hamid, 55 miles (88km) away near the Algerian frontier, but the journey is nearly always done in darkness. M'hamid has a Monday souk but don't believe those stories about blue men. At Tagounit, 34 miles (54km) from Zagora, is the Necropolis of Foum Rjam dating from 800BC and still holding hundreds of conical burial chambers, but there's no point in trying to see it in the dark.

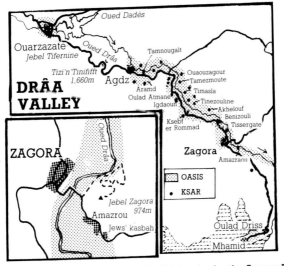

Map labels:
Oued Dadès
Ouarzazate
Jebel Tifernine
Oued Drâa
Tamnougalt
Tizi'n'Tinififft
1,660m
Agdz
DRÂA VALLEY
Aramd
Oulad Atmane
Igdaoun
Ouaouzagour
Tamezmoute
Timasla
Tinezouline
Akhelouf
Benizouli
Tissergate
Ksebt er Rommad
ZAGORA
Oued Drâa
Jebel Zagora 974m
Amazrou
Jews' kasbah
Zagora
Amazraou
☐ OASIS
• KSAR
Oulad Driss
Mhamid

THE TAFILALT. The road to the Tafilalt begins by the **Source Bleue de Meski,** near the Er Rachidia campsite. The source is one of those picture-postcard delights set in a small cave at the foot of a cliff, and accessible down some steps; the water cascades into a cement basin built by the Foreign Legion.

The Oued Ziz — Berber for 'gazelle,' by the way — flows south through scattered date-palm oases (there are supposedly more than 800,000 palms in the region) into the Tafilalt proper, where it parallels but never meets the Oued Rheris (Gheris) before they cross the somewhere-border into Algeria and fade into the sands. Several ksour line both river banks, mostly in communal occupation by the oasis labourers, but the ksar of Aït Amira by Aoufuss is perhaps the easiest to explore.

Erfoud. The effective capital of the Tafilalt today is Erfoud, a sad little grid-plan outpost of government occupied by 5,000 people. Here are the banks, PTT, **bus** and taxi stands, and the **hotels:** Club-Salam (4*, 100 rms); Sijilmassa (3*, 75 rms), turn right entering town; Tafilalet (2*, 20 rms), Ave Moulay Ismail; with more basic hotels nearby.

Erfoud's usefulness is mainly as a dormitory for excursions into the oases and the desert; buses go several times a day to Rissani, or you can share a grand taxi, hire a car, or buy a place in an organised expedition — or even walk, if **Borj Est** is your destination. This is a ruined fortress of unknown ancestry standing on a 3,069-ft (935-m) mountain to the east of town; leave by the main square and ford the Oued Ziz.

Sandy Desert. A rough track goes direct from Erfoud to Merzouga, 37 miles (60km) south, on the edge of the **Erg Chebbi,** the 'small erg,' but in fact Morocco's largest sand dune and a popular destination with tourists on packaged adventure. From the 400-ft (120m) crest of this Saharan ridge in winter and spring you might see a small lake west of Merzouga.

It's not a mirage; it takes floodwaters from the Ziz but dries to a saltpan in summer, when its flamingo residents migrate.

Sijilmassa. You would not expect to find another Fès or Marrakech in the Tafilalt, but if you had come here in the Middle Ages that's exactly what you would have seen. This collection of oases marked the starting point of Morocco's most important caravan route across the Sahara, with its capital, Sijilmassa, home to 100,000 people and guarded by 600 ksour. It's virtually unbelievable today, as the crumbling city, a mile west of Rissani, was destroyed in the 19th cent and the few surviving foundations are covered by the sand.

Leon l'Africain wrote that Sijilmassa was founded by the Roman general Sigillum Massa, but the Arab geographer El Bekri claimed it was the city of Midrar, a Berber blacksmith of the Meknassa tribe, who was here in 757. Certainly it became the Timbuctoo of the north, trading with the real Timbuctoo in gold, salt, iron, slaves, dates, ivory and ostrich plumes. Sijilmassa saw the creation of the Alaouite dynasty, and sultans careful of usurpers to their throne sent ambitious cousins and younger brothers out here into permanent exile; Moulay Ismail, who created Meknès, built the kasbah whose ruins now form the Rissani souk.

Other traces of history lie in the neighbourhood, the most promising being the crumbling mudbrick of the **Ksar Abbar,** probably 19th cent and occupying 13 or 14 acres (5ha). A fort within a fort, it had 500 negro soldiers armed with cannon guarding...what: the approaches to the Tafilalt, or the ambitious royal relations? Beside it is the Mausoleum of Moulay Ali Cherif, father of Mouley el Rachid, but this was totally rebuilt in 1955 after a flood, and is forbidden territory to non-Moslems.

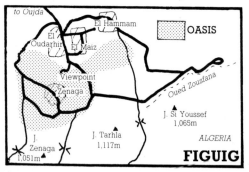

FIGUIG.

Unless you penetrate the deep south, Figuig is likely to be the furthest you travel from civilization in Morocco: 234 miles (376km) from Oujda and 218 miles (350km) from Midelt through spectacular multicoloured scenery. But you're very close to Algeria and almost surrounded by it; I can't quote distances as the frontier is undefined even though it's usually open.

Figuig is a collection of seven ksour, several of which were mortal enemies until recent times, and it lies in an 8 sq-mile (20 sq-km) basin around 2,900 ft (900m) high, containing around 200,000 poor quality date palms and 37,000 people. Each of these ksour has its own protected patch of palms, still guarded by bizarre lookout towers.

The irrigation system in Figuig is also bizarre. The cut-and-cover canals, called *feggaguir* — *foggara* in the singluar — from which the community takes its name, have access wellheads at strategic points, similar to the system used in the Tafilalt, and the unseen and so unmeasurable flow of water could have led to the blood feuds.

The centre of Figuig is an open space with a convenient viewpoint from which you can spy out the land: Zenaga, the largest ksar, is to the south and holds the **Auberge** de la Palmeraie; El Oudahir, to the north, has its narrow alleys, a hot spring and a salty one, and the two basic **hotels**, Meliasse and Sahara. Ksar El-Hammam to the north-east has, as its name suggests, another hot spring; around 92°F (33°8C).

If the early morning heat allows you to walk out to the Col Tarhla near the border you'll be rewarded by a distant view of the real sandy Sahara far to the south, the beginnings of the Grand Erg Occidental: but that's another journey.

THE DEEP SOUTH. South of Laayoune, known as El Aaiun when this was the 73,000 sq mile Spanish territory of Río de Oro, is the domain of the Polisario guerillas — or freedom fighters, depending upon your viewpoint — and definitely not for the casual tourist. If you plan to venture down here, first contact the Moroccan authorities and explain what you have in mind and be prepared for a refusal. Is it the lure of the great sandy desert? Then why not try Tunisia instead — or Algeria, despite its currency regulations? Or are you planning a trans-saharan expedition? You'd be much better advised to stick to the routes through Algeria and Mali or Niger, and brush up with the *Sahara Handbook* by Simon and Jan Glen (Lascelles, £18.95).

I have seen this country only from 30,000 feet altitude from where it looked like a vast slick of butter stretching featureless to the eastern horizon, the only sense of scale coming from the Atlantic waves drawing white streaks on the beach. It is fascinating and fearsome at the same time, but while the Polisario struggles continue, 30,000 feet is as close as I want to get.

Polisario Background. After Moroccan independence in 1956 and the international rejection of colonialism, Spain was under pressure to withdraw from Río de Oro. It agreed in principle, but started mining phosphates there in 1969, the year it was forced out of Sidi Ifni by a Moroccan frontier blockade.

Morocco was expecting to take control of the vast tract of near-empty land, but had not reckoned on the Sahrawi peoples preferring independence. In 1973 they formed the *Frente Popular para la Liberación de Saguía el Hamra* (the oued that 'flows' into Laayoune) *y Río de Oro*, Polisario for short. Then desperately poor Mauritania expressed an interest, for the phosphates would bring untold wealth.

Marche Verde. Hassan II pulled a master stroke in 1975 by urging volunteer civilians, including women and children, to invade Río de Oro on foot, the Green March or *Marche Verde* which began on 6 November of that year. Spain obviously couldn't send troops into the attack, so it pulled out, the following week drawing up an agreement that Río de Oro should be divided between Morocco and Mauritania.

Meanwhile, Polisario was preparing its guerilla war with help from Algeria, and set up the Saharan Arab Democratic Republic, SADR (RASD in French), with its government in exile. Under pressure from Morocco, Mauritania renounced its claim to any part of the Río de Oro in 1979, which Morocco then annexed — causing great concern in Algeria which resented this territorial expansion.

Sand Wall. As tension increased and Polisario began striking at vulnerable points, Morocco agreed in the 1981 Nairobi Summit to a 'controlled' referendum, but set its armed forces to building a phenomenal series of sand walls 300 miles (450km) long, the first around Laayoune and the Boukra phosphate mines, the second along the lower Drâa.

USA Intervention. The battle against Polisario has continued ever since, and is still being fought, though the Moroccans are gradually bringing this vast southern province under their control. But the price has been almost too much; the war drained the economy to such an extent that Morocco had to ask for help from the USA, a delicate manoeuvre for an Arab nation. The US obliged, stating its terms as the reopening of several military bases which had been closed since independence.

Could Morocco, only recently free of French and Spanish subjugation, accept American troops on its soil? It had to, if it was to hold out any hope of gaining the economic rewards that lay in the barren wastes of the River of Gold. In byegone centuries the sultans had played Spaniard against Portuguese, Jew against Christian, Berber against Arab, and even Moor against Moor. Once again the rulers of this turbulent land had to match one foreign power against another, in the hope of extracting something for their own benefit — but that has always been the way of life in Morocco.

Fantasia: Moroccans love these mock battles, and their marquees are distinctive

19: SPANISH ENCLAVES

Ceuta and Melilla

POLITICALLY AND ECONOMICALLY, CEUTA AND MELILLA ARE SPANISH. They are considered as much part of the Iberian homeland as Madrid and Toledo.

But Ceuta and Melilla — and the Canary Islands for that matter — are not in the European Economic Community, so they can still retain their status as tax-free towns. Ceuta in particular seems to live by catering for tourists, most of whom are mainland Spaniards coming over for the day purely to stock up on the duty-frees and with no thought of going into Morocco. An example? Scotch whisky at 600ptas (say £3) for a 75cl bottle in the open-air stalls fronting the ferry terminal car park. But go upstairs and you'll find the same brands for 550ptas.

Frontier Crossing. Morocco resents these continued irritants on what it claims to be its soil and so makes the frontier crossing an arduous affair full of petty irritations. Allow plenty of time in both directions; it took me all day to travel by car and ferry from Tanger to Algeciras.

CEUTA

The Romans called this peninsula 'Seven Brothers' — Septem Fratres — from which came the name the Arabs still use, Sebta. On the map it might look a suitable partner to Gibraltar to share the title of Pillars of Hercules, but sail through the strait on a clear day and you'll see that Gib's African companion can only be Jebel Musa, also known as Ape's Hill and Mount Abyla. Ceuta's Monte Hacho at 595ft (181m) is no contender.

The Phoenicians, Romans, Vandals, Goths and Byzantines came and went, and the Visigoths were in command when the Islamic flood swept west along the African coast. Tarik ibn Zeyad (from whom Jebel Tarik, Gibraltar, is named) sailed from here in 711 to lead the Arab invasion of western Europe (see *Discover Gibraltar*).

Under Islam, Ceuta fell to the various dynasties: Almoravide in 1083, Almohade in 1145, Marinite in 1273 — and was besieged from 1306 to '09 when the Spanish-born Marinite Osman ben Idriss seized the town and called himself Sultan of Morocco.

Ceuta was an important trading station for all the European city states, with merchants from Marseilles being the first to settle here. But in 1415 João (John) I of Portugal brought 50,000 men in 200 ships to seize the town and despite a number of sieges from the Moors it has never been in Arab hands since.

Ceuta Today. Ceuta lost some of its importance with the ending of the Protectorate and the reimposition of the frontier just down the road. An early victim was the railway to Tetouan, now remembered only in the tunnels along the main road; and the population dropped slightly to 70,000, many of whom are military. There is little to see: the 16th-cent Cathedral of Nuestra Señora de Africa, the Museo Arqueológico (0900-1300, 1600-1800 with Spanish, not Moroccan, punctuality), and the Jardines Andaluces (Andaluz Gardens) and Franco's statue on Monte Hacho. And there is a small beach on the south side of the narrow isthmus.

There is keen competition for the **hotels.** Africa (3°, 39 rms), Muelle (Quay) Cañonero Dato; Atlante (2°, 40 rms), Paseo de la Palmeras; Gran H. Ulises (4°, 124 rms), Calle Camoens; Miramar (2°, 17 rms), Ave Reyes Católicos; la Muralla (4°, 83 rms), Pl. Africa; Skol (2°, 14 rms) near Miramar. The **Oficina de Turismo** is on the main quayside.

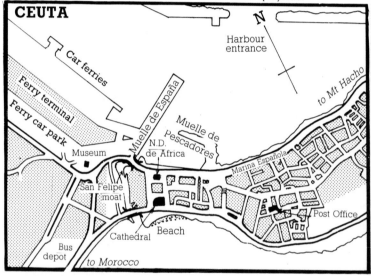

MELILLA

Melilla's early history was parallel with Ceuta's. It was occupied by similar invaders; Phoenician, Carthaginian, Roman, Vandal and Visigoth. After the coming of Islam it was overrun by the Umayyads from Córdoba, the Idrissids, and the Almoravides, but its rise to prominence came when it was the principal port for Fès, and for Sijilmassa, deep in the Tafilalt, and therefore in its trading with the European city states it offered a different kind of merchandise from Ceuta.

When Spain was regaining the last of its territory in 1492, Mlilya — Arabic for 'white,' which describes its bedrock — was lying

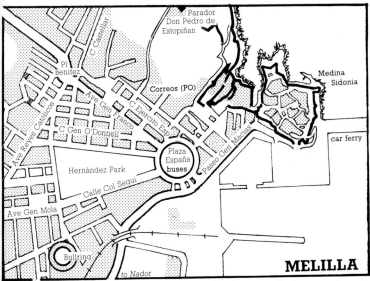

MELILLA

abandoned, though there was no connection between the two events. Spain seized Melilla in 1497 and has never let go, despite a history of sieges and blockades, the most determined being in 1774.

Under the Spanish Protectorate, with the immediate frontier abandoned, Melilla shipped out the mineral wealth of the Rif and became a boom town. But the frontier was back again in 1956, bringing an end to prosperity. The population has dropped from 100,000 at Moroccan independence to little more than half that figure, with the military and the tax-free status being its sole means of existence. Nador has taken over as the Rif's port, and Melilla's airport is purely for Spanish commuter traffic.

Melilla Today. The 16th-cent 'Pueblo' of Medina Sidonia is worth a visit if you can tolerate the two hours required to get through the frontier and back (three hours if you're driving your own car, since you may not leave it in Morocco). Until this century the Pueblo *was* Melilla, a tiny walled city on a rocky headland joined to the rest of Africa by a stubby causeway; look how compact everything is, particularly the tiny Gothic Capella de Santiago (St James's Chapel). Other sights are the 17th-cent church of La Purísima Concepción (Most Pure Conception) and the Museo Municipal (1000-1300, 1600-1800, closed Mon).

There is the same pressure on **hotel** space as in Ceuta. Your choice is mainly from: Anfora (2˚, 145 rms), Calle Pablo Vallesca; Avenida (2˚, 78 rms), Ave del Gen'mo Franco; Cazaza (1˚, 8 rms) Calle Primo de Rivera; Don Pedro de Estopiñan (parador nacional) (3˚, 27 rms), in Alcazaba, overlooking town; España (1˚, 30 rms), Calle Gen Chacel; Miramar (1˚), Paseo Gen. Macias; Nacional (1˚, 30 rms), Calle Primo Rivera; Rusadir San Miguel (2˚, 27 rms), off Pl España. The **Oficina de Turismo** is badly sited on Calle Gen. Aizpuru.

The fishing fleet in the old harbour at Essaouira

INDEX